50 WALKS IN

Warwickshire & West Midlands

50 Walks in Warwickshire & West Midlands

Published by AA Publishing (a trading name of AA Media Limited, whose registered office is Grove House, Lutyens Close, Lychpit, Basingstoke, Hampshire RG24 8AG; registered number 06112600)

© AA Media Limited 2024
Fourth edition
First edition published 2001

Mapping in this book is derived from the following products:
OS Landranger 139 (walks 1–6, 15, 16, 20, 22, 26, 27, 30)
OS Landranger 140 (walks 27, 30, 31, 35, 38–39, 42, 45, 47, 50)
OS Landranger 150 (walks 11–14)
OS Landranger 151 (walks 13–14, 18–19, 25, 28–29, 32–34, 36, 37, 41, 43–49)
OS Landranger 163 (walk 36)
OS Landranger 164 (walk 24, 36)
OS Explorer 205 (walks 17, 23)
OS Explorer 220 (walks 7–10)
OS Explorer 232 (walk 21)
OS Explorer 221 (walk 40)

© Crown copyright and database rights 2024 Ordnance Survey. 100021153.

Maps contain data available from openstreetmap.org © under the Open Database License found at opendatacommons.org

ISBN: 978-0-7495-8377-4

A CIP catalogue record for this book is available from the British Library.

AA Media would like to thank the following contributors in the preparation of this guide:
Clare Ashton, Tracey Freestone, Lauren Havelock, Nicky Hillenbrand, Lin Hutton, Graham Jones, Ian Little, Richard Marchi, Nigel Phillips and Victoria Samways.

Cover design by berkshire design company

Printed and bound in the UK by Oriental Press, Dubai.

A05851

We would like to thank the following photographers, companies and picture libraries for their assistance in the preparation of this book. Abbreviations for the picture credits are as follows:
Alamy = Alamy Stock Photo
Trade Cover, Steve O'Prey/Alamy
Back Cover Advert, SolStock/istockphoto; 9, Edward Webb/Alamy; 12/13, Gary Parker/Alamy; 26/27, Jon Lewis/Alamy; 41, Martin Hill/Alamy; 63, Colin Underhill/Alamy; 121, lovethephoto/Alamy; 143, Dave Porter/Alamy; 169, CHRISTOPHER MICHAEL KEMP/Alamy; 176, SolStock/istockphoto

AA

50 WALKS IN
Warwickshire & West Midlands

CONTENTS

The walks

HOW TO USE THIS BOOK

Each walk starts with an information panel giving all the information you will need about the walk at a glance, including its relative difficulty, distance and total amount of ascent. Difficulty levels and gradients are as follows:

Difficulty of walk

- Easy
- Intermediate
- Hard

Gradient

▲ Some slopes

▲▲ Some steep slopes

▲▲▲ Several very steep slopes

Maps

Every walk has its own route map. We also suggest a relevant Ordnance Survey map to take with you, allowing you to view the area in more detail. The time suggested is the minimum for reasonably fit walkers and doesn't allow for stops.

Route map legend

--→--	Walk route		▨	Built-up area
①	Route waypoint		▨	Woodland area
----	Adjoining path		🚻	Toilet
●	Place of interest		🅿	Car park
⌂	Steep section		⊞	Picnic area
☀	Viewpoint		)(	Bridge
▥	Embankment			

Start points

The start of each walk is given as a six-figure grid reference prefixed by two letters referring to a 100km square of the National Grid. More information on grid references can be found on most OS Walker's Maps.

Dogs

We have tried to give dog owners useful advice about how dog friendly each walk is. Please respect other countryside users. Keep your dog under control, especially around livestock, and obey local by-laws and other dog control notices.

Car parking

Many of the car parks suggested are public, but occasionally you may have to park on the roadside or in a lay-by. Please be considerate about where you leave your car, ensuring that you are not on private property or access roads, and that gates are not blocked and other vehicles can pass safely.

Walks locator map

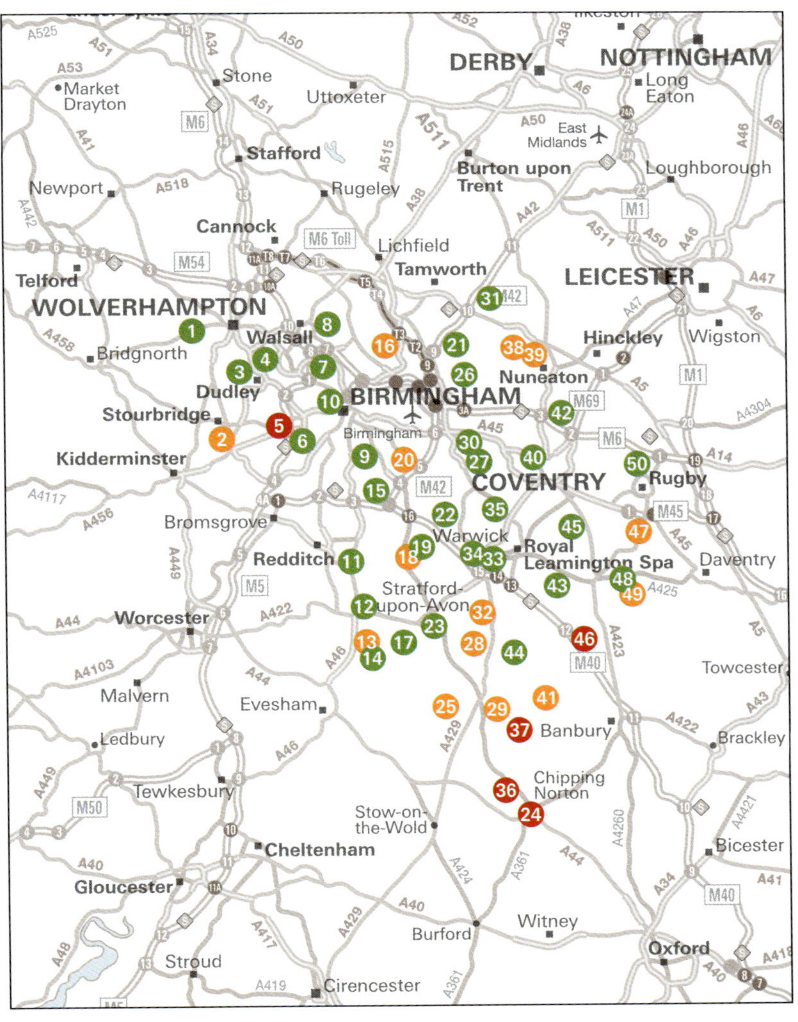

EXPLORING THE AREA

The sparkle of early morning sunlight on a country river as it meanders through beautiful countryside; the reflections of sailing boats on a country lake; relaxing with a pint in the garden of an old English pub in a picturesque village; the sight of colourful narrow boats making their way through a flight of lock gates; the visual impact created by an historic castle. These are just a few of the experiences to enjoy in Warwickshire and the West Midlands. These two counties form the picturesque and historic heart of England, and an ancient cross in the village of Meriden supposedly marks the spot regarded as the very centre of the country. There may be few seriously high hills in this fertile plain, but it is an area full of attractive walking in rolling countryside, blessed with a fascinating history and many wonderful places and buildings to visit.

William Shakespeare

Warwickshire is Shakespeare's county, and the footprint of the famous Bard appears almost everywhere. William Shakespeare is probably the most famous playwright the world has known. He was born and brought up around the beautiful Warwickshire town of Stratford-upon-Avon, and many of his plays draw upon his own experiences in the area. In his youth, Stratford was an important market town and this gave Shakespeare the opportunity to note the manners, dress and speech of the tradesmen, farmers, milkmaids, lawyers and others who attended on market day. Stratford was a centre of government and rural business matters, with one of the finest grammar schools in the country. Today, the swans gather by Clopton Bridge to be fed by the tourists who come to visit the home of the Bard.

Historic Homes

Warwickshire has a history that embraces the Civil War, and many castles and large country houses are scattered over the county. Warwick Castle is the home of the Earl of Warwick; Kenilworth Castle was a stronghold for lords and kings of England in the 11th and 12th centuries; Ragley Hall is the home of Lord Hertford; Coughton Court is the home of the Throckmorton family and history connects it with the Gunpowder Plot; Baddesley Clinton Manor House contains a number of priests' holes used to hide the clergy from Cromwell's men; Packwood House has a garden of yew trees that represent Christ, the four evangelists, the apostles and the multitude at the sermon on the mount; Upton House is a fine William and Mary mansion; Compton Wynyates is one of the most beautiful Tudor houses in the country; and Charlecote House is where Shakespeare is said to have been caught poaching deer.

Industrial Heritage

The West Midlands is dominated by the great industrial city of Birmingham and embraces the Black Country, a region whose limitless energy has helped shape the destiny of Britain. The West Midlands was central to Britain's development during the Industrial Revolution. Canals were built to transport coal, ironware, glass, pottery and textiles across the country, and it remains a vibrant area of business. Today, there are fine parkland areas intermixed with the urban sprawl, and many preserved historic sites to discover. So enjoy a little of everything as you explore these central regions of England on foot.

PUBLIC TRANSPORT

Most of the villages in these walks are accessible by public transport, and start near railway stations. For train times visit www.nationalrail.co.uk. For times of buses and maps of public transport routes visit www.traveline.org.uk.

WALKING IN SAFETY

All these walks are suitable for any reasonably fit person, but less experienced walkers should try the easier walks first. Route-finding is usually straightforward, but you will find that an Ordnance Survey walking map is a useful addition to the route maps and descriptions; recommendations can be found in the information panels.

Risks

Although each walk here has been researched with a view to minimising the risks to the walkers who follow its route, no walk in the countryside can be considered to be completely free from risk. Walking in the outdoors will always require a degree of common sense and judgement to ensure that it is as safe as possible.

- Be particularly careful on cliff paths and in upland terrain, where the consequences of a slip can be very serious.
- Remember to check tidal conditions before walking on the seashore.
- Some sections of route are by, or cross, busy roads. Take care, and remember that traffic is a danger even on minor country lanes.
- Be careful around farmyard machinery and livestock, especially if you have children with you.
- Be aware of the consequences of changes in the weather, and check the forecast before you set out. Carry spare clothing and a torch if you are walking in the winter months. Remember that the weather can change very quickly at any time of the year, and in moorland and heathland areas, mist and fog can make route-finding much harder. Don't set out in these conditions unless you are confident of your navigation skills in poor visibility.
- In summer remember to take account of the heat and sun; wear a hat and carry water.
- On walks away from centres of population you should carry a whistle and survival bag. If you do have an accident that means you require help from the emergency services, make a note of your position as accurately as possible and dial 999.

Countryside Code
Respect other people:

- Consider the local community and other people enjoying the outdoors.
- Co-operate with people at work in the countryside. For example, keep out of the way when farm animals are being gathered or moved, and follow directions from the farmer.

- Don't block gateways, driveways or other paths with your vehicle.

- Leave gates and property as you find them, and follow paths unless wider access is available, such as on open country or registered common land (known as 'open access land').

- Leave machinery and farm animals alone – don't interfere with animals, even if you think they're in distress. Try to alert the farmer instead.

- Use gates, stiles or gaps in field boundaries if you can – climbing over walls, hedges and fences can damage them and increase the risk of farm animals escaping.

- Our heritage matters to all of us – be careful not to disturb ruins and historic sites.

Protect the natural environment:

- Take your litter home. Litter and leftover food don't just spoil the beauty of the countryside; they can be dangerous to wildlife and farm animals. Dropping litter and dumping rubbish are criminal offences.

- Leave no trace of your visit, and take special care not to damage, destroy or remove features such as rocks, plants and trees.

- Keep dogs under effective control, making sure they are not a danger or nuisance to farm animals, horses, wildlife or other people.

- If cattle or horses chase you and your dog, it is safer to let your dog off the lead – don't risk getting hurt by trying to protect it. Your dog will be much safer if you let it run away from a farm animal in these circumstances, and so will you.

- Everyone knows how unpleasant dog mess is and it can cause infections, so always clean up after your dog and get rid of the mess responsibly – bag it and bin it.

- Fires can be as devastating to wildlife and habitats as they are to people and property – so be careful with naked flames and cigarettes at any time of the year.

Enjoy the outdoors:

- Plan ahead and be prepared for natural hazards, changes in weather and other events.

- Wild animals, farm animals and horses can behave unpredictably if you get too close, especially if they're with their young – so give them plenty of space.

- Follow advice and local signs.

For more information visit www.gov.uk/government/publications/the-countryside-code

ALONG THE CANAL AT WIGHTWICK

DISTANCE/TIME	4.5 miles (7.2km) / 1hr 30min
ASCENT/GRADIENT	59ft (18m) / ▲
PATHS	Canal tow path, disused railway track and field paths
LANDSCAPE	Open countryside near urban residences
SUGGESTED MAP	OS Explorer 219 Wolverhampton & Dudley
START/FINISH	Grid Reference: SO870983
DOG FRIENDLINESS	Off lead along tow path and disused railway, otherwise under control
PARKING	On-street parking near Mermaid pub, Wightwick
PUBLIC TOILETS	None on route

This is a journey into the 18th and 19th centuries – a time when the canals and railways preceded our modern, noisy road network. The walk follows the tow path of the Staffordshire and Worcestershire Canal and a stretch of disused railway line to Compton.

At the end of the 19th century, James Brindley helped to revolutionise Britain's transport system by building a series of remarkable canals that linked virtually all of the major cities in Britain. The Staffordshire and Worcestershire Canal was one of his early constructions, built to link the Severn at Stourport with the Trent at Great Heywood and carry coal from the Staffordshire coalfields. Brindley's waterways were built on the contour principle, following the lie of the land. This approach avoided straight lines of canal, deep cuttings, massive embankments and large groups of lock gates.

Work on the Staffordshire and Worcestershire Canal began in 1766 and was eventually completed in 1772. When you walk along the tow path you can imagine the dirty barges of the late 18th and early 19th centuries being hauled along by horses. Commercial traffic finally ceased on the canal in 1960 and in 1978 the whole waterway, including its buildings and its signs, was designated a conservation area.

Steam trains effectively replaced canal barges, but there were gaps in the rail network. The Kingswinford branch was built by the Great Western Railway to fill one of these, allowing through traffic from Bridgnorth to Wolverhampton. It opened in 1925 but was never a great success for passengers. It became a freight-only line in 1932, carrying people again briefly during World War II, when it was used to transfer wounded soldiers from the Normandy landings. The last train ran in 1965. The lines were dismantled and the Kingswinford Railway Walk was introduced to allow people to use the former line for leisure.

Today pleasure boats use the canal, and its tow path combines with the disused railway to provide a fine urban walk away from the noise of the busy road traffic.

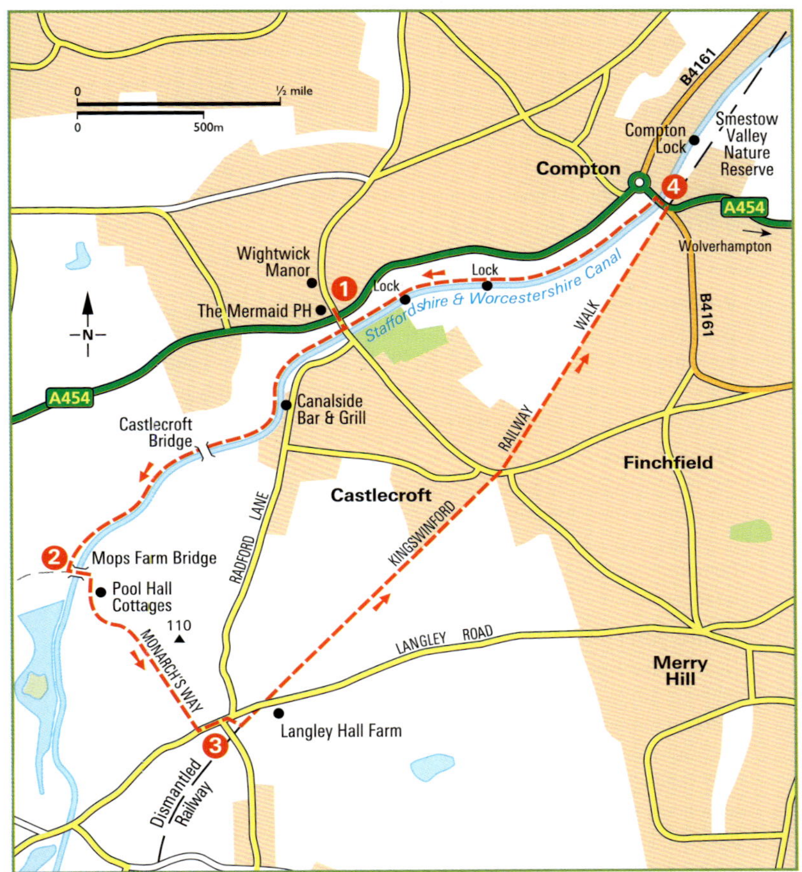

1. From The Mermaid pub, cross the A454 at the pedestrian crossing to take the lane opposite. Don't cross the bridge, but bear right, descending to the tow path of the Staffordshire and Worcestershire Canal. Turn right (southwest) along the path, and after passing the Canalside Bar and Grill (on the far side of the canal), you reach open countryside. This stretch of the canal is similar to a river and you are likely to see anglers fishing for perch, roach, chub, bream or carp. Continue beneath bridge No. 55 (Castlecroft Bridge) and along the tow path until you come to bridge No. 54 (Mops Farm Bridge).

2. Leave the tow path and cross the bridge. Go right past Pool Hall Cottages and follow the waymarkers of the Monarch's Way, heading southeast. At first, the path is to the right of the field hedge; later it crosses over to the left-hand side until you come to a gap leading out onto Langley Road.

Go left up the road, and immediately past the junction, bear right at the postbox, go through a fence gap into the picnic area and descend steps to the dismantled railway. Head left and follow the Kingswinford (South Staffordshire) Railway Walk. This is easy walking and you are likely to meet other walkers and even cyclists. Follow the course of the railway for about 2 miles (3.2km). You will eventually pass beneath the road bridge near

Castlecroft via a kissing gate; following this there are moments when the scene opens up. Continue along the Kingswinford Railway Walk until you come to Compton. Leave the disused railway line and descend to the A454, going left.

3. Cross the road and then the canal bridge to descend to the tow path. Pass beneath bridge No. 59 and take it back to bridge No. 56, passing a couple of lock gates. Go beneath bridge No. 56 and leave the canal, walking onto the pavement of Windmill Lane. Continue towards the main A454 road and cross over to return to The Mermaid pub in Wightwick.

Where to eat and drink

Eating out in the small garden of The Mermaid pub, watching the world go by, is the perfect way to end the day. Children and dogs are also welcome. If you visit Wightwick Manor, you can enjoy a quiet, leisurely lunch in the tea room. Many of the ingredients are grown in the kitchen garden.

What to see

You may not see a horse-drawn coal barge as you stroll the tow path of the Staffordshire and Worcestershire Canal, but you are likely to meet a colourful narrowboat making its way through one of the lock gates. Compton Lock, just beyond Compton village, was the first lock to be built on this canal.

While you're there

Nearby Wightwick Manor was built in 1887 for the Mander family, paint manufacturers from nearby Wolverhampton. The half-timbered house was donated to the National Trust in 1937. The influence of the 19th-century decorative artist William Morris is clear to see. Original Morris wallpapers, Pre-Raphaelite pictures, stained glass by C E Kempe and De Morgan tiles are on display. There are also fine gardens laid out with terraces and pools by Thomas Mawson.

LINKING PEDMORE AND HAGLEY PARK

DISTANCE/TIME	4.5 miles (7.2km) / 2hrs
ASCENT/GRADIENT	279ft (85m) / ▲ ▲
PATHS	Field paths, farm tracks and pavement, several stiles
LANDSCAPE	Fields, woods and suburban housing
SUGGESTED MAP	OS Explorer 219 Wolverhampton & Dudley
START/FINISH	Grid Reference: SO913821
DOG FRIENDLINESS	On lead at all times through residential areas, off lead on Wychbury Hill
PARKING	On-street parking on and around Pedmore Lane
PUBLIC TOILETS	None on route

For much of this walk, there are fine views into Worcestershire over the Clent Hills, and the best of these is from the Obelisk, with Hagley Hall in the valley below. From the suburban West Midlands, town paths take you into the countryside, then link with farm tracks and the North Worcestershire Path, following part of the Monarch's Way over Wychbury Hill.

Set below the range of the Clent Hills, on the outskirts of the village of Hagley, is one of the stateliest houses in England. Hagley Hall was the last of the great Palladian houses to be built. It was designed by Sanderson Miller and built between 1754 and 1760 for George, the 1st Lord Lyttelton (who was secretary to the Prince of Wales), on the site of an earlier house. The impressive building is constructed of brown stone, a rich colour that contrasts well with the Clent Hills in the background and the hall's raised lawns. Its roof balustrades run the length of the four square-towered wings.

In 1925, a serious fire caused a great deal of damage to the interior of the building but, thankfully, it has since been restored to its former glory. The entrance hall is decorated with lovely stucco work and the dining room, one of the rooms most badly affected by the fire, has an impressive rococo ceiling. Rich tapestries and fine Van Dyke paintings are the main feature of the gallery. The 2nd Lord Lyttleton was a founder member of the notorious Hellfire Club of 18th-century aristocratic libertines. Littleton was a great gambler and on one occasion gambled the whole of Hagley Hall against a single painting. Luckily, he won the bet and kept his home.

The hall is set in some 350 acres (142ha) of imaginatively landscaped deer park, with an Ionic temple, a weathered rotunda and a folly in the form of a Gothic ruin. The Obelisk was built in 1758. Behind, the Clent Hills rise to 997ft (304m), forming the perfect backdrop for the views that will follow you along this walk. Today, Hagley is home to Lord and Lady Cobham and is now a location for conferences, business meetings, fairy-tale weddings and dinner parties. It can also be visited on a guided tour.

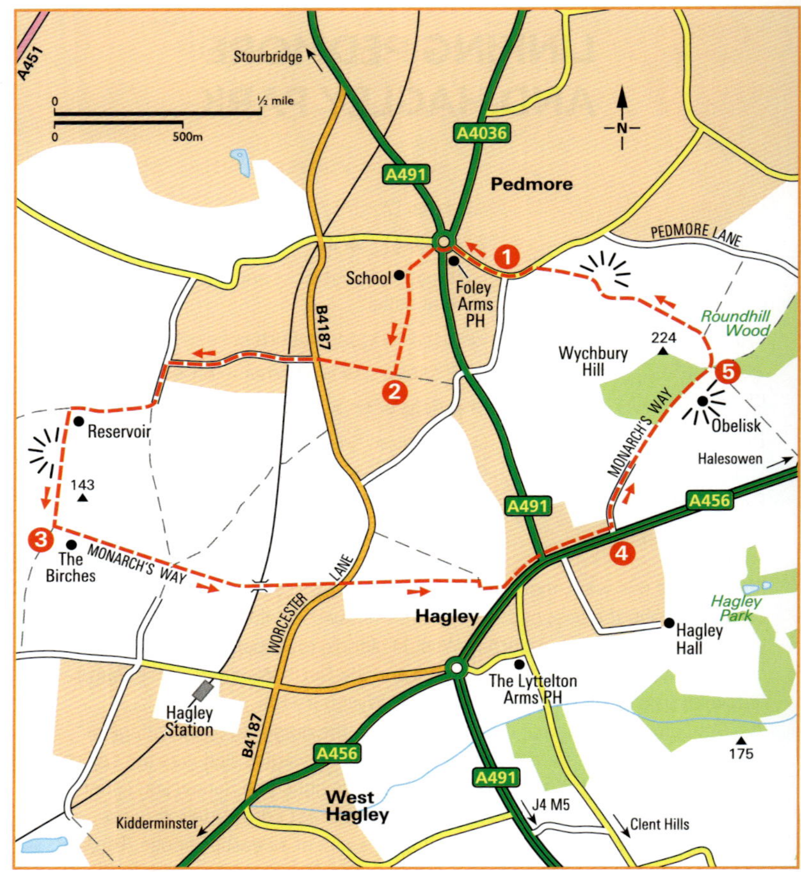

1. From Pedmore Lane, walk into the centre of Pedmore to a roundabout junction with the A491. Go around the island, cross the A491 and continue down the public bridleway signed 'Hagley Road'. Follow this path along the back of houses and past a primary school then more houses, bearing right at a path junction.

2. At the footpath T-junction, go right and continue on footpaths to the B4187 (Worcester Lane). Cross the lane and the main line railway bridge into Quarry Park Road. Continue along the path, following the public bridleway sign to Ounty John Lane, eventually turning left onto a stone track until you come to open countryside. When you reach the track junction go right, soon passing a Severn Trent reservoir. At the end of the reservoir, go immediately left and walk along a farm track over undulating ground, with views to the right towards the hills and Bewdley.

3. At the junction of paths by The Birches copse, go left (east) over a stile along the North Worcestershire Path, Monarch's Way. Initially this is to the left of The Birches, then it veers to the other side of a field hedge, via a stile, descending to cross the railway line once again. It then continues straight ahead through a small housing estate in Hagley, first along the road and then on a footpath beyond No. 60. Eventually the Way comes to a road corner on the B4187 (Worcester Lane). Cross the road, following the footpath sign opposite, and take the hedged path via a stile and continue ahead at the bottom of a series of fields, crossing two stiles, until you reach the busy A456. Go left beside the road, walking to the left of the traffic island and cross the A491 (Stourbridge Road).

4. After following the pavement along the A456 for about 350yds (320m), go left up Monument Lane. Take the lane to the end, then continue on the Monarch's Way via two gates as it climbs towards the Obelisk on Wychbury Hill. Beyond a stile the path goes to the left of the monument and along the side of Roundhill Wood to a junction of footpaths by the trees.

5. Take the path on the left through a kissing gate and a belt of trees and, through a gate, continue down a fenced path, turning right to return to Pedmore Lane.

Where to eat and drink

There are two pubs in the vicinity. The Foley Arms in Pedmore is at the start and finish of the walk, offers decent food, and has a spacious beer garden. The Lyttelton Arms, close to Hagley Hall, is a pub, bar and restaurant with its own courtyard and garden. Nearby Hagley Park has a café open seven days a week with a patio and picnic areas.

What to look out for

Back in the 18th century, Hagley Hall was praised for its fine gardens. Then, in the 19th century, the Kidderminster–Birmingham road (the present-day A456) was built, cutting off Wychbury Hill from the main garden, leaving the garden ornaments of the Obelisk and the Temple of Theseus on the wrong side of the road.

While you're there

Hagley Park is open to visitors and worth a visit or head to the Clent Hills ccuntry park run by the National Trust, which covers some 425 acres (172ha), to the south of this walk. Much of the area is covered with deciduous woodland, gorse and heather. Stroll up to Adam's Hill and the Four Stones where you will be rewarded with a magnificent view that, on a clear day, embraces the Shropshire, Abberley, Malvern and Welsh hills.

A WALK AROUND DUDLEY

DISTANCE/TIME	4.3 miles (7km) / 2hrs
ASCENT/GRADIENT	328ft (100m) / ▲ ▲
PATHS	Parkland paths and pavements, several stiles
LANDSCAPE	Nature reserve and streets around Dudley
SUGGESTED MAP	OS Explorer 219 Wolverhampton & Dudley
START/FINISH	Grid Reference: SO949907
DOG FRIENDLINESS	Off lead in park, otherwise under control
PARKING	Dudley Zoo and Castle car park, Discovery Way, Dudley
PUBLIC TOILETS	In Dudley

The Black Country originally took its name from the dark, coal-stained soil that characterises this corner of the county where the old boundaries of Worcestershire, Shropshire, Staffordshire and Warwickshire meet. It truly earned the name in the 18th and 19th centuries, when the Industrial Revolution took off. The mines, factories and furnaces belched out their blackening soot, so the sky was 'black by day and red by night'. This walk offers the opportunity to explore the unique history of Dudley and the surrounding countryside, including the Wren's Nest National Nature Reserve.

You could be forgiven for expecting the capital of the Black Country to be an old industrial town with little to offer the visitor, but Dudley is a large, vibrant place with a fascinating history that reveals an amazing contrast of English heritage. From Saxon times up to the Civil War, the town developed much like any other in Britain. In the Middle Ages, it became a country market town, with a town hall and small shops dotted around its central market place. The arrival of coal mining and iron working in the 17th century brought massive changes to the area and Dudley steadily expanded to become the main business centre of the Black Country.

It was here in the 1620s that Dud Dudley first experimented with using coal (as coke) for smelting iron. Another Dudley man, Abraham Darby, at Coalbrookdale, developed the process and the town's later ironworks dominated the area until the middle of the 20th century. The Black Country Living Museum reveals how tough life would have been during the early days of the Industrial Revolution. Today, mining activities are a thing of the past. The 1817 Regency Gothic Church of St Thomas the Apostle, with its towering spire, dominates the town's skyline. A number of other attractive old buildings remain, including the landmark Crown Inn, with its unusual bartizan (corner turret with windows), and Baylies's Charity, a charity school built in 1820.

The Wren's Nest National Nature Reserve, Britain's first National Nature Reserve for Geology, is famous for its fossils, the best-known being a trilobite christened the 'Dudley Bug' or the 'Dudley Locust'. It forms the centrepiece of the town's coat of arms and is a symbol of the limestone mining industry.

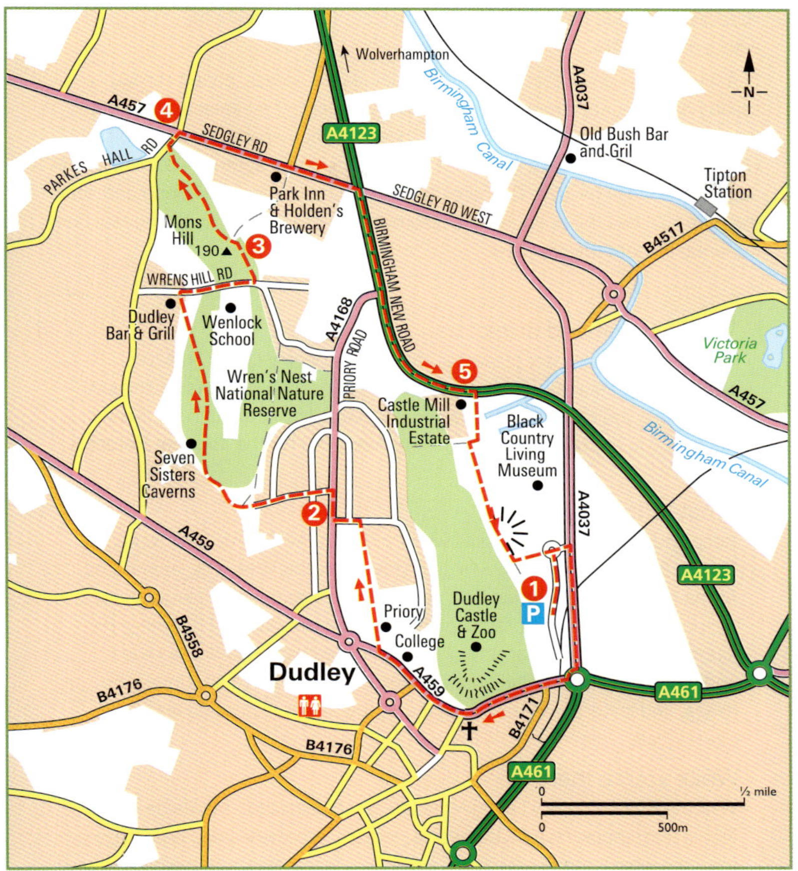

1. From the car park, return to the A4037, turn right and right again at the roundabout to head up Castle Hill. Bear right, along Broadway, down past the college. You'll soon reach the 12th-century priory ruins in Priory Park. Go right and wander through to the far end of the park, then go left down Woodland Avenue, turn right along the A4168 (Priory Road), crossing to the other side.

2. Turn left down Cedar Road and continue past a school to enter the southern part of Wren's Nest National Nature Reserve. Continue ahead for 100yds (91m), turn left up the long flight of steps and continue along the higher footpath, first left and then right. This path leads near to the Seven Sisters Caverns. Continue ahead past the school on your left and you will eventually emerge onto Wrens Hill Road near the Dudley Bar and Grill. Go right along the road and just past the houses, to a gate on the left.

3. Follow the path that takes you over craggy Mons Hill. Eventually, where the path divides, take the left fork, initially down steps, until you near some houses. Reaching Parkes Hall Road, turn right along the road until you come to the A457 (Sedgley Road West).

4. Turn right and follow the A457 for about 750yds (686m), then go right along the A4123 (Birmingham New Road). After 440yds (400m) of easy walking, the

road arcs left, and beyond a bus stop look out for the Castle Mill industrial estate on the right.

5. A few paces up the Castle Hill industrial estate access, go left through a scruffy barrier onto a footpath, then continue along the Limekiln Walk path through the woodland by Castle Hill. There are many paths through this woodland, but try to keep to the left-hand paths going southwards near to the edge of the trees for over 0.5 miles (800m). This is pleasant walking and soon the path reaches the open, with a view over the Black Country Living Museum. Continue back to the car park.

Where to eat and drink

Light refreshments are offered at the Black Country Living Museum and Dudley Castle. Old Bush Bar and Grill at nearby Tipton is a canalside pub where you can enjoy the narrowboat world from the garden. Real ale fans will enjoy The Park Inn, the brewery tap for the adjacent Holden's Brewery.

What to look out for

Keep your eyes open for fossils when you visit the Wren's Nest National Nature Reserve. Around 425 million years ago, this area was submerged, forming part of the Silurian Sea, and a wide range of sea creatures including trilobites and brachiopods inhabited the coral reefs. Today, the site has been stripped largely of its fossils – collecting is discouraged and hammers are definitely not allowed. However, there are lime kilns to see, and children will enjoy exploring the Seven Sisters Caverns and Cherry Hole.

While you're there

Visit the Black Country Living Museum, a reconstructed canalside village with a pub, shops, chapel, ironworks, miner's experience and boat trips from the wharf into the Dudley Tunnel, with its caverns and basins. Dudley Zoo, in the grounds of Dudley Castle, is also a magnet for children of all ages. There are seals in the moat, llamas roaming the slopes below the keep, a tropical rain forest, as well as great views to enjoy.

4 ALONG THE BIRMINGHAM CANAL AT TIPTON

DISTANCE/TIME	2.1 miles (3.4km) / 1hr 45min
ASCENT/GRADIENT	328ft (100m) / Negligible
PATHS	Towpath, park paths and pavements
LANDSCAPE	Canal and urban park
SUGGESTED MAP	OS Explorer 219 Wolverhampton & Dudley
START/FINISH	Grid Reference: SO953925
DOG FRIENDLINESS	Off lead on stretches of canal towpath, otherwise under control
PARKING	Car park opposite Tipton railway station
PUBLIC TOILETS	None on route

To walk along the Birmingham Canal in the Black Country is to walk through social history. The area's spirit, culture and character remain, a place full of quirky traditions and obscure language, though inevitably much of it has moved with the times. This walk, which passes the relics of a landscape once blackened by industry, reflects the years of change and upheaval here but it also reminds those who complete the route that Tipton was the birthplace of a particularly famous son of the town.

William Perry was born at Tipton in 1819. His parents were members of the local canal community. A bout of rickets during infancy had weakened Perry's right knee, which bent inwards, but Perry was a natural fighter. He began his sporting career around 1835 when he was in his mid-teens. At that time, fighting was often undertaken with just bare fists and only the toughest and fittest survived to claim the prize money. Perry's nickname came about following a particularly vicious fight at nearby Oldbury. The blows were so fast and furious that he became known as 'The Slasher.' Many fights followed, some with as many as one hundred rounds or more and there were varying amounts of prize money.

The Fountain Inn at Tipton, directly on the route of this walk, was Perry's headquarters from the start of his career until 1851. A plaque on the wall of the pub recalls that it was erected by the Black Country Society. The Fountain was eventually given Grade II-listed status in recognition of the pub's famous link with Perry, who regularly held court here. William Perry ended up champion prize-fighter of England but age and the consequences of a life in the ring forced him to quit in 1857, aged 38. He then ran a pub, the Bricklayers Arms in Walsall Road, Wolverhampton. A bronze statue of this great man of Tipton, whose name is still celebrated today, can be seen in Coronation Gardens, close to the canal and the pub. William Perry died on Christmas Eve 1880, aged 61. He was buried at St John's Church, Dudley; his remains were later removed and placed in the foundations of the statue.

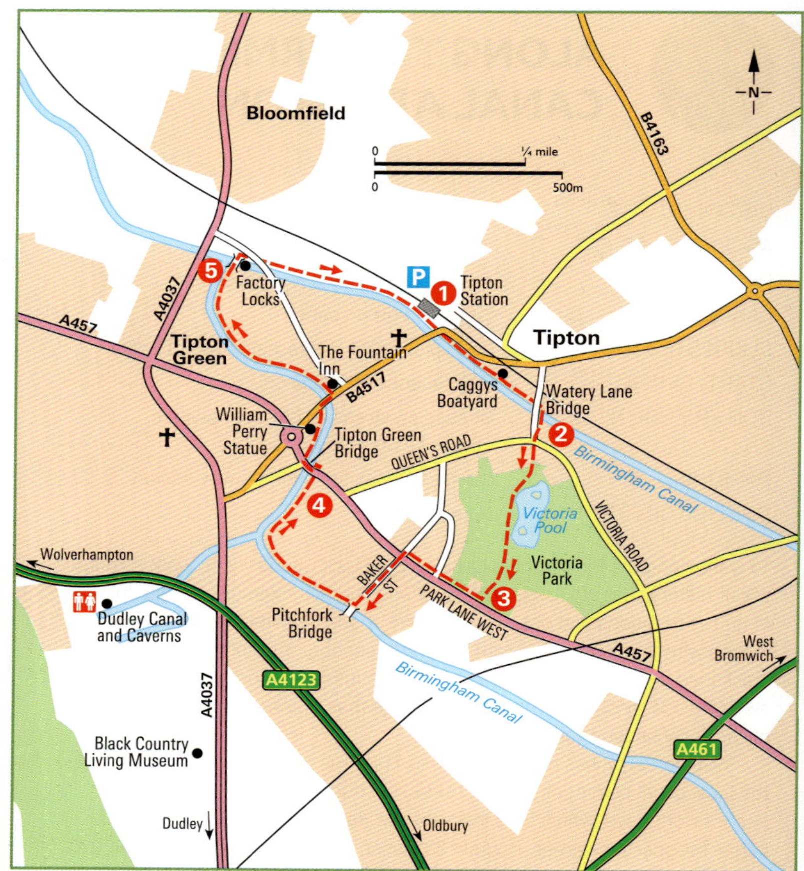

1. From Tipton railway station, make for the towpath of the Birmingham Canal and turn left. A row of bungalows can be seen on the opposite bank. Soon, you reach a boatyard. A railway line is visible over to the left. Cross two footbridges and pass beneath the next canal bridge (1880). Narrow boats and fishermen are often seen along this stretch. Go under Watery Lane Bridge and then swing left, off the towpath. At the road turn left. Looking back along the canal reveals a striking view of the rooftops of Tipton and the church near the start of the walk.

2. Go down the steep slope signposted Dudley and Burnt Tree and on reaching the road where Victoria Road and Queens Road meet, go straight over into Victoria Park. Make your way through the park, choosing your own route. Pass the main lake, known as Victoria Pool, and on its southern side keep right with the skate park on your right. Look for an obvious exit to the A457 and turn right on reaching it.

3. Follow the pavement, with the greenery of Victoria Park glimpsed on your right. Continue along Park Lane West, cross Hill Street and at Manor Road turn left, cross the main road carefully into Baker Street. Make for the Birmingham Canal at Pitchfork Bridge, keep right and follow the towpath to a sign for

Tipton Junction. The towpath is lined on this stretch by a mix of industrial units and period buildings, some of which are now apartments.

4. Walk along to Tipton Green Bridge, pass under it and turn immediately right. At the road turn right to cross the canal and enter the park. Ahead is a statue of William Perry, the Tipton Slasher. Make for the corner of the park and exit to the road by railings. Re-cross the canal to reach the Fountain Inn. Rejoin the towpath at the pub, keeping the waterway on the left, following the sign for the canal cycleway (Wolverhampton). Houses and apartments line the towpath, followed by factories.

5. Cross the footbridge at Old Factory Bridge, following it as it bends to the left. Next, turn left to go back on yourself, under the footbridge and continue on the towpath. Along this stretch is another glimpse of Tipton in the vicinity of the railway station, framed by trees. Pass under Wood Street footbridge and walk along the towpath to the station at the start of the walk.

Where to eat and drink

The Fountain Inn is a traditional canalside pub offering homecooked food, including various snacks. There are many pubs and cafés to be found within the vicinity of the walk and a handy fish and chip shop on Park Lane West.

What to look out for

Opened in 1901 and named after the monarch who died that year, Victoria Park is a fine example of urban public gardens, with its network of paths, bowling green, lake, war memorial and play area, including a skate park. The park is usually busy on summer afternoons and weekends – as it should be.

While you're there

The Birmingham Canal once carried the products of industrial Britain around the Midlands and across the country. Today the canal is a leisure facility, and you will see narrowboats negotiating their way up the canal in the summer.

LLIAM
ERRY

THE LEASOWES AT HALESOWEN

DISTANCE/TIME	4 miles (6.4km) / 1hr 30min
ASCENT/GRADIENT	394ft (120m) / ▲ ▲ ▲
PATHS	Pavements, field paths and tow path, many stiles
LANDSCAPE	Nature reserve and open countryside around urban area
SUGGESTED MAP	OS Explorer 219 Wolverhampton & Dudley
START/FINISH	Grid Reference: SO975839
DOG FRIENDLINESS	Off lead along tow path, otherwise under control
PARKING	Leasowes Lane car park, off A458
PUBLIC TOILETS	None on route

The Leasowes was a mixed farm of arable and pasture when William Shenstone (1714–63) inherited it from his uncle in the early 1740s. William freely admitted he would rather be known as a poet than as a farmer, and he set about transforming the surrounding fields into a *ferme ornée* – an ornamental farm, or what was the Romantic movement's answer to landscape gardening. Shenstone was not a rich landowner, however, so many of the innovations he made were borne of necessity rather than extravagance. He transformed the local water courses into cascades and pools, planted trees and installed benches and even strategically sited 'ruins' to enhance the pleasurable aspect.

In 1755, a collection of his poems became a bestseller, and Shenstone could relax into the role of garden innovator. It wasn't until after his death, however, that *A Description of The Leasowes* was published by Robert Dodsley, and the landscape's fame spread far and wide, attracting salubrious visitors such as Benjamin Franklin, Thomas Jefferson and even John Wesley.

The arrival of the Dudley No. 2 canal in 1779 finally interrupted the scene, and from then on Shenstone's vision began to fade. The parklands came into municipal ownership in 1932, and the Ruined Priory survived until demolition in the 1960s, but it had to wait until 2008 for the centre piece, Virgil's Grove, to be restored with the aid of a Heritage Lottery Fund grant.

Today, The Leasowes is recognised as an important milestone in landscape design, with English Heritage listing and a management plan to ensure this important parkland is retained for future generations.

The Monarch's Way, which forms part of this walk, is a 625-mile (1,006km) long-distance footpath. It is based on the route that King Charles II took during his escape after defeat by Cromwell in the final battle of the Civil War at Worcester in 1651. For six weeks Parliamentary troops chased the King, who managed to flee to mainland Europe. The Way passes through Boscobel, Stratford upon Avon, the Cotswolds, Mendips and the South Coast from Charmouth to Shoreham.

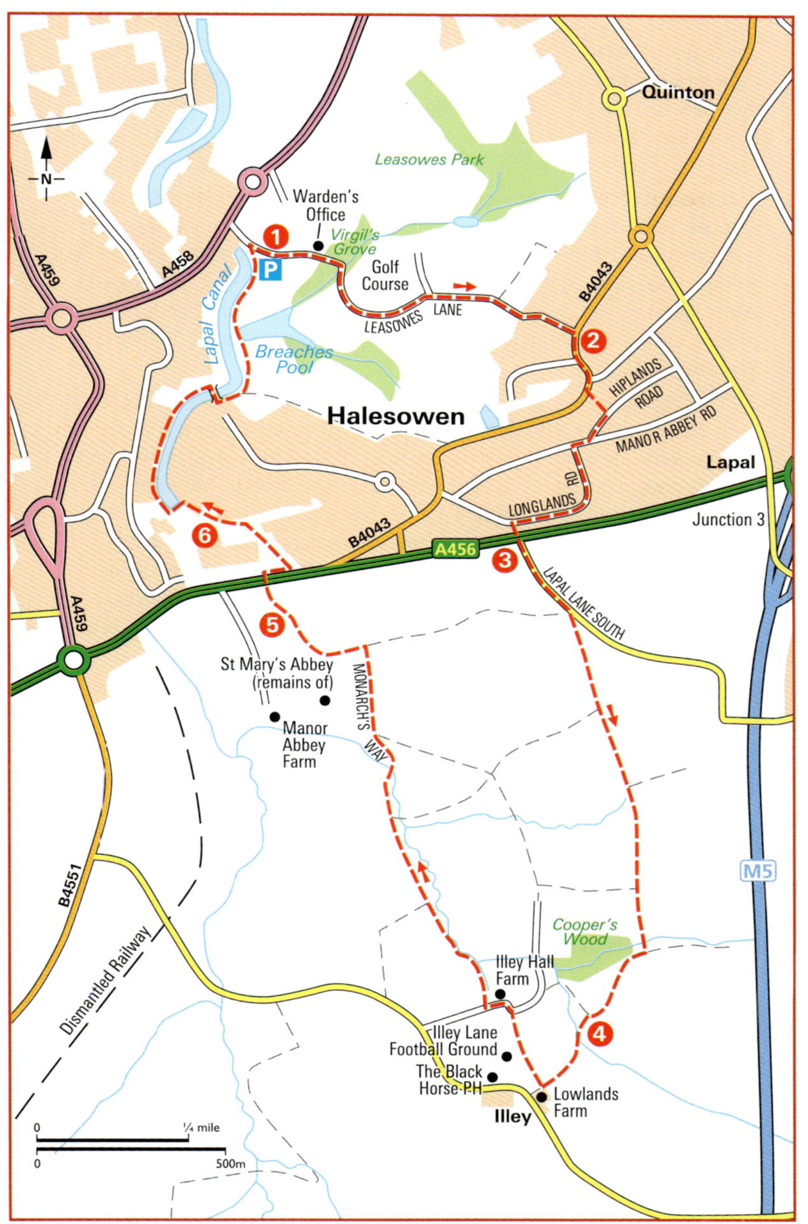

N
Quinton
Leasowes Park
A459
A458
Lapal Canal
Warden's Office
Virgil's Grove
Golf Course
P
1
Breaches Pool
LEASOWES LANE
B4043
2
Halesowen
HIPLANDS ROAD
MANOR ABBEY RD
Lapal
LONGLANDS RD
Junction 3
B4043
A456
3
6
LAPAL LANE SOUTH
A459
5
St Mary's Abbey (remains of)
MONARCH'S WAY
Manor Abbey Farm
M5
Cooper's Wood
B4551
Dismantled Railway
Illey Hall Farm
Illey Lane Football Ground
The Black Horse PH
Illey
4
Lowlands Farm
¼ mile
500m

1. Leave the car park at the north end by walking east past the Warden's base, uphill along a tarmac driveway. At the junction, near a couple of houses, bear right through a gateway and continue along the driveway past a small pool, then between the greens below Halesowen Golf Club clubhouse. Where the tarmac track arcs to the left near the clubhouse and through a gate, turn right. At the top of the hill the drive leads into Leasowes Lane and a residential area.

2. At the end of the lane go right along Manor Lane (B4043). After passing Stennels Avenue, the road bends right. Go left up a narrow public footpath to the right, just past Priory Road. Follow this fenced footpath into Hiplands Road; go right, then right again into Manor Abbey Road at the T-junction. In about 20yds (18m), go left down Longlands Road and continue as it bends right. After passing Lavina and Christopher roads, go left through a public footpath barrier to reach the A456.

3. Cross the busy road at the pedestrian crossing and proceed down Lapal Lane South opposite. After about 275yds (251m), go right over a stile and into open countryside. Follow the direction of the fingerpost signed to Illey, and take the path up along the left edge of a large field. Now go left over a second stile and bear right to the hedged path, heading southwards. Where another path joins from the left, the path becomes a track. At a junction of paths, continue ahead, then walk through trees to the left of Cooper's Wood. At the end of the wood, over a stile, go right. Cross over another stile, then bear quarter-left to a stile to cross pasture. Over a stile the path arcs right, and then left over another stile onto a track.

4. Follow this track and in about 100yds (91m) go right over a pair of stiles (if you walk to the end of the track you reach a road and will find The Black Horse pub on the corner opposite). Continue to the right of a field hedge with Illey Lane football ground on the other side. At the field corner, go left over a stile and walk around the bottom end of the football field, leaving via the football club gate onto the farm drive near Illey Hall Farm. Go left along the farm drive for 30yds (27m), then right over a stile and take the path to the left of the field hedge. Follow this path, soon merging with the Monarch's Way, over several fields and stiles, later crossing to the other side of the hedge via a stile where there is a stream to the right. The path arcs right to a bridge and becomes a farm track arcing left towards Manor Abbey Farm. Bear right as you approach the farm, picking out a field corner stile and continuing across a large field.

5. Cross the stile and go left, then bear right over a footbridge to a pair of stiles that take you back to the side of the A456. Go right for 25yds (23m), then over the road at the crossing. Go right again, then left to follow the tarmac footpath at a sign, 'Leasowes Park and Breaches Pool'.

6. This path passes along the back of residential properties. Continue ahead to the right of a chain-link fence and soon the path becomes the tow path of the Lapal Canal (formally known as the Dudley No. 2). The canal is covered with water plants, and there are houses up to the right. After about 400yds (366m), a bank crosses the canal, just before a former lock. Cross this and head along the tow path, now to the right of the canal (there is visible water here), with The Leasowes to your right. In 150yds (137m) stop to enjoy the fine view over Breaches Pool, then continue up the tow path and return to the car park.

Where to eat and drink

A local favourite with walkers is The Black Horse pub in Illey. The food is classic pub fare and there are usually some special offers. The Sunday roasts are also popular. Occasionally, there is a mobile fast-food van at the Leasowes car park, where you can get snacks.

What to look out for

Near the start of the walk, you pass one of the restored pools from William Shenstone's *ferme ornée* parkland. Take a detour left at this point and you will find more pools and waterfalls in Virgil's Grove, one of the features of the 18th-century walk around this magnificent landscape. The restoration works in 2008 followed Shenstone's plans as closely as possible to recreate the The Leasowes as contemporaries would have experienced it.

While you're there

Visit the remains of St Mary's Abbey. The abbey was founded in 1215 by monks of the Premonstratensian Order, who were granted the Manor of Hales by King John. In 1538, the abbey surrendered to the Crown. It was demolished and the land granted to Sir John Dudley by Henry VIII. Near by, earth mounds and breached dams mark the place where it is believed there was once a flight of five fish ponds, built by the monks to breed fish and supplement their diet.

WOODGATE VALLEY COUNTRY PARK

DISTANCE/TIME	3.5 miles (5.7km) / 1hr 30min
ASCENT/GRADIENT	49ft (15m) / ▲
PATHS	Grassy footpaths and tracks
LANDSCAPE	Country park
SUGGESTED MAP	OS Explorers 219 Wolverhampton & Dudley; 220 Birmingham
START/FINISH	Grid Reference: SO994829
DOG FRIENDLINESS	Off lead around park
PARKING	Woodgate Valley Country Park
PUBLIC TOILETS	Country Park Visitor Centre

Birmingham is surrounded by country parks and Woodgate Valley Country Park is one of these vital green spaces. This walk takes you past an urban farm complex and along the side of the babbling Bourn Brook, which runs the length of the valley to the River Rea at Cannon Hill Park.

The park comprises some 450 acres (182ha) of meadows, hedgerows and woodland on the western edge of Birmingham. It was originally a mixture of farms and smallholdings and every effort has been made to retain its rural appeal. Threatened by development, it was designated a Country Park in 1984. A programme of hedge and tree replanting has taken place, and the visitor centre opened in 1987.

The woodland, ponds and meadows have now become home to a vast range of wildlife and hundreds of species of plants and flowers. The meadowlands near the start of this walk, known as Pinewoods, are a treat to stroll through on a warm summer's day. Pheasants, kingfishers, cuckoos, chiffchaffs, whitethroats and willow warblers are regular visitors. When the plants are in flower, butterflies arrive during the summer. Look out especially for the red admiral and the small tortoiseshell.

Although it is close to so many urban roads, you can still enjoy peace and tranquillity away from the noise of traffic. Houses surround it, yet very few can be seen when you are walking the footpaths along the side of Bourn Brook.

Beneath the parkland are the remains of part of the Lapal Tunnel on the Dudley No. 2 Canal, which connected Halesowen with Selly Oak. It is one of the longest canal tunnels in England and a reminder that the industrial side of Birmingham is never too far away, even if you can't actually see it.

The canal was built in 1790 despite fierce local opposition as industrial expansion in the West Midlands was proceeding at a frightening pace. Measuring only 9ft (2.7m) wide and 9ft (2.7m) from water level to ceiling, it gradually fell into disuse with competition from the railways. Following mining subsidence in 1917, the tunnel was closed and finally sealed off in 1926.

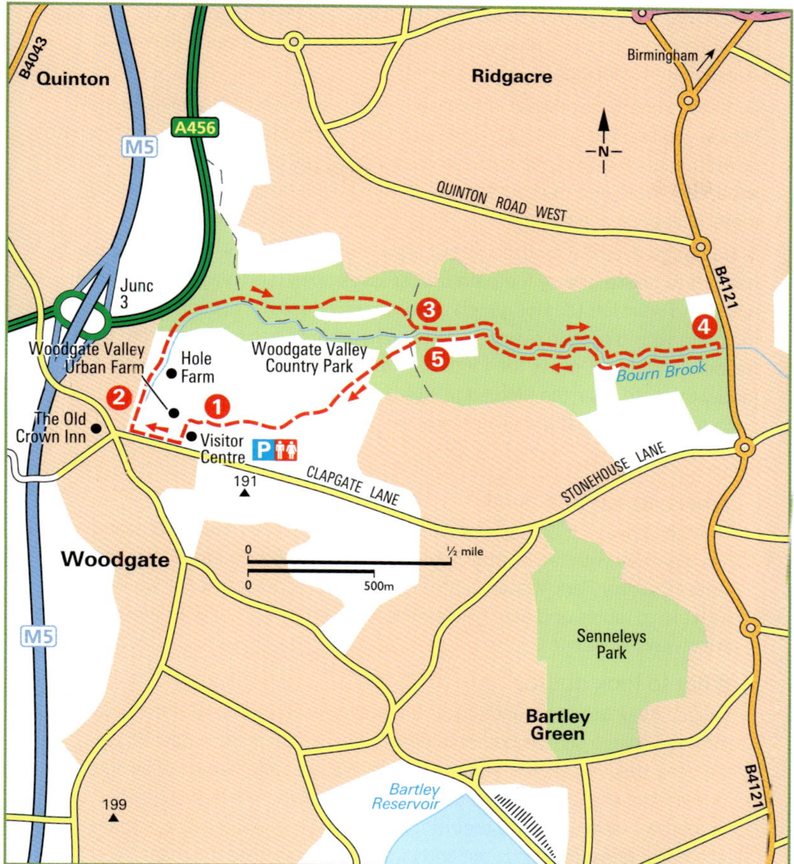

1. From the bottom of the visitor centre car park, head to the main road, and then right along the pavement, down the hill for 100yds (93m), bearing right at the roundabout. Turn right down Watery Lane, signposted to Bourn Brook, Harbourne and Selly Oak.

2. When you reach the farm access gate, bear left along the tarmac footpath by the side of a stream – the Bourn Brook – with the bridleway up to the left. This path arcs right, passing two footbridges over the brook. At the second footbridge, do not cross it but bear left past the large oak tree and a bench seat and walk along a footpath that arcs away from the stream towards an area of trees. In about 100yds (93m), bear right and in a few more paces right again, beyond a white-tipped marker post. The path dips back into the woods briefly before emerging in an open area. Follow the grassy path down the left-hand side of the clearing. At a junction of paths, by a bench, take the right-hand option, crossing the meadow.

3. Another footpath comes in from the left, and you then reach another junction of footpaths at which you continue ahead. Soon another path merges from the left and you bear right towards a rather high footbridge over the stream. Do not cross it; instead bear left and follow the footpath on the left side of Bourn Brook. This leads into the trees and there follows a very pleasant stroll through the park, always close to the bank of the stream (ignore a subsequent footbridge).

4. All too soon you will hear the noise of traffic on the B4121 ahead. Just before you reach the road, go right over the footbridge and follow the footpath down the other side of the stream. The path passes close to housing, but this is barely visible and the country feel is maintained until you reach the high footbridge once again.

5. Do not go over the footbridge, but leave the Bourn Brook behind and bear half left to take a grassy footpath that crosses open land diagonally with houses to your left (do not go left towards the houses). Through a tree belt maintain your direction over a second open area, diverging away from the houses. At the end, cross the footbridge in the far corner and bear right to follow the path near the field edge, firstly in woods, then passing by a football pitch to arrive back at the visitor centre.

Where to eat and drink
The Old Crown Inn on Carter's Lane is a traditional community pub and has a garden with tables and climbing frames for the children. Woodgate Valley Country Park Visitor Centre is a popular eating place for walkers, with picnic tables and benches in the park area where children and dogs are always welcome.

What to look out for
Despite its urban surroundings, there are several remnants of the old rural landscape still visible. Hole Farm's former farmhouse now houses the pony trekking centre, and the nearby Watery Lane was once a route for salt carriers, crossing the country from Lincolnshire to Wales. The hedgerows here can trace their origins to the 13th century. The ancient lane encountered towards the end of the walk was once the main thoroughfare in the area, and maybe over 500 years old.

While you're there
Visit the rare and unusual breeds of farm animals at the Woodgate Valley Urban Farm, who live alongside more familiar domestic breeds and pets. The farm is a registered charity, maintained by volunteers from the local community. If pony trekking is your scene, Hole Farm Pony Trekking Centre offers facilities for riders of all ages and abilities.

7

SANDWELL VALLEY COUNTRY PARK

DISTANCE/TIME	4.5 miles (7.2km) / 2hrs
ASCENT/GRADIENT	66ft (20m) / ▲
PATHS	Lakeside paths and tracks
LANDSCAPE	Country park with many lakes
SUGGESTED MAP	OS Explorer 220 Birmingham
START/FINISH	Grid Reference: SP035927
DOG FRIENDLINESS	Off lead in park
PARKING	RSPB Sandwell Valley Visitor Centre
PUBLIC TOILETS	None on route
NOTES	The car park and visitor centre at RSPB Sandwell Valley are closed on Mondays, but the nature reserve is open

Once upon a time there was a 12th-century Benedictine monastery on the site of an earlier hermitage in the area now called Sandwell Valley Country Park. The monastery was closed down in 1525 on the directions of Cardinal Wolsey, then in 1705 Sandwell Hall was erected on the site for the Earl of Dartmouth, incorporating some of the old priory buildings. The hall was demolished in 1928 with the development of Hamstead Colliery, which came to dominate the whole area. When the pit was nationalised in the 1940s, it was one of the largest in South Staffordshire, outside Cannock Chase, with nearly 1,000 men working underground here and at the nearby Sandwell Park Colliery.

The collieries closed in the early 1960s and the land has been transformed into an urban oasis, with the earthworks and spoil from the site became a series of artificial lakes. Sandwell Valley Country Park is now a fascinating area of lakes and 2,000 acres (810ha) of parkland developed from the old colliery sites and the remains of the Sandwell Hall Estate. The park has become a major leisure facility, with three golf courses, walking routes, a Millennium Cycle Route and two off-road cycle paths, which have been specially designed for mountain bikes.

Wildfowl flock to the area in large numbers and the Royal Society for the Protection of Birds (RSPB) has established a nature reserve nearby, which covers some 25 acres (10ha) of the reclaimed Hamstead Colliery site. The Sandwell Valley Sailing Club occupies the former pithead buildings.

Sandwell Park Farm was also part of the Earl of Dartmouth's estate and was extensively restored in 1981. It now forms part of the Sandwell Valley Country Park.

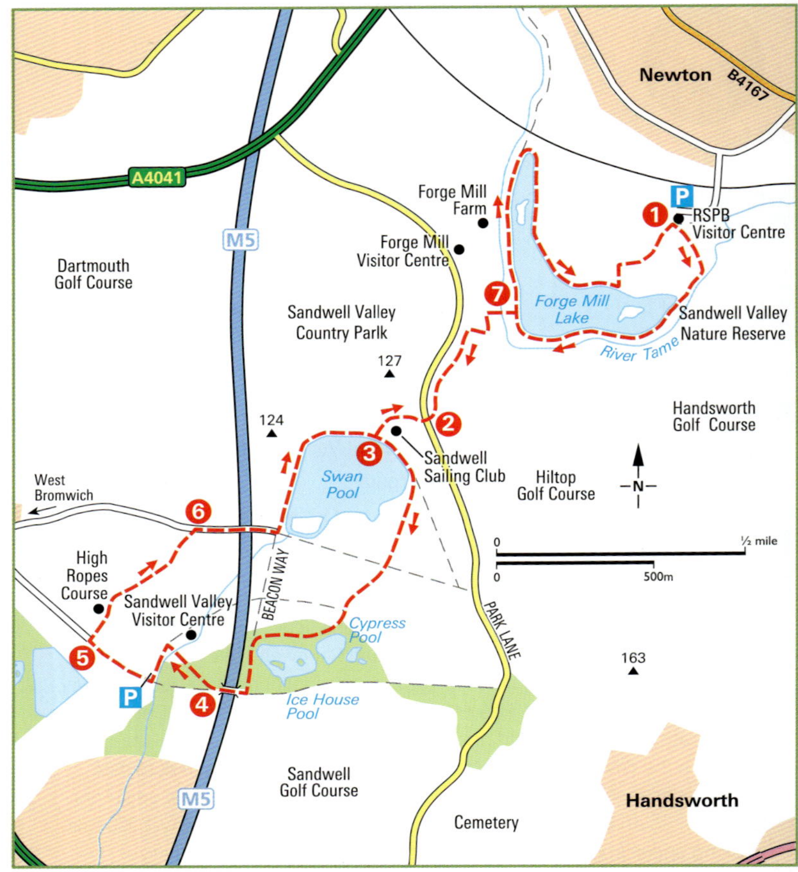

1. Leave the RSPB car park by going left of the visitor centre building onto a footpath. This leads down to a path along the dike crest between the River Tame and Forge Mill Lake. Continue along this footpath as it arcs gently right – look out for the many birds on the lake, as well as Canada geese and ducks on the river. As you work your way around the lake, you will come to a gateway where you go left over a bridge across the River Tame. Turn immediately left to continue on a tarmac path/cycleway that leads down to Forge Lane.

2. Cross the busy lane with great care, and walk to the right of the Sandwell Valley Sailing Club, then bear left until you come to the shore of Swan Pool.

3. Here, turn left and stroll around the side of the pool for 150yds (137m), then bear left again on a footpath, via a kissing gate that leads across meadowland away from the water's edge, initially alongside the pool's fence. Through a kissing gate, cross the track and continue ahead on a hedged footpath heading generally southwest. At a junction of paths, go left through a barrier and head on through the trees, then go right to follow the narrow path to the north bank of both Cypress and Ice House pools. Continue ahead to leave the lakes and emerge on a concrete lane by the side of the M5. Go left along this lane and at a junction, bear right and take the footbridge to cross over the M5.

4. Across the bridge go right down steps, now on the Beacon Way, and wind amid trees on the path up to Sandwell Valley Country Park car park.

5. Leave the car park and continue along the lane, turning right opposite a car park through a kissing gate. Walk ahead along the signed public footpath heading northeastwards within a belt of trees. You will see a high ropes course to the left. When you reach the end of the hedged area, bear left and proceed along a tarmac path towards the motorway, until you reach a junction.

6. Go right here along Salters Lane and return over the M5, via a footbridge. Take the tarmac path that goes to the left of Swan Pool and continue left past the sailing cub to busy Forge Lane. Cross the lane and take the footpath back to the bridge over the River Tame to reach the junction of footpaths by the edge of Forge Mill Lake.

7. Go left and walk around the lake, leaving the River Tame and going right just before the railway bridge. Keep close to the lake shore until turning left at a sign – this path takes you back to the RSPB visitor centre.

Where to eat and drink
Sandwell Valley Visitor Centre has a tea room and there's an outdoor picnic area. To quench your thirst, you could visit one of the many pubs in West Bromwich, 3 miles (4.8km) west.

What to look out for
The RSPB reserve in Sandwell Valley Country Park is an important home to a wide variety of birds and attracts around 150 species each year. Volunteers often staff the various viewing hides. Highlights in the reserve may include goosander and snipe in winter, lapwings and little ringed plover in spring and whitethroats through the summer. Look out too for a hobby, hunting for larger insects around the pool edges.

While you're there
Take the opportunity to travel into West Bromwich. It is the centre of the Metropolitan Borough of Sandwell and is an attractive town, with a fine modern centre. Situated in the old part of town is the superb timber framed Old Manor House, dating from the 13th century.

8 PARK LIME PITS AND WALSALL'S CANAL

DISTANCE/TIME	4.75 miles (7.7km) / 1hr 45min
ASCENT/GRADIENT	66ft (20m) / ▲
PATHS	Field paths and tow paths
LANDSCAPE	Canalside and urban parkland
SUGGESTED MAP	OS Explorer 220 Birmingham
START/FINISH	Grid Reference: SP041990
DOG FRIENDLINESS	Off lead along tow path, otherwise under control
PARKING	Hay Head Wood Nature Reserve car park
PUBLIC TOILETS	None on route

As you explore the history of the Black Country, it becomes clear that Walsall was very much at the hub of the Industrial Revolution in 19th-century Britain. Each large town in the area had its role to play, and limestone, used in the iron foundries and for cement production in the construction of canal buildings, was mined in the countryside around Walsall. The town also became England's centre for the manufacture of leather goods and fine saddlery – the nickname of the local football team is the Saddlers. Much of old Walsall has disappeared, but it has become a vibrant modern town, surrounded by numerous parks, which offer a link with its industrial past.

John Wilkinson, a pioneering 'ironmaster' opened up Hay Head Wood for limestone excavation in the 18th century. The rock was transported along two canals – the Wyrley and Essington, and the Rushall. The Wyrley and Essington was completed in 1797, with nine locks designed to lift the lime-laden barges some 65ft (20m) up to the Longwood Junction near Aldridge. This contour canal, affectionately known as the Curly Wyrley, follows the lie of the land and winds its way from Hay Head Park up to Lime Pits Farm and Park Lime Pits Local Nature Reserve, then on to the north of Birmingham.

From 1417 to the mid-19th century, limestone was burnt at Park Lime Pits and was dispatched across Britain via the Rushall Canal and the wider canal system. Following the demise of the lime industry, the pits were closed in 1865 and planted with trees. The pits have been flooded and today the area is a haven for wildlife. More than 100 bird species have been recorded here, including moorhens and grebes at the pools, while bullfinches and buntings inhabit the stubble fields, which are specially managed to encourage wildlife.

Whilst walking up around the Park Lime Pits Local Nature Reserve, keep an eye out for views of Rushall Hall and St Michael's Church. The hall was mentioned as the Manor in the Domesday Book but was dismantled after the Civil War. It was rebuilt in 1846. St Michael's Church was built in 1856 and its fine spire was added in 1867.

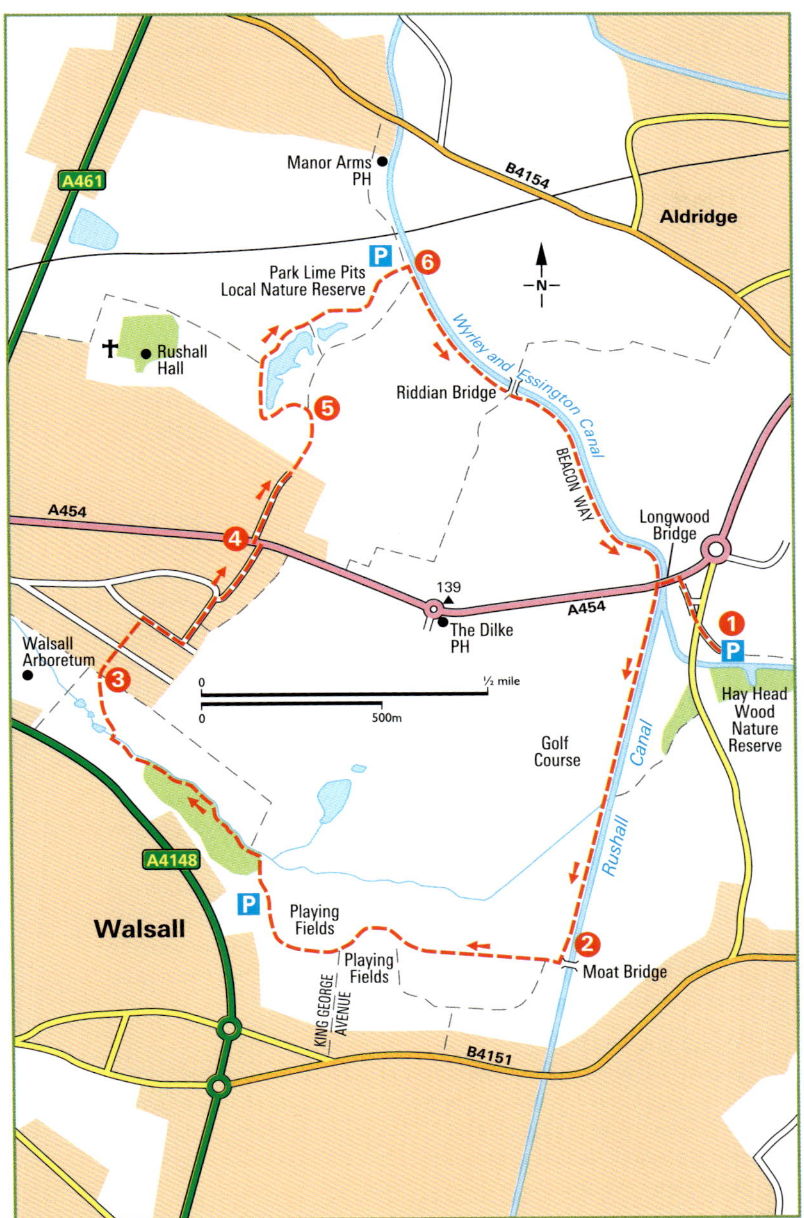

1. From the car park proceed over Longwood Lane, now on the Beacon Way, through a lay-by and on to the Longwood Bridge. Cross it to descend left to the tow path of the Rushall Canal. Go right (southwest) and walk past the canal junction, now off the Beacon Way, along the side of the very straight part of the canal.

2. After 1,100yds (1km) you will come to Moat Bridge (do not cross). Turn right and continue along a well-defined track through trees and between playing fields. The path arcs left to the end of King George Avenue. Keep ahead past another cricket pitch before swinging right to a municipal depot and parking area. Cross the car park, heading for an exit on the opposite side by a dog waste bin. Join a tarmac path, keeping to the left side of a stream. After about 700yds (640m), turn right over a stone footbridge, and then left along the right-hand side of a children's play area up to reach a tarmac footway.

3. Head right up the footway to leave the park area between the houses. Cross over Buchanan Road and continue up the footpath until you reach Argyle Road. Turn right and follow the road as it arcs round to the left. Now turn right on Fernleigh Road and follow this to the main A454.

4. Turn left then go immediately right up Mellish Drive. Walk to the end of Mellish Drive, cross Stencills Road to a kissing gate. Continue into open countryside on the footpath. When you reach a waymarked junction of footpaths, bear left through the fence gap into the trees of Park Lime Pits Local Nature Reserve .

5. Follow the footpath to the main pool where you go left up steps to follow the path along the pool edge. At the far end of the pool descend steps and bear left up further steps to progress into the open, looking southwest to see Rushall Hall and St Michael's Church. Take the left fork and continue northeastwards alongside a hedge until you reach Lime Pits car park via a kissing gate by the side of the Wyrley and Essington Canal.

6. At the canal, turn right and walk along the tow path, joining up with Beacon Way. In about 0.5 miles (800m) you come to Longwood Bridge. Walk under the bridge and exit with the Beacon Way signs to the A454. Cross the canal and bear right to return to the car park at the nature reserve.

Where to eat and drink

The Manor Arms, near Park Lime Pits Country Park, is a canalside pub serving food and real ale. It is unusual that it has no bar counter, with beer taps and glasses set against the rear wall. Alternatively, you could try The Dilke along the A454 (Aldridge Road) or one of the many pubs, restaurants and eateries in Walsall itself.

While you're there

The Walsall Arboretum, off the corner of Lichfield Street and Broadway North, was formed in 1874 by the Walsall Arboretum and Lake Company. They rented 7 acres (2.8ha) of land from the landowners, Lord Hatherton and Sir George Mellish, to provide a facility for croquet, archery and quoits, with two lakes for angling and boating.

SAREHOLE MILL AND THE RIVER COLE

DISTANCE/TIME	3.25 miles (5.2km) / 1hr 30min
ASCENT/GRADIENT	Negligible
PATHS	Parks, woodland, riverbank, pavements
LANDSCAPE	Rural enclaves and urban
SUGGESTED MAP	OS Explorer 220 Birmingham
START/FINISH	Grid Reference: SP098817
DOG FRIENDLINESS	Under control near busy roads
PARKING	Sarehole Mill car park, next to Sarehole Mill, on B4146
PUBLIC TOILETS	None on route

John Ronald Reul Tolkien was born in South Africa in 1892 to British parents. Following his father's death as a result of rheumatic fever, young Tolkien and his mother and brother settled in the Worcestershire hamlet of Sarehole, then outside Birmingham. The area was very different in those days – a good deal more rural and remote. 'It was a kind of lost paradise,' Tolkien told a Guardian journalist in an interview in 1966. 'There was an old mill that really did grind corn with two millers, a great big pond with swans on it, a sandpit, a wonderful dell with flowers, a few old-fashioned village houses and further away a stream with another mill...'

While at Sarehole, Tolkien's imagination was fuelled by the nearby watermill and its complex machinery. This local landmark later became the model for the mill at Hobbiton in *The Lord of the Rings*. Tolkien found himself fascinated by the miller and his son, who could often be seen covered in bone dust. He described them as 'characters of wonder and terror to a small child.' John Morris Jones, a local historian and contemporary of Tolkien, described Sarehole in the author's day as a place where you would hear the occasional blast of a poacher's shotgun: 'There are game-birds, rabbits and hares in plenty. The [River] Cole is clear and well-stocked with fish, as are the millponds. The air is fresh, for the westerly wind blows away the smoke from the reeking town four miles away in the next county.'

Tolkien returned to Sarehole in the 1930s and found the place much changed. The countryside where he had played contentedly as a child was disappearing under concrete and Sarehole was no longer the sleepy rural settlement he remembered. It may have altered beyond recognition but even today there are surviving pockets of trickling streams and leafy paths that give the impression in places that you could be deep in the countryside.

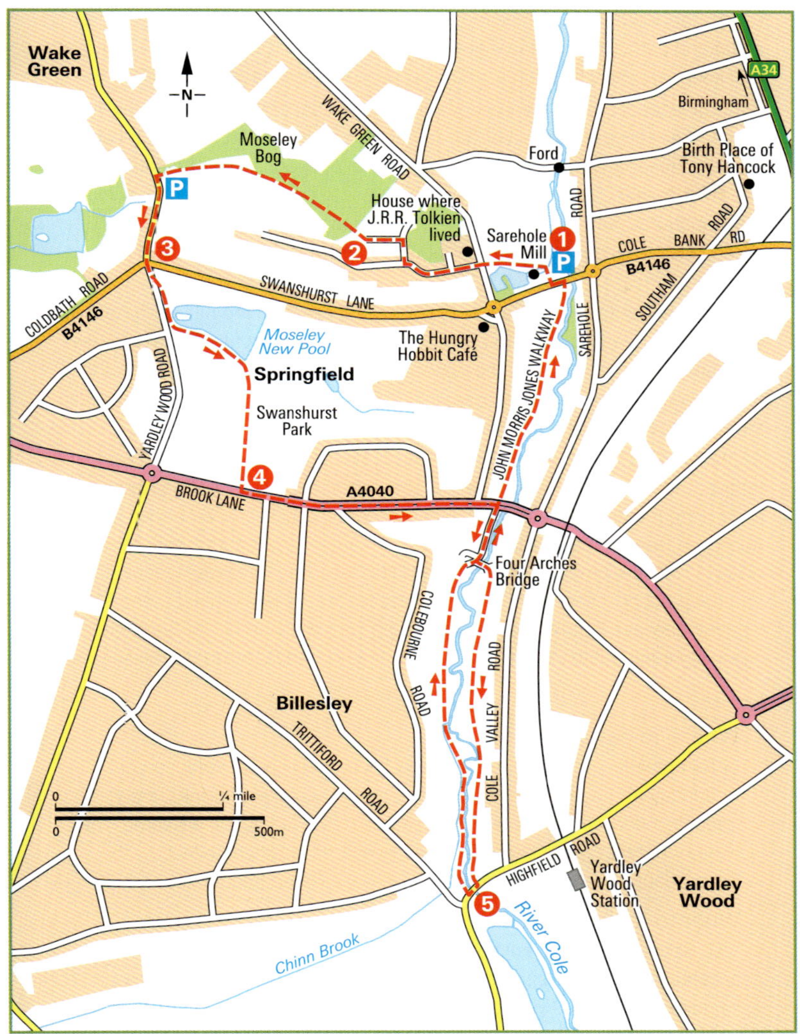

1. With your back to the road, cross the car park, bearing left to a footbridge. Keep left in the field, passing Sarehole Mill and its distinctive chimney. Pass a pond, part of the mill, on the left and make for a gate ahead leading out to Wake Green Road. Number 264, the house where Tolkien lived, is diagonally right. It is privately owned and not open to the public. Cross over into Thirlmere Drive and follow the road to Pensby Close. Pass several lock-up garages and turn left just before some flats.

2. Bear right at a line of bungalows and follow the path into woodland. Ascend a short flight of steps, then down ten steps to turn right over a footbridge. This is Moseley Bog, one of Tolkien's childhood haunts. Turn immediately left and follow the boardwalk through the wood, keeping to the main path. When it divides, take either route as they rejoin shortly. At the next fork, by a footbridge, keep left. Climb some steps, turn right at the top and follow the woodland path. On reaching a grassy clearing, cross it to another obvious path and keep left. Pass through a small car park to the road and turn left.

3. At the island, cross Swanshurst Lane and continue briefly on Yardley Wood Road. After 100yds (91m), veer left to follow a path parallel to the road and keep Moseley New Pool on your left. Skirt the pool and when the path bends left at its corner, bear right between the trees to reach the vast grassy expanse of Swanshurst Park. Follow the obvious path, with the tower of a local fire station visible close by on the right. Draw level with the building and at the road turn left.

4. Follow Brook Lane, pass a row of shops and descend the hill. Turn right into Coleside Avenue and cross the River Cole at the Four Arches Bridge. Follow the path as it bears right on the opposite side, keep the river on your right and eventually reach the next road (Highfield Road). The walk turns right for several paces, crossing the Cole.

5. Once over, turn right to follow the riverside path. At one point, the walk follows the path between a stream on the left and the river on the right. Cross a concrete footbridge, keep right with both watercourses now on the right. Approach the next bridge. Do not cross it; instead turn left and walk beside the water. Cross the next bridge, keep right and return to Coleside Avenue. Follow it to the junction, cross over with care and follow the path ahead (John Morris Jones Walkway). Follow the riverbank path with the chimney of Sarehole Mill gradually edging into view. Cross over at the lights and return to the car park.

Where to eat and drink

At Sarehole Mill Museum, Pizza in the Courtyard is open Wednesday to Sunday for lunch. As well as pizzas, there's a range of drinks, ice creams and sweet treats. Well behaved dogs, on leads, are welcome. The Hungry Hobbit Café is several minutes' walk from Sarehole Mill, by the roundabout where Cole Bank Road and Wake Green Road meet.

What to look out for

Visit Sarehole Mill Museum to see the operational machinery and bakehouse that have been carefully restored to working order. Entry is by guided tour only, Friday to Sunday. The mill also plays host to several special events and tours, including Middle-earth themed days.

While you're there

From Sarehole Mill turn left and walk along Cole Bank Road, then left into Southam Road. On the right is No. 41, where the comedian Tony Hancock was born in May 1924. The plaque outside the family home describes him as a 'comedian of genius.' There is a statue of Hancock, who died in Australia in 1968, in Birmingham city centre.

10

BIRMINGHAM'S JEWELLERY QUARTER

DISTANCE/TIME	4 miles (6.4km) / 1hr 45min
ASCENT/GRADIENT	16ft (5m) / ▲
PATHS	Tow paths and pavements
LANDSCAPE	City centre buildings, factories and canals
SUGGESTED MAP	OS Explorer 220 Birmingham
START/FINISH	Grid Reference: SP064877
DOG FRIENDLINESS	On lead at all times, beware of any construction work in the town centre
PARKING	Northwood Street pay-and-display car park
PUBLIC TOILETS	At entrance to Jewellery Quarter car park on Vyse Street

Birmingham's growth in the Industrial Revolution was vast and overwhelming. The quiet country town of the 16th century had been subsumed by one of the world's first manufacturing cities by the middle of the 18th century, though it wasn't until 1889 that Queen Victoria recognised its city status with a royal charter.

Foremost amongst those who created this industrial powerhouse was Matthew Boulton (1728–1809), whose partnership with Scottish engineer James Watt (1736–1819) developed a pioneering steam engine. Boulton was first and foremost a manufacturer, with a speciality in buttons and buckles. From his huge Soho Manufactory on the north side of the town he expanded into coins, silver plate and other items.

Boulton's enterprise was hampered by its distance from the nearest Assay Office in Chester, which tested and hallmarked precious metals items. Goods were lost, damaged, copied or stolen on the journey between Birmingham and Cheshire. Teaming up with the cutlers of Sheffield, Boulton petitioned for new local offices. When Sheffield and Birmingham received their new Assay Offices by an Act of Parliament in 1773, their new hallmarks were a crown (for Sheffield, it later became a rose), and an anchor (for Birmingham).

Today, Birmingham's Assay Office is one of the busiest in the world, handling over 12 million items every year. More than 400 jewellery businesses work in the area north of the city centre, which is still known as the Jewellery Quarter. Its buildings, canals and churches reflect the fortunes of the city as a whole, with wealth, decline and regeneration a continuous theme.

This walk also takes in some of the newer parts of the city centre, with the new library an outstanding feature, alongside Brindley Place and the 1980s Gas Street Basin. The canalside paths take you swiftly and quietly from bustling street to bustling street, in a way that seems unique to Birmingham.

1. From the car park, walk down Northwood Street and go left into Caroline Street. At the end of the street, continue ahead into the churchyard of St Paul's Church, known as the Jeweller's Church, then walk up Ludgate Hill. Proceed over the Birmingham and Fazeley Canal and cross the footbridge over Great Charles Street Queensway. Continue up Church Street and into Colmore Row to see the impressive Birmingham Cathedral (St Philip's).

2. With your back to the cathedral, turn left and walk along Colmore Row into Victoria Square, passing by the Museum and Art Gallery, Town Hall and Council House. Bear right into Paradise Forum, then cross the walkway into Centenary Square to pass the Hall of Memory war memorial, the Library of Birmingham and The Rep Theatre. Bear left, across Broad Street, beware of the trams, into Bridge Street. Go right in 100yds (91m) just after the Hyatt Hotel to descend to the Worcester and Birmingham Canal, and the Gas Street Basin. Go left past The Canal House, and cross the canal, via a mooring pontoon and a footbridge, before going right along the tow path past The Tap and Spile pub and beneath Broad Street to Water's Edge, then you'll pass the National Sea Life Centre in Brindley Place.

3. Continue ahead over a footbridge and beneath a footbridge numbered 68, along the tow path beneath Sheepcote Street Bridge to St Vincent Bridge. Cross it and cescend to the tow path on the other side of the Birmingham Main Line Canal, heading back towards the city centre.

4. Bear left at the Old Turn Junction and walk along the tow path on the left-hand bank of the Birmingham and Fazeley Canal, passing the National Indoor Arena and beneath Tindal Bridge – ahead is the BT Tower. Descend past a flight of eight canal locks and, just before the ninth lock, go left through a gap in the wall and up steps, signed 'Jewellery Quarter', into Newhall Street.

5. Go left along Newhall Street, which becomes Graham Street, then right along Frederick Street past the Argent Centre to see the Jewellery Quarter Chamberlain clock tower. Turn left into Warstone Lane, then just after passing the gateway to the Warstone Lane Cemetery go right up a pathway into the cemetery, past the catacombs, to Pitsford Street.

6. Turn right towards Vyse Street, then left to the main Jewellery Quarter. Continue right into Hockley Street and then go to the right of The Jewellers Arms pub down Spencer Street. Bear right into Caroline Street, then go left to return along Northwood Street to the car park.

Where to eat and drink

There are numerous eating places around Brindley Place and the Gas Street Basin. In the Jewellery Quarter, the Jeweller's Arms is a real ale pub or seek out the Hylton Café in Hylton Street for no-nonsense traditional British café food served with panache.

What to look out for

Narrowboats line up along the wharves that extend from the Gas Street Basin. Boats stop here from all over the English canal network. Now mostly leisure craft, some of the more exotic looking ones are residential. If you have the chance, why not help a boat's passage through the nine locks on the Birmingham and Fazeley Canal. It can take over an hour to travel the few hundred yards from one end of the flight to the other.

While you're there

There are many distractions on this route, including the National Sea Life Centre at Water's Edge, Brindley Place. It has more than 60 displays, including an Otter Sanctuary and Kingdom of the Seahorses. You can also take a boat trip around the canals on one of several waterbus tours that cruise around the inner-city canal network. Ozzy the mechanical bull, created for the Birmingham 2022 Commonwealth Games, is in residence at New Street station. He was named by public vote – after Black Sabbath frontman and local hero, Ozzy Osbourne.

11

A LOOP FROM STUDLEY PRIORY

DISTANCE/TIME	5 miles (8km) / 2hrs 15min
ASCENT/GRADIENT	49ft (15m) / ▲
PATHS	Field paths and parkland
LANDSCAPE	Gentle rolling countryside
SUGGESTED MAP	OS Explorer 220 Birmingham
START/FINISH	Grid Reference: SP071637
DOG FRIENDLINESS	Under control at all times
PARKING	Pool Road car park in Studley
PUBLIC TOILETS	Bottom of High Street in Studley

Although mentioned in the Doomsday Book, very little of ancient Studley remains. The village is built on the old Roman Ryknild Street, which became the main turnpike into Birmingham in 1721. The River Arrow still meanders gently through pastureland below the residential areas.

The mill, a castle, manor house and church are the only old buildings to survive. Washford Mill has become a public house. The present extraordinary neo-Norman and neo-Gothic Studley Castle was actually built in 1834 as the home of the Goodricke family, and is now a prestigious hotel. Of its 13th-century predecessor nothing remains. The manor house, which is now called Mountbatten House, used to be the headquarters of the Royal Life Saving Society before it moved down the road to Broom, near Alcester. The 700-year-old Church of the Nativity of the Blessed Virgin Mary, on the other side of the river away from the village, features a Norman door, an old rood, some ancient stairs and a stone coffin lid displaying a superb cross. A fascinating brass relates the story of a commendable 17th-century local man who left money for 48 penny loaves for the poor to be distributed every Sunday.

Needle-making became the main occupation in Studley from the early 17th century, when Elizabeth I allowed a group of Hugenot refugees from France to settle in the area. They brought with them the craft of precision-making needles, which had been developed by Continental manufacturers in the late medieval period. Their expertise helped the local industry develop and soon Studley was one of the largest producers of needles in Britain and known worldwide. From the mid-19th century, surgical needles were greatly in demand. By the end of the 19th century, industrial techniques had taken over and there were more than 3,000 workers involved in the needle-making business. Since then, the industry has declined, though there is still the need for precision needles and they continue to be made in some of the local factories. It is this industry we must thank for Studley having more public houses than most villages – to supply refreshment to the factory workers.

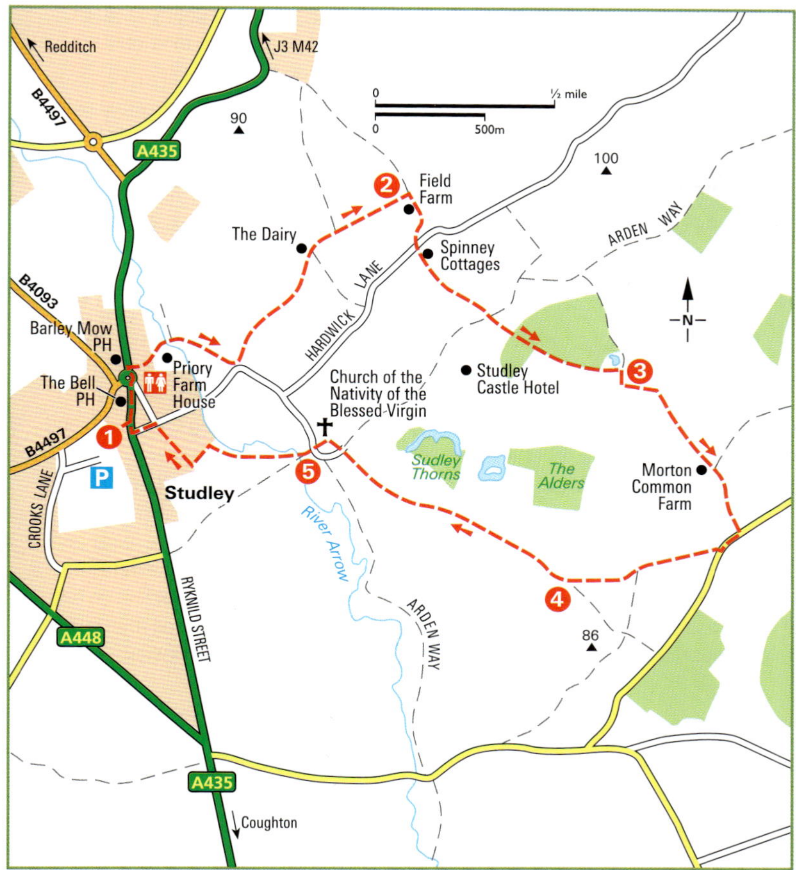

1. From the Pool Road car park, walk down the footpath beside the Studley Community Infants School and continue ahead down Needle Close to the Alcester road (the A435), then go left to the roundabout. Cross over the road and go down the drive to the left of the toilets to Priory Court Farm House, then via a kissing gate on a footpath to the left of houses. Cross the footbridge over the River Arrow. Go through a kissing gate and bear right to another into a large field, aiming towards a third kissing gate at the corner of the field opposite. Don't go through it but head left to cross the pasture diagonally, aiming to the left of a field gate in the hedge to a waymarker, then go right alongside the hedge for about 0.5 miles (800m).

2. Through a kissing gate and then a hand gate, go right between the buildings of Field Farm and walk along the farm drive. In about 100yds (91m), go right through a gate crossing the corner of the field onto Hardwick Lane via a kissing gate. Cross the lane and, through a gate, walk between Spinney Cottages, then through a kissing gate. Continue ahead over parkland until you come to a driveway near some glasshouses, reaching it via three hand gates. Cross the driveway, go through a gate and walk to the right of a cottage to enter the wood via two gates. Follow the footpath through the trees and

through another gate, then continue ahead by the field edge until you reach the end of the woodland. Join a farm track, passing a pond on the right.

3. Drawing level with a pond on the left, go right on a track and after 90 paces, go left across the field. Through the hedge gap, cross the next cultivated field diagonally to a footbridge. Go through a gate, continue alongside a wire fence to a gate, then alongside a hedge, to pass to the left of Morton Common Farm. Reaching the farm drive, follow it to a road. Go right along the road for about 150yds (137m), then right again over a footbridge and go half left through a wood. At the farm gate, bear right and walk alongside the stream until you reach a farm track.

4. Through a field gate continue right along the track. In about 0.5 miles (800m), it arcs right; turn left here by an old oak to cross the middle of the field, then continue along a hedge path towards Studley's Church of the Nativity of the Blessed Virgin Mary. Go through the overflow graveyard via two gates, and enter the main churchyard via another, passing the church and leaving via the gate with the lamp over it onto a lane.

5. Go briefly left, and cross the lane to go through a kissing gate. Descend through pastureland, cross the footbridge over the River Arrow, then bear right and walk along the river bank towards Studley. A kissing gate leads into the end of Wickham Road. Head left along the side of the housing estate and bear right into Gunners Lane. Continue ahead, and after a path section go left up Castle Road to the Alcester road. Cross and go briefly right and then left to ascend Needle Close, to return to the car park at the start of the walk.

Where to eat and drink

The 400-year-old Barley Mow is a very popular eating place with walkers and local people, and children are welcome if with an adult.

What to look out for

The humps in the field across the lane from Studley's church were probably the sites of the simple houses of the original village. The priory, founded in the 12th century, has long gone, and all that remains is the house called Priory Farm House, opposite The Barley Mow.

While you're there

Spare time to visit the Church of the Nativity of the Blessed Virgin Mary in Studley, which still has some of its original Norman features, such as the north wall – a fine example of herringbone masonry. It's an unusually long way out of the village, but it wasn't always this isolated. There was once a village surrounding the church, but from the Middle Ages onwards it gradually moved closer to the old Ryknild Street. Various reasons have been offered – perhaps plague wiped out the occupants of the old site, maybe it flooded too much, or a combination of these factors, along with better trading opportunities offered by proximity to the main road.

THE ROMAN TOWN OF ALCESTER

DISTANCE/TIME	5.5 miles (8.8km) / 2hrs 15min
ASCENT/GRADIENT	269ft (82m) / ▲ ▲
PATHS	Pavements, field paths, woodland tracks and farm lanes, several stiles
LANDSCAPE	Gentle rolling farmland, woodland and rural town
SUGGESTED MAP	OS Explorer 205 Stratford-upon-Avon & Evesham
START/FINISH	Grid Reference: SP088572
DOG FRIENDLINESS	Under control at all times
PARKING	Bleachfield Street car park
PUBLIC TOILETS	Bulls Head Yard car park

Alcester is one of the most delightful towns in Warwickshire. This former Roman settlement has sadly lost its ancient abbey, but the abbot's splendid ivory crozier, similar to a sheperd's crook, was discovered in the rectory garden and is now displayed in the British Museum. From time to time, new Roman relics also come to light, such as the Roman milestone commemorating the Emperor Constantine (AD 306–337), which was excavated in the town in 1966. The Romano-British town, which flourished between the 2nd and 4th centuries, is now completely covered by the modern town.

Following the turnpiking of the Stratford to Alcester road in 1753, Alcester became a busy stopping point on the main stagecoach route linking London and Holyhead via Shrewsbury. Few of the town's old coaching inns survived the developments of the 1960s, but the Bear Hotel is a reminder of those days. Horse-drawn coaches gave way to trains, but today Alcester's old station, now a private home, is all that remains in the age of the car.

The town centre is now bypassed and so Alcester has had space to breathe. A regular in the Britain in Bloom competition, the town's residents adorn its streets each year with beautiful flowers. The great tower of St Nicholas dominates the centre, with its clock face set at an angle on the corner of its tower. The Market Hall was originally built in 1618, when it was simply a pillared edifice, but a timber-framed upper storey was added in 1641. In 1874, the arches were filled in and today it is occupied by the Town Hall.

The walk takes you through the old part of Alcester and down Malt Mill Lane into Oversley Green. Beautiful Oversley Wood is a remnant of the original Forest of Arden, and if you walk through here in spring you will be greeted by a carpet of bluebells and may even spot a shy muntjac deer. The route also goes close to the delightful villages of Exhall and Wixford, with their black-and-white buildings, then returns over Primrose Hill, which rises 250ft (77m) above the Arrow Valley, offering a fine view of Ragley Hall to the left. Once over the busy A46, you will pass several beautiful thatched cottages as you walk down Primrose Lane on the way back into Oversley Green.

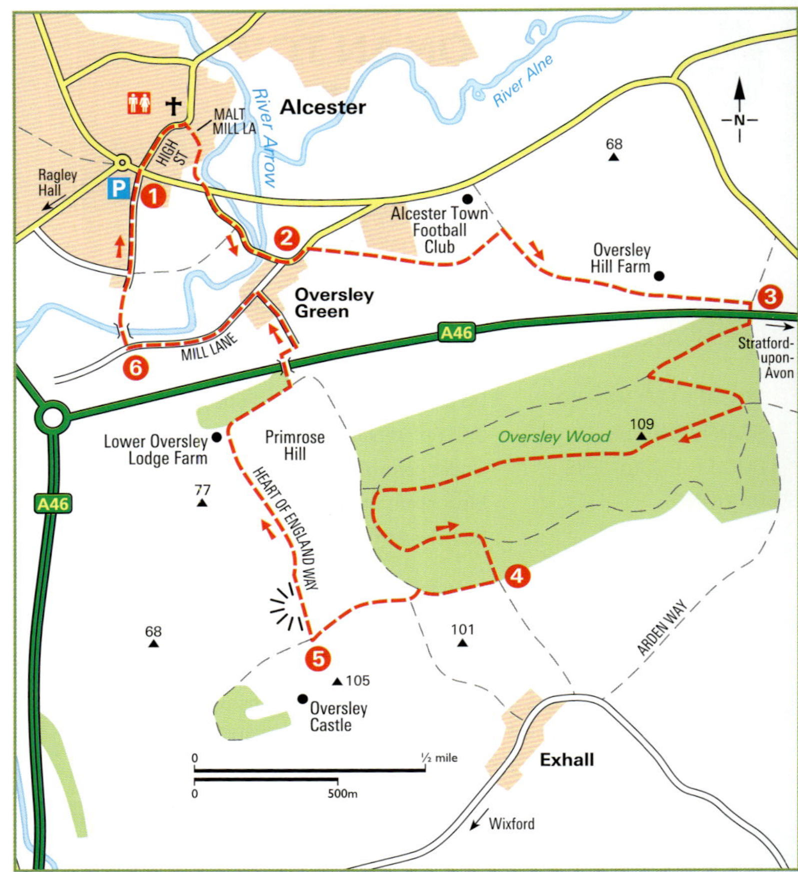

1. From the car park, enter Bleachfield Street and turn left onto Stratford Road. Cross the road and wander up High Street. Bear right past impressive St Nicholas Church and, at the corner of the road, turn right down Malt Mill Lane. At the bottom of the lane, go left through the public gardens and follow the tarmac footpath by the side of the River Arrow to reach the Stratford Road again. Cross the road and go down the lane opposite into Oversley Green village, crossing the bridge over the River Arrow.

2. Keep left through the village on Stratford Road, and 80yds (73m) after passing a road to the right, go right through a gate along a hedged footpath behind a row of houses. Cross a field via two kissing gates and walk past a football field, to reach a kissing gate at a junction of paths. Do not go through it but go right here along the field edge, then through a field gate and across pastureland to join a track. Follow this through a kissing gate below Oversley Hill Farm to reach a Severn Trent substation.

3. Continue ahead across a stile and through a gate to go right, under the A46 road bridge, and bear right through the gateway into Oversley Wood. Take the metalled track into the wood for about 400yds (366m), then go left. In a further 400yds (366m), the metalled track arcs right. In 50yds (46m), at

a path crossroads, go right on a grass path steeply uphill and continue westwards over the crest of the hill. Descend past a viewpoint bench back to the main metalled track. Now go left for 650yds (594m), then right at a bench onto a wide path to leave the wood over a stile.

4. Go right through dense vegetation and walk along the edge of Oversley Wood to its corner. Continue ahead along the hedged track until you reach a farm lane, with Oversley Castle on the hillock to the left.

5. Go right along the lane and join the Heart of England Way. Walk up the lane towards some large grain silos by the side of Lower Oversley Lodge Farm. From the farm complex, go right along the concrete lane and left through a gate down to the footbridge over the busy A46. Cross, turn right then left and walk down Primrose Lane. At the T-junction, go left along Mill Lane for about 650yds (594m).

6. After passing a fourth park home, go right down a path and cross a footbridge over the River Arrow. Continuing ahead, the path becomes a lane by houses, with allotments to the right. Walk up Bleachfield Street back to the car park.

Where to eat and drink

Alcester has a number of pus and eating places. The Royal Oak and the Bear Hotel are both on the High Street and date back to the 18th century, serving food and real ales. There are also several cafés and restaurants in the town centre.

What to look out for

The lovely Church of St Milburga, on the edge of Wixford village, is tucked away up a high banked lane and is almost hidden from view by the oldest yew tree in Warwickshire. Look for the 1411 Crewe brass, which lies on top of a tomb in the south chapel. The tomb shows Thomas Crewe, who looked after the affairs of the Countess of Warwick, wearing armour.

While you're there

Take the opportunity to visit Ragley Hall, along the Evesham Road, set in 400 acres (165ha) of parkland. The home of the Marquess and Marchioness of Hertford, it was designed by Robert Hooke in 1680, and is one of the earliest and most handsome of England's great Palladian houses. The magnificent great hall contains some outstanding baroque plasterwork by James Gibbs and a large mural up the stairway. The stables house a carriage collection, and 'Capability' Brown designed the gardens. There is also an adventure playground for children.

BIDFORD-ON-AVON AND THE RIVER AVON

DISTANCE/TIME	7 miles (11.3km) / 3hrs
ASCENT/GRADIENT	190ft (58m) / ▲▲
PATHS	Field paths, farm tracks and country lanes
LANDSCAPE	Riverside and rolling countryside
SUGGESTED MAP	OS Explorer 205 Stratford-upon-Avon & Evesham
START/FINISH	Grid Reference: SP098518
DOG FRIENDLINESS	On lead at all times
PARKING	Car park southeast of roundabout in Bidford-on-Avon
PUBLIC TOILETS	At recreation ground

William Shakespeare (1564–1616) is believed to have been a regular visitor to Bidford-on-Avon. The old 13th-century Falcon Inn, which stood opposite the church, was one of his favourite taverns. He reputedly got drunk at the inn and slept it off under a crab apple tree on his way back to his home in Stratford-upon-Avon. He recounts his drinking exploits in the local villages in a rhyme that finishes '…Papish Wicksford, Beggarly Broom and Drunken Bidford'. Sadly, the old inn fell into disrepair and was subsequently renovated and turned into flats some years ago. The crab apple tree has long disappeared.

Bidford can trace its origins back to Saxon times when it was called Byda's Ford, though Roman legions had earlier tramped the area. The ford would have been on their great Ryknild Street. As you stroll back along the river bank into Bidford-on-Avon, you'll enjoy a superb view of St Laurence's Church and the mainly 15th-century Bidford Bridge. Lean on its parapet and watch the placid waters of the Avon flow by the willow beds below – this is Shakespeare country at its very best.

The fine 13th-century Church of St Laurence stands above the River Avon. Its first incumbent was Rogenus Capellanno in 1260, and inside you can see a beautiful church plate that was presented to the church in 1660 by Duchess Dudley. You can climb the tower that rises above a small avenue of lime trees. From the top, there are exceptional views of the town's beautiful eight-arched bridge and the Avon, with the Cotswold Hills forming a scenic backdrop.

This walk takes you along the River Avon, passing a lovely weir at Barton where The Cottage of Content pub is a famous watering hole for walkers. You may wish to continue into Welford-on-Avon to see the timbered black-and-white thatched cottages that line its streets. Your return is along the Heart of England Way.

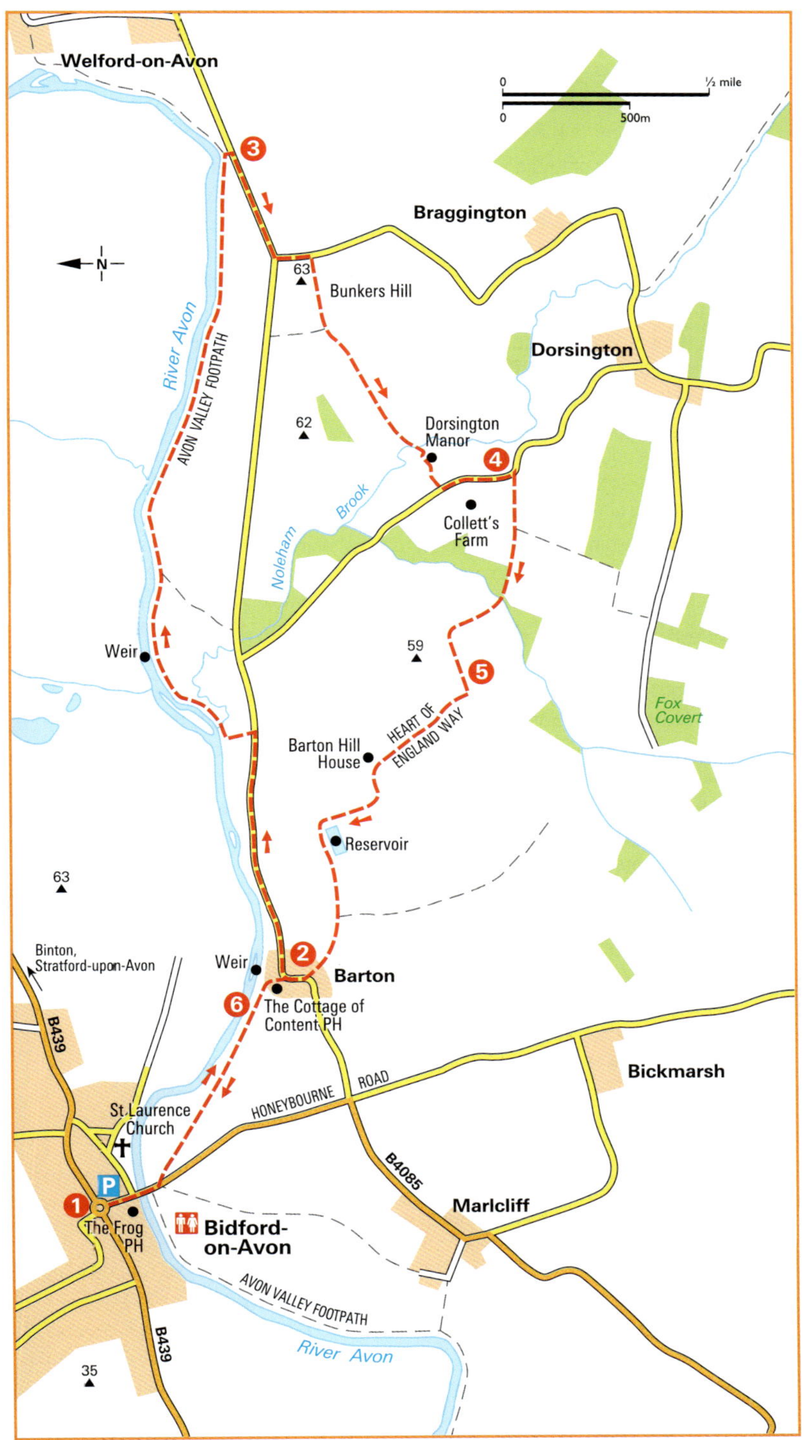

Welford-on-Avon
3
Braggington
½ mile
500m
63
Bunkers Hill
Dorsington
River Avon
AVON VALLEY FOOTPATH
62
Dorsington Manor
4
N
Noleham Brook
Collett's Farm
Weir
59
5
Fox Covert
HEART OF ENGLAND WAY
Barton Hill House
63
Reservoir
2
Weir
Barton
6
The Cottage of Content PH
Binton, Stratford-upon-Avon
B439
Bickmarsh
HONEYBOURNE ROAD
St Laurence Church
B4085
P
Marlcliff
1
The Frog PH
Bidford-on-Avon
AVON VALLEY FOOTPATH
B439
35
River Avon

1. Cross Bidford Bridge and go left through a kissing gate by a farm gate. Follow the Heart of England Way waymarkers through three kissing gates over a series of fields to the River Avon. Continue by the riverside until you reach a weir and lock gates, then go right up to the road in the hamlet of Barton – The Cottage of Content pub is on the right.

2. Leave the Heart of England Way and head left along the road for about 0.5 miles (800m). Go left through a gateway opposite Willow Cottage, down to the river's edge, and follow the Avon Valley Footpath by the side of the Avon for the next 1.5 miles (2.4km). After passing two benches, bear right to a kissing gate and climb the steps up Cress Hill until you come to a road, through a kissing gate.

3. Turn right along the road, bearing left at the road junction by Bunkers Hill. In 125yds (114m), go right through a kissing gate and take the footpath on the left of the field hedge. This leads, via four gates and two drives, past a swimming pool, then continues over a series of fields and a gate until through a kissing gate you cross a footbridge over Noleham Brook, passing Dorsington Manor on your left to reach the Dorsington road. Go left along the road for 300yds (274m) to where it bears left.

4. Go right to rejoin the Heart of England Way, taking a track past Collett's Farm to a gate. Through this, continue ahead and follow the waymarkers as the track crosses a stile to skirt a young copse and lake, then through a gate and over a footbridge, before continuing ahead to follow a hedge uphill. Go left at a waymark post and follow the path for about 250yds (229m).

5. Turn right at a waymark post and walk towards Barton Hill House. Pass to the left of the buildings and bear left, then shortly right. Follow the track past a large storage pond. Continue on the track as it arcs right and gently descends into Barton. At the road, go right and then ahead through a gate by The Cottage of Content pub, and take the wide track down to the Avon.

6. Walk along the riverside footpath, retracing your steps back to the car park in Bidford-on-Avon.

Where to eat and drink

The Cottage of Content pub at Barton is a regular stopping-off place for walkers on the Heart of England Way – dogs on leads and children are allowed in the bar and front garden (open Thursday to Sunday). At The Frog, along the High Street in Bidford-on-Avon, you can enjoy a pleasant bar snack by the river. Children and guide dogs (only) are welcome.

What to look out for

Linger in the 'Bard's villages' of Barton, Dorsington and Marlcliff and take time to enjoy the attractive cottages. Marlcliff, by the River Avon, is a charming mix of old, thatched buildings and more modern ones that blend in perfectly.

A WALK FROM DORSINGTON

DISTANCE/TIME	3.5 miles (5.7km) / 1hr 45min
ASCENT/GRADIENT	165ft (50m) / ▲
PATHS	Tracks, field paths, quiet road
LANDSCAPE	Rolling countryside near the Warwickshire/ Worcestershire border
SUGGESTED MAP	OS Explorer 205 Stratford-upon-Avon & Evesham
START/FINISH	Grid Reference: SP133496
DOG FRIENDLINESS	On lead on farmland
PARKING	Limited spaces in the vicinity of the church at Dorsington
PUBLIC TOILETS	None on route

On 24 April 1965, the first official long-distance trail in Britain was formally opened. At Malham Tarn House in North Yorkshire, the Pennine Way was introduced to a generation of walkers who had been waiting eagerly for the new route to open. The trail had been a long time in the making and the battle to bring it to fruition was protracted and arduous. The Pennine Way was the brainchild of Tom Stephenson, a much-respected figure in walking circles and a former secretary of the Ramblers' Association. In a 1935 article in the Daily Herald, 'Wanted – a Long Green Trail,' he described the thinking behind his idea.

More than half a century later, Britain has a whole host of long-distance trails. In addition to those that have formal backing and support, there are countless other themed walks of varying lengths around the country. There is even a trail dedicated to William Shakespeare. One route that for many years has been a popular choice with long-distance walkers is the 100-mile (160km) Heart of England Way. It's followed in the initial stages of this walk, starting in the village of Dorsington. It cuts an impressive route through the West Midlands and the Cotswolds and forms a border of sorts between the grand walking country of the north and the gentler countryside of the south and east of England.

The Heart of England Way was almost 13 years in the making. It was conceived in 1978 by various walking clubs and in the early stages of planning, was very much a voluntary effort. In time, however, the Countryside Commission and several local authorities added their weight by negotiating with landowners and farmers. Eventually, in October 1990, the Heart of England Way was officially opened at Alcester.

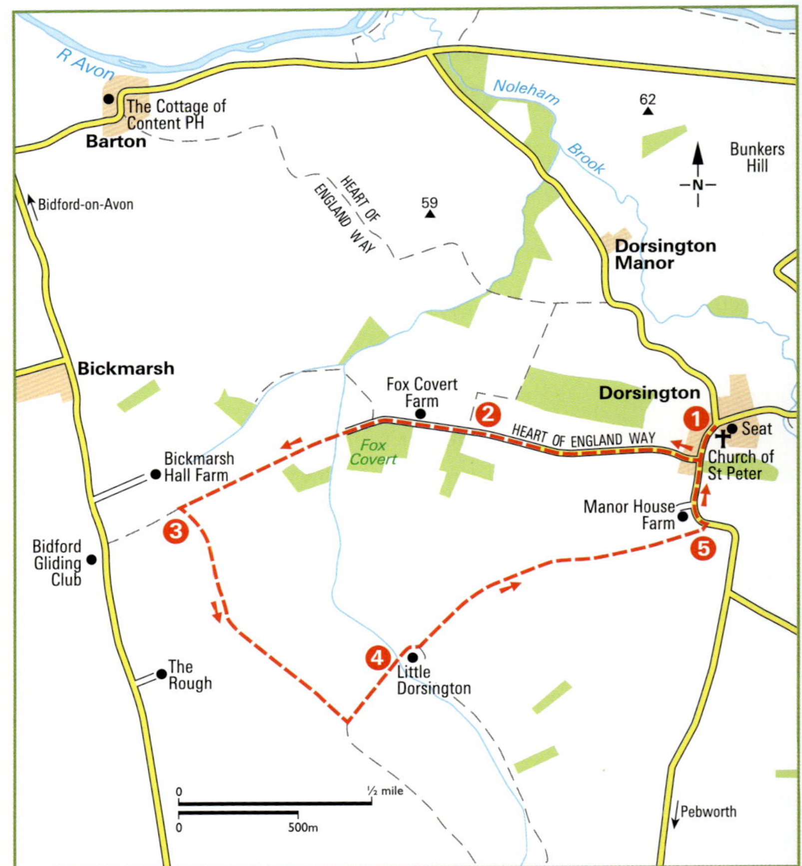

1. From St Peter's church in Dorsington, follow the road signposted to Pebworth and Long Marston. On reaching wrought iron gates at the entrance to the Moat House on the left, turn right and follow the lane (Heart of England Way). On the right is the Dorsington Arboretum. Pass a sign for Udde Well Pond, a conservation area, and continue on the single-track lane between hedgerows and farmland, with pleasant views over pastoral Warwickshire, close to where it meets Worcestershire. Pass double gates at the entrance to a house and keep ahead on the right of way, which becomes a rough track.

2. When the Heart of England Way turns right, continue ahead on the track, passing a solitary stone-built house called Fox Covert. Pass through gates, break cover from the trees and look for the chimneys of Bickmarsh Hall Farm in the distance. On drawing level with its farm buildings and silos, turn left to cross a field.

3. The farmland track should be in line with the farm entrance. Cross a ditch on the far side of the field, enter the next pasture and on the right are the buildings of The Rough farm. Continue on a track and when you draw level with a clump of trees over on the right and a solitary dwelling away to the left across the field, turn left towards it. This is Little Dorsington.

4. Keep to the left of the building, cross a footbridge and go through a gate to cross a stream. Pass through a meadow to a waymarked gate and follow the right-hand fence, curving right. Make for a gate and turn immediately left to a second gate. Follow a grassy path between fences to the next gate and then ahead across the field to a further gate, avoiding the exit in the far left corner. Continue in the next pasture, with hedgerow on the left, and pass through the next gate. Make for the far right corner of the field and exit through a single gate beyond a footbridge. Keep to the right-hand boundary in the next field to reach a further gate and pass alongside Manor House Farm on the left.

5. Follow the hedge to a gate leading out to road and turn left. Pass the entrance to the farm on the left and return to Dorsington. On reaching the village pass some thatched cottages on the left before finishing the walk.

Where to eat and drink

There are no refreshment points on this walk though the surrounding villages offer plenty of choice. Try the Cottage of Content pub at Barton or the Frog in Bidford-on-Avon. Stratford-upon-Avon is nearby and includes a wide range of pubs, tea rooms and restaurants.

What to look out for

Have a closer look at Dorsington's striking 18th-century church of St Peter, which can be found in the centre of the village and was rebuilt in 1754 following a fire. The church includes a perpendicular tower and an embattled western tower. The village itself was originally in Gloucestershire.

While you're there

Outside the church at Dorsington is an oak tree planted to mark the jubilee of King George V on 6th May 1935. The seat that encircles the tree was presented by Mr and Mrs Hugh Roberts of Dorsington Manor, to mark the coronation of George VI on 12 May 1937 – exactly two years and six days after the jubilee celebrations. There is also a George VI postbox in the village.

A CIRCUIT FROM EARLSWOOD LAKES

DISTANCE/TIME	5.5 miles (8.8km) / 2hrs 15min
ASCENT/GRADIENT	98ft (30m) / ▲
PATHS	Lakeside paths and field paths, many stiles
LANDSCAPE	Woodland, lakes and rolling countryside
SUGGESTED MAP	OS Explorer 220 Birmingham
START/FINISH	Grid Reference: SP109739
DOG FRIENDLINESS	Dogs shoud be on leads when near wildfowl
PARKING	Malthouse Lane car park
PUBLIC TOILETS	None on route

Earlswood is delightfully set in the Forest of Arden. The three man-made lakes here, known as Terry's Pool, Engine Pool and Windmill Pool, were completed in 1821 to supply water to the nearby Birmingham–Stratford-upon-Avon canal. It took five years to build the reservoirs – at a cost of about £300,000.

The canal has not been in commercial use since 1936 but, being so close to the sprawling West Midlands conurbation, it has developed into a major leisure facility, which is also true of Earlswood Lakes. Visit on a sunny Sunday morning and Windmill Pool will be full of the boats of the Earlswood Lakes Sailing Club, while the banks of Engine Pool will be covered with anglers. The 10ha (25-acre) reservoir has no fewer than 80 timber platforms for anglers, who are keen to catch one of the huge carp that thrive in these waters. Bream, roach and perch can also be found in the other two pools.

Terry's Pool is a wildlife reserve that is home to a wealth of birds, mammals and plants. Walkers out close to dusk might see bats, muntjac deer and possibly even otters, though you'd be very lucky to spot the otters. Otters were driven to the brink of extinction in England in the middle of the 20th century, but numbers have recovered in the last couple of decades. During spring and summer, Terry's Pool is a riot of colour, home to the bright flowers of yellow flag iris, great willowherb and betony.

New Fallings Coppice and Clowes Wood contain areas of ancient woodland that are the breeding grounds for an amazing 49 species of bird. These include all three species of woodpecker that are found in England, along with several tit species, warblers, kestrels, tawny owls and even the elusive woodcock – a large wading bird with short legs and a long bill.

The walk starts from Terry's Pool and takes in these woods, as well as farmland, a golf course and country roads, before returning for a a lovely stroll around the lake.

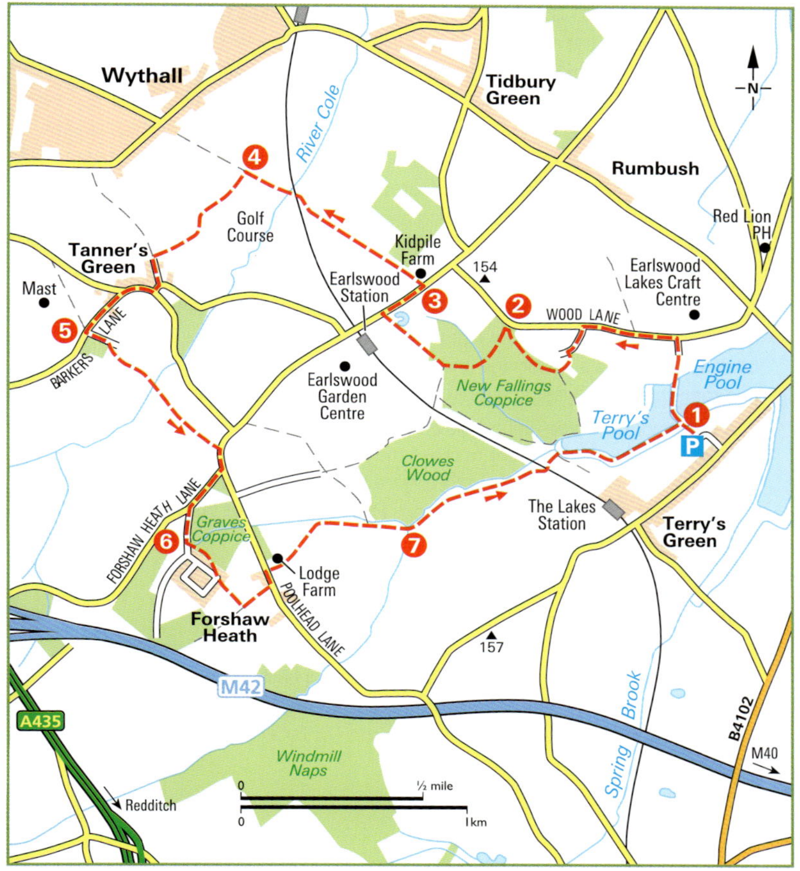

1. From the car park, go through a kissing gate and over a footbridge to cross the embankment between the lakes. After a metal bridge, bear right and then left over a wooden footbridge. Continue to Wood Lane. Go left for 400yds (366m), then left along a campsite driveway. Walk past the log cabin, and at the woodland edge go right over a footbridge and bear left, along the side of New Fallings Coppice.

2. Cross a stile, turn left and bear right at a fork. After a footbridge, keep straight ahead. Just before the path swings left, leave it by bearing right to join a trail along the coppice boundary to a fence gap. Through this, follow a path across a field. This becomes a hedged path that leads to a road. Turn right along the road for 200yds (183m).

3. Just before Kidpile Farm, go left through a gap beside a gate. Initially, the path is to the left of the hedge, then enters trees via two kissing gates and a footbridge, before continuing on the right. After a kissing gate, bear half right to pass, via another kissing gate, under the railway. Continue up the side of a field, soon joining a hedged path beside Fulford Heath Golf Club.

4. Go left through a kissing gate and take the waymarked footpath across the golf course. After the maintenance yard, bear right to a kissing gate. Through this, bear left. Reaching a road at the golf club entrance, turn right towards Wythall. After 125yds (114m), go left down Barkers Lane.

5. In a further 250yds (229m), go left along a driveway signed 'Forshaw Heath' and right over a stile. Over the next stile, cross a field to a footbridge. Once over this, bear right. Cross a plank footbridge and walk straight across a large field. Turn right along Forshaw Heath Lane, right at the next junction and then left into Juggins Lane.

6. In 300yds (274m), turn left through Graves Coppice, exiting via a footbridge. Continue through a field and, after the second stile, turn left to Poolhead Lane. Go left for 100yds (91m), then right over a stile by Lodge Farm. Bear half left after a stile, cross a footbridge and then recross via a second bridge. Go left and then through a kissing gate straight ahead to walk beside Clowes Wood.

7. After about 0.5 miles (800m), having crossed two gated footbridges, go through a gate and bear right to cross the railway. After a kissing gate, take the footpath ahead to a stile. Go through a kissing gate and over a footbridge, then turn right to emerge beside Terry's Pool. Continue for 700yds (640m), then go right to return to the car park.

Where to eat and drink

The café at Earlswood Garden Centre, offering breakfast, lunch, snacks and drinks, is nearby, as is The Red Lion, dating back to the 18th century. The menu is full of hearty favourites and pub classics, with a well-stocked bar that can be enjoyed either in the garden or by a crackling log fire. Dogs are allowed in the bar area.

AROUND SUTTON PARK

DISTANCE/TIME	8 miles (12.9km) / 3hrs
ASCENT/GRADIENT	230ft (70m) / ▲ ▲
PATHS	Footpaths, tracks and road in parkland
LANDSCAPE	Undulating parkland
SUGGESTED MAP	OS Explorer 220 Birmingham
START/FINISH	Grid Reference: SP113962
DOG FRIENDLINESS	Off lead in park
PARKING	Visitor centre car park in Sutton Park, via Sutton Park Town Gate entrance on Tudor Hill
PUBLIC TOILETS	Sutton Park Visitor Centre

Sutton Park comprises 2,400 acres (970ha) of wild and wooded countryside of moorland, meadows, lakes and groves and is one of the largest urban parks in the country. The old Roman Ryknild Street runs across one corner of the park, and the Normans once hunted deer here. In 1997, English Nature designated Sutton Park a National Nature Reserve (NNR) in an effort to preserve this wonderful landscape. It is now surrounded on all sides by residential properties, but it remains an important area for Birmingham and the local Sutton Coldfield community. It's a valuable space, offering many leisure pursuits. However, it is still possible to escape from the crowds and find peace and quiet.

It is the park's diversity of habitats that earned it NNR status. Many areas, like the heathland, wetland and ancient forest, represent habitats that were once widespread but have now completely disappeared from the rest of the West Midlands. For this reason, it is the home of a large number of resident birds, as well as providing an important stopover for migrants and other visitors. Around the pools, you might see tufted duck, pochard and even snipe, especially near Longmoor Pool.

The nearby market town of Sutton Coldfield was important in the Middle Ages and owes a great deal to local benefactor John Veysey, who became bishop of Exeter in 1519. He lived at Moor Hall, north of the town and now a hotel, and built a number of notable buildings in and around the town. He also founded a school and paved the streets. Veysey is buried in Holy Trinity Church and there is a fine effigy of him on his tomb. It depicts him as a young man, even though he is reputed to have lived to the ripe old age of 103. The church also contains some interesting old brasses. In particular, there is one of Josias Bull in a gown of fur, along with small brasses of his five children. William Wilson, a mason for Sir Christopher Wren, made the marble busts of Henry Pudsey and his wife.

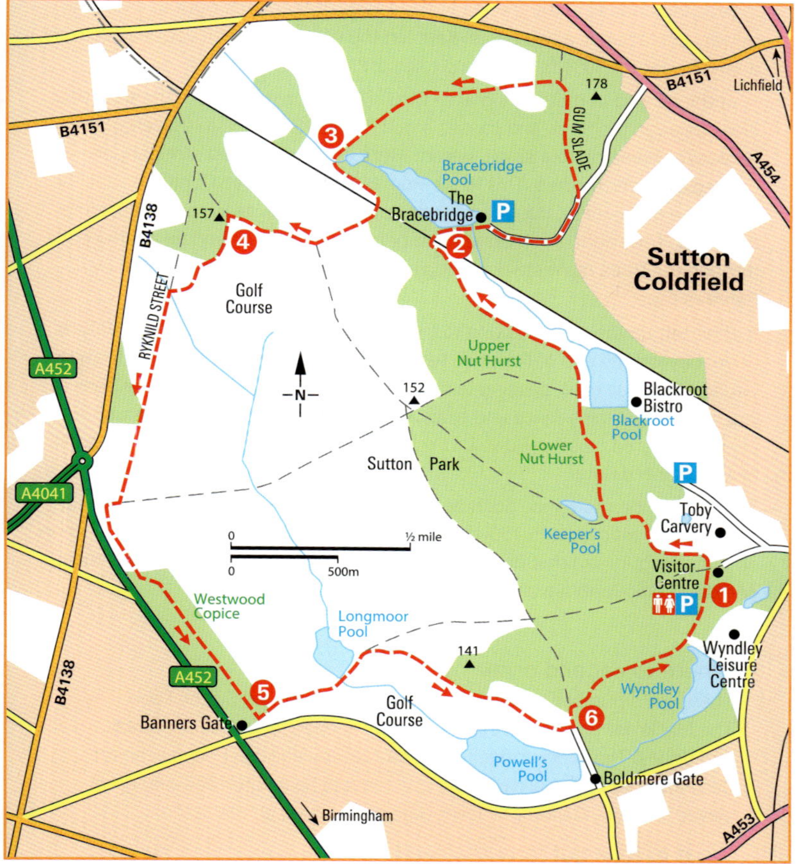

1. Walk from the car park to the entrance road, and go left and shortly right at a five-way junction to follow the tarmac lane up to Keeper's Pool. At the corner of the pool turn right and follow its edge, continuing northwards uphill through the trees on a path until you descend to reach Blackroot Pool. Walk close to the left edge of the pool for about 220yds (201m), then follow the path bearing left (northwest) and keep ahead through the woodland of Upper Nut Hurst. In about 0.5 miles (800m), bear right and cross the railway bridge, via two gates, to get to Bracebridge Pool.

2. Turn right along the edge of the pool and at the end, bear right along a track just before the Bracebridge restaurant. Continue along the tarmac lane and through the car park until you reach a T-junction by housing. Turn left, and in 150yds (137m) leave the road and go left by a large oak tree on a wide path, which soon bears right by ancient oaks in the woodland of Gum Slade. Continue ahead to a junction of paths, then go left and up to a grassy clearing. Cross it and continue ahead on a gravel track. Where this bears right continue ahead, ignoring minor cross paths, and descending gently. Maintain your direction then continue ahead on a track that arcs left and descends to cross a footbridge at the end of Bracebridge Pool.

3. Bear left, following the track into the woods. It then arcs right to cross the railway line again, via two gates. Keep on the wide track until you reach a road, then go right for 500yds (457m) up to a parking area on the left.

4. At the far end of the parking area turn left by a post, and take the path that dives through the trees and passes a golf green. Now keep to the left of the fairway, descending to a small stream. Here, turn left on to a straight path flanked by silver birches. This is the Roman Ryknild Street. Continue, initially within the golf course, but later across heath, until you reach a track leading to an exit. Turn right and then left just before the exit gate and follow the path through the trees of Westwood Coppice until you come to the car park by Banners Gate.

5. Bear left up the road, passing to the right of Longmoor Pool. About 100yds (91m) beyond the end of the pool, turn right along a path. Join a path from the left and continue on it, passing to the right of a copse of silver birches. Soon you walk alongside a fence and trees, drop through a tree belt and cross an open grass area close to Powell's Pool to reach the roadway, via the car park near Boldmere Gate.

6. Go left at the road, then soon bear right, along the edge of Wyndley Wood, and join a tarmac lane. In 150yds (137m), bear right at a four-way lane junction on to a straight road that descends to pass a footbridge and ford at the end of Wyndley Pool. Continue ahead to return to the visitor centre.

Where to eat and drink

There are a number of cafés and kiosks dotted around Sutton Park. The Blackroot Bistro near Blackroot Pool is open for breakfast, lunch and drinks. The Bracebridge Restaurant at Bracebridge Pool has an art deco-inspired dining area, plus a covered and heated terrace, and great views. The Toby Carvery at Town Gate serves food all day.

What to look out for

The beautiful Bracebridge Pool was built for Sir Ralph Bracebridge in order to maintain a plentiful supply of fish. In 1419, he obtained a lease on the manor and chase of Sutton Coldfield from the Earl of Warwick.

While you're there

The Wall Roman Site Baths and Museum lies 9 miles (14.5km) north of Sutton Coldfield, near Lichfield. Here, you will see the excavation of the most complete public bathhouse of a Roman staging post, known as Letocetum. It's situated just off Watling Street, the great arterial road that connected the Roman port at Richborough, near Canterbury, with London and the northwest.

BLACK-AND-WHITE BUILDINGS IN WELFORD

DISTANCE/TIME	3 miles (4.8km) / 1hr 15min
ASCENT/GRADIENT	49ft (15m) / ▲
PATHS	Village footpaths and field paths
LANDSCAPE	Residential village area
SUGGESTED MAP	OS Explorer 205 Stratford-upon-Avon & Evesham
START/FINISH	Grid Reference: SP148522
DOG FRIENDLINESS	Under control at all times
PARKING	On side roads near the Bell Inn, Welford-on-Avon
PUBLIC TOILETS	None on route

This walk takes you on a journey back in time to the delightful black-and-white buildings in the villages of Welford-on-Avon and Weston-on-Avon. Picturesque Welford-on-Avon was established in Saxon times by the monks of Deerhurst Abbey (near Tewkesbury, in Gloucestershire). There must be more black-and-white thatched cottages here than almost any other village in England. Three particularly stunning examples are Ten Penny Cottage, the Owl Pen and Daffodil Cottage. Welford also has three pubs – the Shakespeare, The Bell Inn and The Four Alls, all of which welcome walkers.

Since the 14th century, there has been a 65ft (20m) maypole on the village green. It must have been taken down some time after the Civil War, when such frivolities were made illegal, but seems to have been restored soon after. Following a lightning strike, the original wooden pole was replaced by an aluminium ship's mast. Welford is proud of its traditions, and the village children still dance around the maypole in July each year.

Welford's church has a register that records the flooding of the River Avon in 1588 – this was due to the same storm that wrecked the Spanish Armada. Joseph Green, the vicar here in 1735, discovered and made copies of Shakespeare's will, one of which is now held in the British Museum.

In the sanctuary of the church, two fighting men are depicted in full armour. Sir John Greville, of nearby Milcote Manor, is shown with his head resting on a horned sheep and flowers at his feet, while his son, who fought in the Battle of the Spurs in 1513, wears an heraldic coat and holds his hands in prayer.

William Shakespeare has connections with neighbouring Weston-on-Avon. John Trapp was vicar in this tiny village between 1660 and 1669. He was also a master at Stratford Grammar School for a time, and it is believed that he and his wife knew the Shakespeare family.

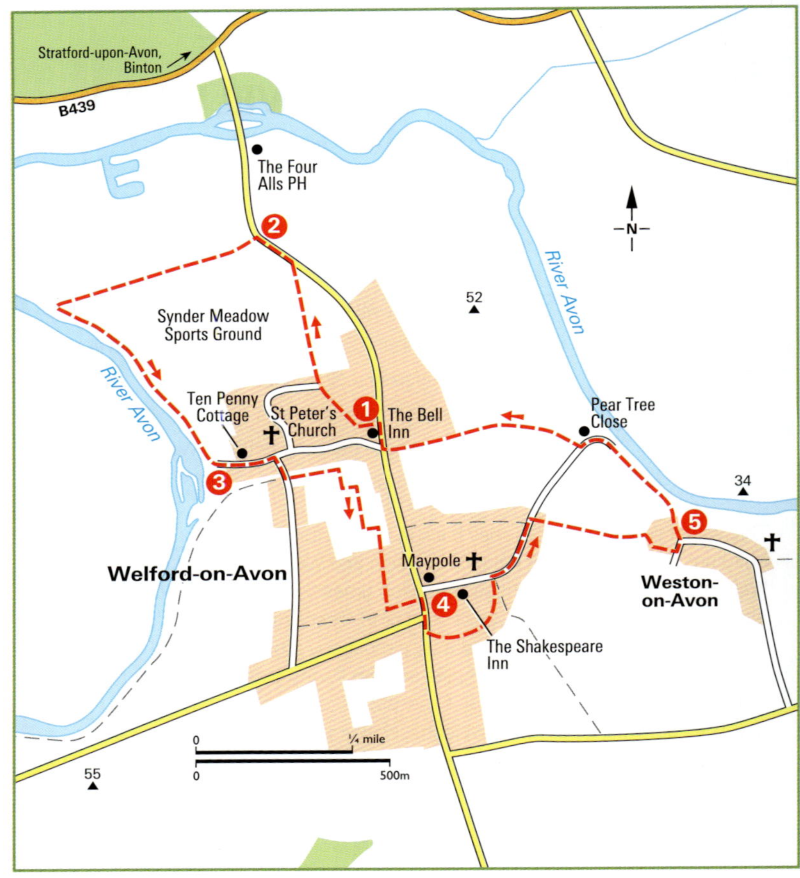

1. Facing the Bell Inn, take the footpath to the left of the pub's car park. At the end of the path, near Daffodil Cottage, go right along a footpath past the back of some houses and through a kissing gate until you come to the end of Church Lane, by Applegarth House. Continue through the gate and follow a path at the back of more houses to reach the main road once again, then go left along the pavement for about 100yds (91m).

2. Go left again into the entrance gate of Synder Meadow Sports Ground. Walk along the track, then through a kissing gate into the sports ground, and soon out via a gate in the fence on the right to continue along the footpath down to the River Avon. At the river, go left and follow the bank for 500yds (457m).

3. Go through the kissing gate and over a footbridge at the end of the field and left up Boat Lane, lined with beautiful old thatched black-and-white cottages. Look out for Ten Penny Cottage. Near the top of the lane is St Peter's Church; go right here along Headland Road. Opposite Mill Lane, turn left along a footpath at the back of houses. After a kissing gate, you will pass by the extension to the graveyard of St Peter's Church and continue to a junction of paths. Keep ahead here, and at the next junction go left and through a kissing gate. Walk up to the High Street to emerge opposite the Maypole general store, near the maypole.

4. Turn right along the pavement for 100 paces, then cross over and go down another waymarked footpath, Frog Lane, past more beautiful cottages and through a kissing gate. Walk through to Pool Close then bear left to Chapel Street (the chapel is on the left). Go right along Chapel Street, then right again through a kissing gate along a footpath just after Millers Close. Go through another kissing gate and walk along the field edge towards Weston-on-Avon.

5. At the crossroads, keep ahead to descend a bridlepath set just above the River Avon. Follow it as it arcs left to come out on Duck Lane by a house called Pear Tree Close. At the next residential drive, go right up the hedged path and walk west to High Street, where you will emerge at the junction with Church Street. The Bell Inn is on the right.

Where to eat and drink
There are three pubs in Welford-upon-Avon. The Bell Inn, at the start of the walk, is colourful with flowers during the summer months. The Shakespeare Inn lies just beyond the maypole in Chapel Street, and The Four Alls is close to the weir and Welford Bridge. They can all get very busy during the summer when many visitors come to admire the flower-adorned village.

What to look out for
Visit the neighbouring village of Binton to see the memorial to Captain Robert Falcon Scott. The famous explorer, whose brother-in-law, Lloyd Bruce, was the vicar in Binton, spent time here before his final expedition to the South Pole in 1912. Binton commemorated the exploits of the great man in the church's west window.

While you're there
St Peter's Church in Welford has a Saxon font bowl and carved wooden screen dedicated to the 'Fallen of the First World War'. In nearby Weston's 15th-century church, you can find out about the 'Wicked Loddy'. Was he really the notorious Lodvic Greville, son of Sir Edward Greville of Milcote Manor, pressed to death with stones in 1589 for murder?

HENLEY-IN-ARDEN AND THE STRATFORD CANAL

DISTANCE/TIME	5.5 miles (8.8km) / 2hrs
ASCENT/GRADIENT	180ft (55m) / ▲ ▲
PATHS	Field paths, farm tracks and tow path, several stiles
LANDSCAPE	Rolling countryside
SUGGESTED MAP	OS Explorer 220 Birmingham
START/FINISH	Grid Reference: SP152658
DOG FRIENDLINESS	Off lead along tow path, otherwise under control
PARKING	Prince Harry Road car park in Henley-in-Arden
PUBLIC TOILETS	Station Road in Henley-in-Arden

This walk takes you over the top of The Mount for a great view over Henley-in-Arden, and then descends on country lanes past Preston Bagot Manor House on the way to the Stratford-upon-Avon Canal. Henley-in-Arden has a superb mile-long (1.6km) street which offers a glimpse of the medieval world. It is lined with mostly 15th-, 16th- and 17th-century timber-framed buildings, with roofs at every level, ancient windows and a wide variety of old doors. It has been described as a museum of English domestic architecture.

Peter de Montfort was Henley's Lord of the Manor until he fell in battle on Evesham Field in 1265. Following the battle, the town was burnt to the ground, but a new Henley rose from the ashes. The town maintains a Court Leet that has jurisdiction over petty offences and civil affairs. While this has been abolished in most towns, the Henley-in-Arden Court Leet has survived and each year the Burgesses elect a High and Low Bailiff, a Mace Bearer, a Constable, an Ale Taster, two Brook Lookers, a Butter Weigher and two Affearors (assessors). These ceremonial roles were dying out by the early 20th century, but were revived in 1915 by the then Lord of the Manor, W J Fieldhouse. His title was later bought by the Pittsburgh millionaire Joseph Hardy, who established a charitable trust that now runs the heritage centre in the town.

Peter de Montfort lived at the castle that used to stand behind the Church of St Nicholas in Beaudesert Lane, and the hill is known locally as The Mount in his memory. The church has a memorial tablet to the Revd Richard Jago, father of the esteemed 17th-century poet Richard Jago.

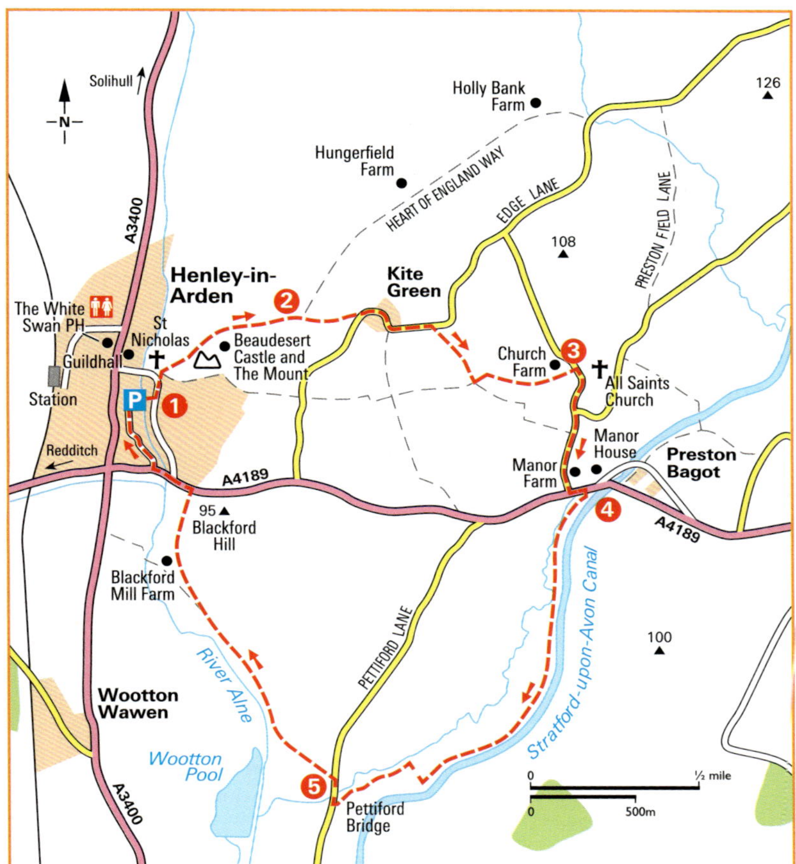

1. Leave the car park at the rear, walk through the park, cross the footbridge walk up to Alne Close. Turn left, and at the end you come to Beaudesert Lane, with the Church of St Nicholas opposite. Go right through the kissing gate to the right of churchyard, and follow the Heart of England Way for a steep but short ascent to the top of the Mount. Continue over the old earthworks of the former castle until you reach the corner of the top far field. Go right over the stile and continue along the footpath that runs to the right of the hedge.

2. In about 220yds (201m), cross a stile and go left over another stile. Diagonally cross the next field to a stile, then follow the path to a gate leading onto a lane in Kite Green. Turn right, then go left along the lane for about 0.25 miles (400m). Just past Barn View, turn right through a gate and shortly through a kissing gate onto a footpath, following the left-hand edge of a field. At end of the field go through two kissing gates and proceed in an easterly direction towards Church Farm.

3. After three kissing gates, go through the gate to the right of the farm buildings onto a lane. Turn right and follow the lane, passing by Manor Farm to reach the A4189 Henley–Warwick road. Go left along the road for about 220yds (201m), then cross it.

4. Immediately before the canal bridge, descend onto the tow path of the Stratford-upon-Avon Canal, via two gates, and take this back towards Henley-in-Arden. Continue past canal bridge No. 49. Leave the canal at bridge No. 50 and go right along a lane. In 180yds (165m), this bends sharp left, bringing you to a road near the Pettiford Bridge. Turn right over the bridge.

5. In 50yds (46m), go left through a kissing gate into pastureland. The path arcs right, diagonally over a field. Over a plank footbridge and through a kissing gate in the far corner, you reach the banks of the River Alne. Take the riverside path then, at a hedge gap junction, bear right and shortly take the right-hand footpath and proceed ahead, passing to the right of Blackford Mill Farm buildings via a kissing gate and a gate. Continue on field paths to the left of Blackford Hill to reach the A4189 road in Henley-in-Arden via a kissing gate. Cross the road going left, then right onto Prince Harry Road which leads back to the car park.

Where to eat and drink

There are a number of good pubs in Henley-in-Arden, including some superb old coaching inns. The White Swan, a restored 16th-century coaching inn opposite the Guildhall, is a regular stop-off for walkers completing the 100-mile (161km) Heart of England Way, which passes through its archway. Well-behaved children and dogs are welcome in the bar and the large rear gardens.

What to look out for

The half-timbered Guildhall, to the north of St John's Church in Henley-in-Arden, dates from 1448 and is one of the town's best-known and most familiar features. This building is where the Court Leet meets annually every November to elect its officers and report on the work of the previous 12 months.

While you're there

The Stratford-upon-Avon Canal was completed in 1816 to link up with the Worcester and Birmingham Canal at King's Norton. In 1850, the Great Western Railway Company purchased the canal and all its assets. It gradually became derelict and eventually unnavigable. The National Trust took up a lease on the canal and, following a huge restoration programme, it was finally re-opened by British Waterways in 1964.

PRESTON BAGOT AND ALL SAINTS CHURCH

DISTANCE/TIME	4 miles (6.4km) / 2hrs
ASCENT/GRADIENT	345ft (105m) / ▲
PATHS	Field paths, brief stretch of road, canal towpath
LANDSCAPE	Rolling farmland bisected by canal
SUGGESTED MAP	OS Explorer 220 Birmingham
START/FINISH	Grid Reference: SP187677
DOG FRIENDLINESS	On farmland and country lanes
PARKING	Village hall car park or vicinity in Lowsonford
PUBLIC TOILETS	None on route

All Saints Church at Preston Bagot, passed on the route of this walk, sounds as if it stands in the middle of a village, occupying a traditional setting at the heart of the community, in common with thousands of other churches around the country. This is not the case. The church lies surely in one of the loneliest locations anywhere, situated on a peaceful hillside above the Stratford-upon-Avon Canal. There has been a settlement here since Roman times, confirmed by the discovery of pottery remains. The present church is Norman, though there have been many changes to the look of it over the centuries.

The original structure of this church was constructed of local rubble and was no more than a basic building. However, it is said that some of the faced stones near the foundations and on the corners could have come from the ruins of a nearby Roman villa. Much of the original structure survives, though you have to peer closely to see it. To the right of the door, scratched on a stone, is a finger sundial and the font just inside the south door is 15th century. The cross wall with its Romanesque style arch is 19th century.

Of particular note are the five windows on the east, south and west walls. They depict Simplicitas, Christ, Mary, Martha and St Celia and were made by Morris & Co of Birmingham, the factory established by William Morris. The figure of Christ is by Henry Dearle, a glass painter who ran the stained-glass department following Morris' death in 1896. The other figures are the work of Burne-Jones. All the figures were at one time in the old Meeting House in Bristol Street in Birmingham but fortunately were stored elsewhere before the building was destroyed by bombing in World War II. In the 1930s, an unmarked grave was discovered beneath the altar, containing two bodies lying north and south, side by side and seemingly holding hands. There was no sign of a coffin. Some theories suggest this grave was originally outside the church but became part of the interior when All Saints was extended eastwards. It has also been suggested that the shallowness of the grave indicates a hurried burial and that those who died were victims of plague. All Saints contains a memorial to those who fell in the Great War, serving as a reminder of more recent momentous events in our long history.

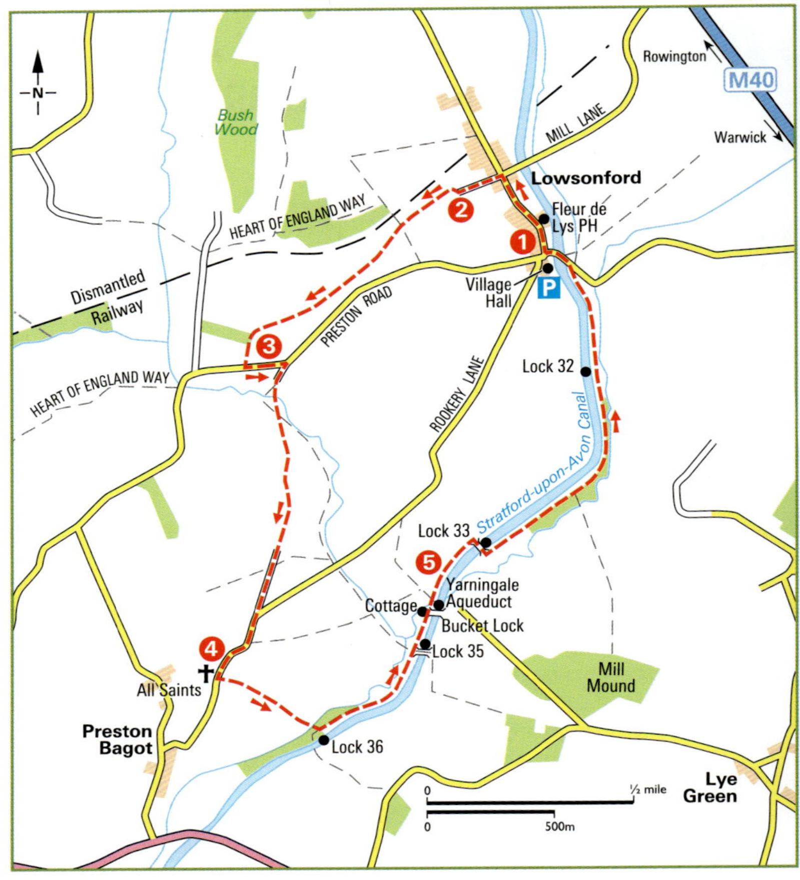

1. Leave the village hall car park and walk northwards along the road through Lowsonford, passing the Fleur de Lys pub on the right. Head down to the next main junction, by a telephone box and a turning for Rowington, and turn left to follow part of the route of the Heart of England Way.

2. Follow the trail, ascending to a house. Keep right, cross a stile and maintain the same direction to the next field boundary. Beyond the next stile, head up the field slope. At the gate and stile, cross over to a junction of rights of way. Cross over to join a path to the left of a track and gate. Follow the narrow path between trees, hedges and fencing. Cross a stile where you emerge from tree cover, keep ahead to the next stile and then continue ahead across a large field. Cross a footbridge on the far side, followed by two stiles, with a small pasture in between, then turn left along a field path.

3. Cross a stile to reach the road, turn left and when it bends left, turn sharp right by some white railings. There is a sign here 'unclassified county road'. Cross a ford via a concrete footbridge and continue along Preston Fields Lane. Pass some houses, merge with another road and keep ahead. Look for twin lock-up garages on the right. Avoid footpaths on the left and right and ahead now is All Saints church.

4. Almost opposite the church entrance is a kissing gate giving access to a field path. Follow it down the slope and in the second pasture, keep the hedgerow to the right. Make for the bottom corner of the elongated field and look for a gate and waymark. Cross a small river, turn right in the trees and head up the bank to the towpath of the Stratford-upon-Avon Canal at lock 36. Turn left. Pass lock 35 and continue to Bucket Lock. Beyond it is Yarningale Aqueduct.

5. Continue to lock 33 and cross to the opposite towpath. Keep ahead with woodland to the right and farmland over to the left. Pass lock 32, continue to the outskirts of Lowsonford and at bridge 41, leave the towpath to cross the canal via the road bridge. Return to the village.

Where to eat and drink
The Fleur de Lys at Lowsonford is a well-established pub on the banks of the Stratford-upon-Avon Canal. Expect some popular beers and a good menu, including fish and chips, pies and various snacks.

What to look out for
At the start of the walk is Lowsonford village hall, recalling an integral part of our rural communities. This one dates back to the mid-1930s and one of its first truestees was Basil Darby, a descendant of Abraham Darby, the renowned iron-master. Darby's widow served the hall for many years as chairman and trustee and the meeting room is named in her memory.

While you're there
During the walk you'll pass a charming and unusual barrel-roofed cottage beside the Stratford-upon-Avon Canal. These structures are quite rare; this one was built for the lock keeper at Bucket Lock. The reason for this style of architecture has never been fully explained though some sources suggest the cottages were constructed by builders who only knew how to build bridges and tunnels. A barrel-roofed cottage can also be seen from the bridge at the end of the walk.

BRUETON PARK AND THE GRAND UNION CANAL

DISTANCE/TIME	7 miles (11.3km) / 3hrs
ASCENT/GRADIENT	33ft (10m) / ▲
PATHS	Field footpaths and tow paths, many stiles
LANDSCAPE	Parkland, canalside and residential areas
SUGGESTED MAP	OS Explorer 220 Birmingham
START/FINISH	Grid Reference: SP162789
DOG FRIENDLINESS	Off lead along tow path, otherwise under control
PARKING	Brueton Park car park
PUBLIC TOILETS	Parkridge Visitor Centre

This enjoyable circuit starts in Brueton Park and encompasses a stroll along the Grand Union Canal. Brueton Park was gifted to Solihull in 1944 by the prominent local businessman and councillor Horace Brueton. It was formerly attached to Malvern Hall, and the two parks were linked in 1963. Today the two distinct parks form one large park to the southeast of Solihull town centre. The narrow strip of land follows a roughly U-shaped layout and covers an area of approximately 130 acres (53ha).

Brueton Park incorporates a local nature reserve, and many species of mature trees including oak, ash and conifers can be found. Brueton Park Lake, which was formed by damming the local River Blythe, can be found at its southern end. Wildlife enthusiasts will find much of interest, with abundant birdlife on and surrounding the lake. The Parkridge Nature Centre in the middle of the park was opened in 2002 by the Warwickshire Wildlife Trust, when the park also received Local Nature Reserve status in recognition for its importance to wildlife. Here you will find an interesting conservation interpretation and education centre that provides workshops, talks and demonstrations, as well as a restaurant.

By contrast, Malvern Park is a formal municipal town centre park, and throughout the year the floral displays are magnificent. It was originally laid out by the Urban District Council in 1926 on land partly forming a section of the estate of Malvern Hall and partly purchased from local farmers (Malvern Park Farm). The buildings of Malvern Hall, dating from about 1690 and a favourite subject for the painter John Constable, are now home to the private Solihull Prep School

Malvern Park Avenue is dominated by a magnificent statue, the Prancing Horse and Man. It was the work of Vienna-born Joseph Edgar Boehm in 1874, and is thought to depict Alexander the Great and his horse Bucephalas. It was purchased at auction by Captain Oliver Bird, of Bird's Custard fame, for his garden in Solihull, but he donated it to the Solihull Council in 1945 and it was placed in Malvern Park in 1953, the Coronation year.

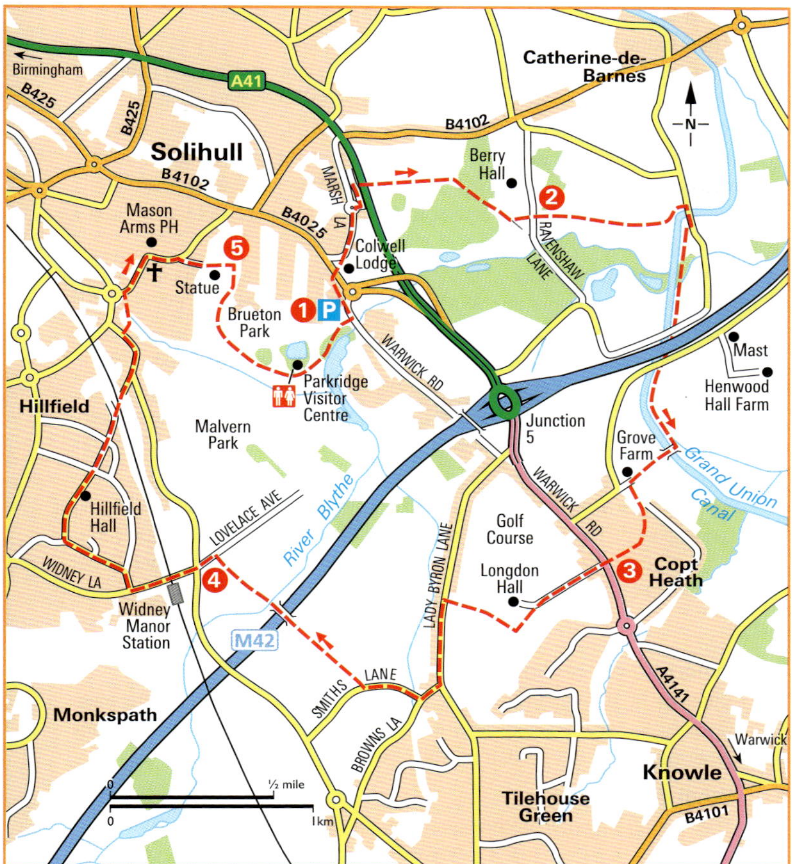

1. Leave the car park and head back onto the main road. Go left through a cul-de-sac, then cross the B4025. Follow the pathway into Marsh Lane and continue to a roundabout. Turn right into Avenbury Drive. Go right through a kissing gate before No. 16. Cross the A41 then go through a kissing gate and take the path on the right of a hedge, via a kissing gate. Follow the path over several fields, then go right through a kissing gate into woodland. Follow a path via a kissing gate. Pass farm buildings and leave via three kissing gates. Continue across a paddock via two kissing gates and cross Ravenshaw Lane.

2. Continue ahead through a kissing gate, walking to the right of a hedge over fields. Go through two further kissing gates, then left through a kissing gate onto a track leading to the canal. Cross a bridge to descend to a tow path. Go left beneath the M42 and Barston Lane. Exit at bridge No. 75, via a stile. Cross a bridge and stile onto a footpath towards Grove Farm. Past the farm, go through a kissing gate and along a driveway. Go left over two stiles, and follow a footpath and lanes, skirting Knowle. Through a gate, the footpath crosses a cul-de-sac onto a path beyond No. 15. At Keepers Cottage, bear right on the lane towards Warwick Road.

3. Cross the road and follow the footpath towards Longdon Hall. Turn right at a junction, following the hedge towards the golf course. Cross this to reach a kissing gate into Lady Byron Lane. Go left, then right into Browns Lane and right into Smiths Lane. After about 325yds (297m), go right over a stile and footbridge into a garden, then over a stile into farmland. Keep to the right of two fields via a stile, then cross a footbridge over the M42 via two stiles. Continue ahead over a stile and footbridge over the River Blythe. Cross another stile and follow a fenced footpath to the right of a field, then go over stile onto Lovelace Avenue.

4. Turn left, crossing Widney Manor Road into Widney Lane. Go beneath a railway bridge, turn right into Alderminster Road then left into Libbards Way. Turn right into Fielding Lane and join Solihull Way. Pass Hillfield Hall, cross Alderminster Road and continue ahead on Fielding Lane, which becomes a walking/cycling route. Go beneath the railway bridge towards Church Hill Road. Bear left, then right up the path beside No. 57. At the end of the path turn right, rejoining Church Hill Road. Pass St Alphege's Church and school.

5. Turn right to enter Malvern Park on a path between Malvern and Cedarhurst. Turn right before reaching ornate gate piers, passing to the right of tennis courts, then bear left into Malvern Park and follow a tarmac footpath until you come to Parkridge Nature Centre. Pass to the right to reach Brueton Park Lake, then turn left and walk along the lakeside to return to the car park.

Where to eat and drink

Opposite St Alphege's Church is The Masons Arms pub, which welcomes walkers. Supervised children are allowed in the bar. There are also many other options in the pedestrianised town centre of Solihull.

What to look out for

The Grand Union Canal, completed in 1805, forms the major part of a London–Birmingham link. Look out for the narrowboats bearing a roses and castle decoration – this is a traditional design. The canal, like most of Britain's navigable waterways, is managed by British Waterways, a state-owned public corporation. In recent years, it has invested millions in maintaining and bringing the ageing canal network into the 21st century.

While you're there

Solihull's High Street still contains some features of Tudor England. St Alphege's Church has a rare altar stone in the crypt and a brass portrait of William Hill (1549), along with his two wives, Isabel and Agnes, and three groups of 18 children.

THE LAKES AT KINGSBURY WATER PARK

DISTANCE/TIME	3 miles (4.8km) / 1hr 20min
ASCENT/GRADIENT	33ft (10m) / ▲
PATHS	Lakeside paths and footpaths, several stiles
LANDSCAPE	Lakes and parkland
SUGGESTED MAP	OS Explorer 232 Nuneaton & Tamworth
START/FINISH	Grid Reference: SP217962
DOG FRIENDLINESS	Under control at all times
PARKING	Pear Tree Avenue car park, off A51
PUBLIC TOILETS	Visitor centre in Kingsbury Water Park

The water park around Kingsbury was once 620 acres (251ha) of old sand and gravel pits, but today it has become a major leisure facility with more than 30 beautiful lakes. This walk takes you across the River Tame into the water park, where you can stroll around a number of the larger pools to enjoy the sight of a wide variety of contemporary sporting activities taking place such as sailing, windsurfing, fishing and horse-riding. There are also several hides where you can do a spot of bird-watching.

The village of Kingsbury sits on a small hill overlooking this wonderland of water. On this high ground is the Church of St Peter and St Paul from where you get a delightful view over the lakes. The church contains a 12th-century nave, a 14th-century tower and a 16th-century belfry. One of its old arches is incised by deep grooves in which it is believed the local bowmen used to sharpen their arrows.

Kingsbury village has been associated with many famous families over the years. In the Middle Ages, the Bracebridge and Arden families were involved in a Romeo-and-Juliet-type feud when Alice Bracebridge married John Arden against the wishes of both families. John's brother's granddaughter was Mary Arden, the mother of William Shakespeare. By the middle of the 19th century, most of the land in the village was owned by Sir Robert Peel. The long-serving MP for Tamworth, one-time Prime Minister and founder of the modern police, lived at nearby Drayton Manor and was buried at Drayton Basset, a few miles up the Tame Valley.

You leave the water park over Hemlingford Bridge, crossing the River Tame in the other direction. This bridge was first built by public subscription in 1783 and takes its name from the Hundred of Hemlingford in which Kingsbury stands (a hundred was an old Saxon local administrative area). On New Year's Day in 1982, the original bridge was destroyed by catastrophic floods that swept down the Tame Valley. Flooding has been a regular feature of the area, with the water frequently rising and spreading over the flood plain between Kingsbury village and the nearby hamlet of Bodymoor Heath.

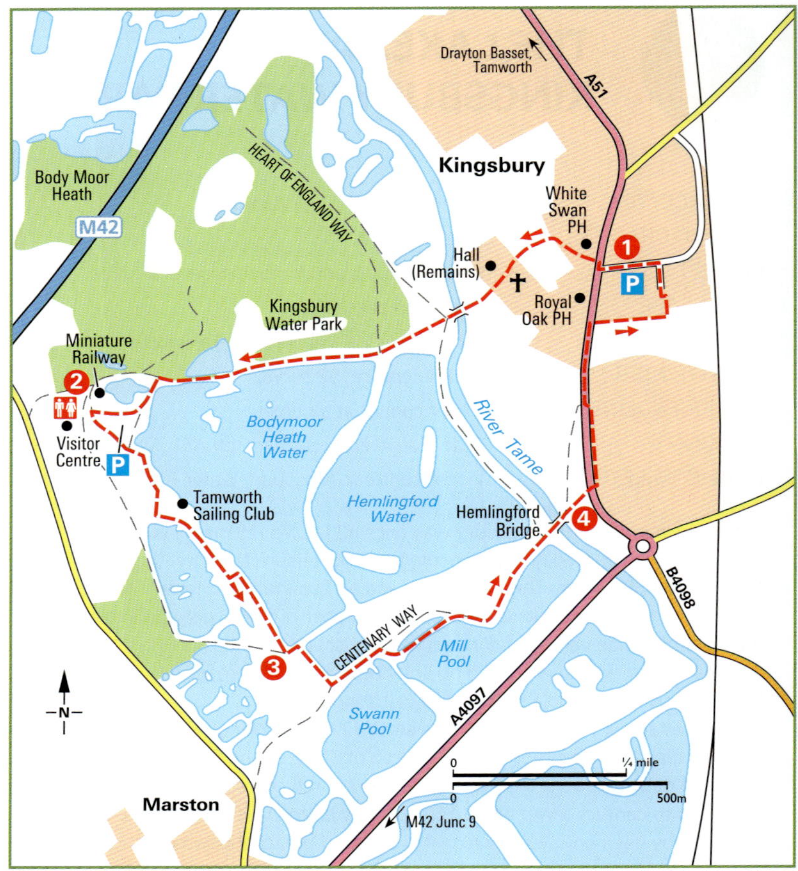

1. From the car park, go left along Pear Tree Avenue to reach the A51 road.
Go right along the pavement of the A51, then cross the road passing in front
of the White Swan pub. About 35yds (32m) beyond the pub, cross over the
road and go left along the well-walked footpath by the side of the churchyard.
Follow the Heart of England waymarkers past the church building and descend
the steps to reach a footbridge over the River Tame. Cross the bridge and walk
ahead along the gravel track to enter Kingsbury Water Park. With Hemlingford
Water close by on your left, cross the footbridge and walk by the side of
Bodymoor Heath Water, leaving the Heart of England behind as you proceed
ahead. Eventually bear left by the miniature railway and keep straight ahead
past a children's play area to reach the visitor centre.

2. From the visitor centre, follow the signs to the watersports clubs along
lanes and footpaths. Shortly the path returns to the side of Bodymoor Heath
Water, then leaves it to pass by the entrance gate to Tamworth Sailing Club.
Continue to the right-hand side of Bodymoor Heath Water, along a tarmac lane,
then back to the water's edge path.

3. At the end of the stretch of Bodymoor Heath Water bear left, then almost
immediately right and follow the waymarkers for the Centenary Way. Turning

left, the waymarkers take you near to Swann Pool and then diagonally across a small car park, between Mill Pool and Hemlingford Water, as your route veers in a northeast direction. Continue on the path until it merges with a lane, then keep ahead to cross Hemlingford Bridge.

4. On the far side of the bridge, continue ahead up the lane to the main road. Cross over and turn left along the pavement towards Kingsbury. After 440yds (402m), reach an area of open land on the right. At the far end turn right, through a kissing gate, to the right of No. 61, onto a clear footpath that goes along the back of some houses. In about 220yds (201m), turn left into Meadow Close, then left again into Pear Tree Avenue to return to the car park.

Where to eat and drink

The White Swan, which you pass on your way into Kingsbury Water Park, is a regular haunt of local rambling groups. The Royal Oak, also on the main road, has a beer garden, children's play area and a large car park. Alternatively, you might like to try the Old Barn Coffee Shop at the visitor centre in the park, which has an outside seating area.

What to look out for

Many wild birds visit the water park and you will certainly see plenty of ducks, swans, coots and moorhens, and especially Canada geese. Look out for herons, kingfishers, common terns, great crested grebes, cormorants, little ringed plovers and lapwings. Some 200 species of bird have been recorded here, and the park has one of the UK's largest inland breeding colonies of common terns.

While you're there

Kingsbury's Norman church stands on a hill overlooking the River Tame where the kings of Mercia were said to have had a palace. Mercia was the main Saxon kingdom at the time of King Offa, who died in AD 796. Close to the church, the crumbling wall round Kingsbury Hall is now part of a farmhouse, which retains its Elizabethan splendour.

BY BADDESLEY CLINTON AND HAY WOOD

DISTANCE/TIME	5 miles (8km) / 2hrs
ASCENT/GRADIENT	16ft (5m) / ▲
PATHS	Field paths and woodland tracks
LANDSCAPE	Rolling Warwickshire countryside
SUGGESTED MAP	OS Explorer 221 Coventry & Warwick
START/FINISH	Grid Reference: SP206706
DOG FRIENDLINESS	On lead at all times
PARKING	Lay-by beside Hay Wood picnic area, Hay Wood Lane
PUBLIC TOILETS	None on route

This lovely walk through the heart of Warwickshire's delightful countryside provides the opportunity to visit Baddesley Clinton Manor. This mansion is one of the finest medieval moated manor houses in the country.

Baddesley Clinton Manor is the former home of the Ferrers family and its wide moat may date back to Norman times. The bridge that spans the moat is comparatively recent, being only 200 or so years old. Many of the Ferrers family were laid to rest in the nearby church. Sir Edward Ferrers, the first of some 12 generations, died in 1535.

The Ferrers family, staunchly loyal to the Roman Catholic faith, were persecuted throughout the 16th century by the Protestant authorities. When Henry Ferrers, who was born in 1549, let the house out in the 1590s, it became a regular refuge for Jesuit priests. On one occasion as many as six were hidden in specially built priest holes, which can still be seen around the house today. The family fell on hard times again during the Civil War, when they were made to pay for their support for Charles I.

Despite a few embellishments over the years, the house has seen little real change since Henry's death in 1633. It stayed in the Ferrers family until 1940, and is now owned and managed by the National Trust.

Nearby Wroxall Abbey was founded by Benedictine nuns in 1135. Owned and occupied by the Bourgoyne family for many years, it was purchased by the architect Sir Christopher Wren as a retreat just three years after he completed his work on St Paul's Cathedral, in London in 1710. His house was replaced by the current Victorian one in the 1860s. Today, only St Leonard's Church and part of the cloisters remain, surrounded by glorious gardens.

You start the walk by crossing the gorgeous Hay Wood. After following tracks and quiet lanes, the route brings you back through the splendid park of Wroxall Abbey. From the abbey parkland you continue past a converted windmill on the edge of the village of Rowington Green and join the Heart of England Way long distance footpath. Fine Warwickshire countryside and footpaths, lined with flowers in the spring, then lead to the church close to Baddesley Clinton Manor.

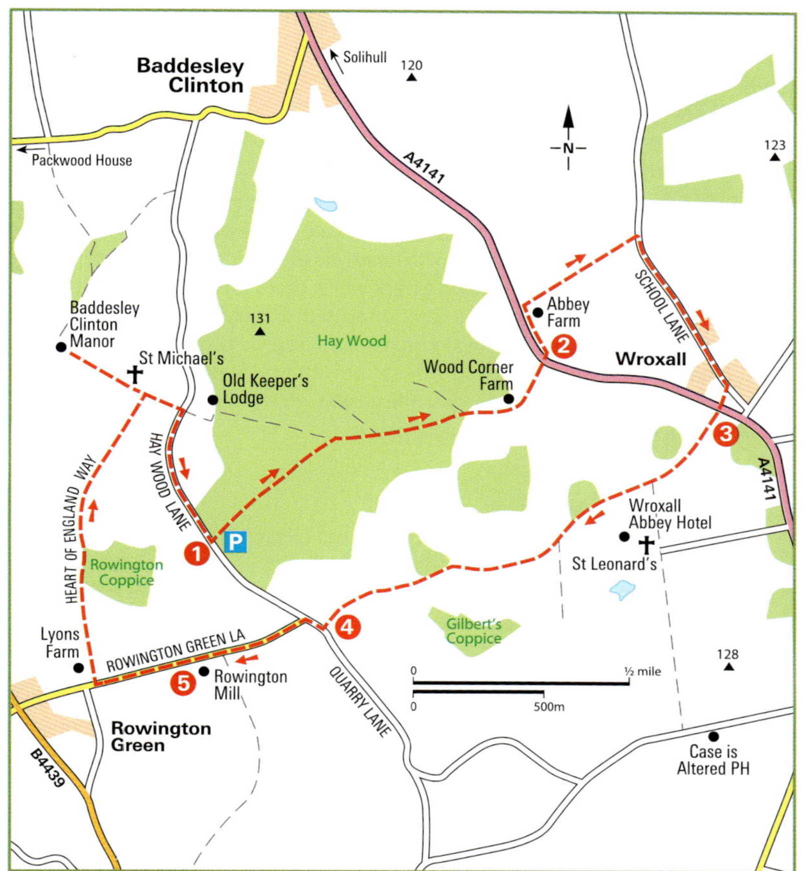

1. From the picnic area lay-by, take the track into Hay Wood. At a crossing of paths, go right along the bridleway. Nearing the edge of the woods, the clear path arcs left and you emerge from the trees via a gate. Cross the field to a gate and pass between the buildings to a double gate. Through these go left then right by Wood Corner Farm, and along the drive to reach the A4141.

2. Cross the road and go left along the pavement of the A4141 for about 220yds (201m), then go right along a bridleway between the buildings of Abbey Farm. Continue along the track until you reach School Lane and walk right along it towards the A4141. About 100yds (91m) before you reach the end of the lane, go right through a gate and cross the corner of a field to reach the A4141 via a kissing gate near the village hall.

3. Cross the A4141, enter Wroxall Abbey park over a stile and through a field gate, then follow the track through the grounds. In about 500yds (457m), the route gives you glimpses of the Victorian mansion (now a hotel) and the old abbey building, which you can see to your left. Where the track peters out continue ahead through two kissing gates and then bear half left towards a kissing gate set in a small area of enclosed woodland. Exit from the woodland via a kissing gate. Follow this path ahead as it descends in a southwesterly direction to a waymark post. Continue ahead to go through another kissing gate and a field gate. Head west-southwest across a large area of pasture, passing to the right of Gilbert's Coppice. Through a kissing gate, bear right along the field edge to a field gate onto Quarry Lane.

4. Turn right along the lane, then bear left at the junction and walk along the quiet Rowington Green Lane for almost 0.5 miles (800m).

5. Pass by the former windmill on the left, now a private house, and just before reaching Lyons Farm, go right through a field gate onto a track which is part of the Heart of England Way. The route takes you to the right of the farm complex, via a gate, and then along a track which bears right. After passing Rowington Coppice you come to a gate. Through this, continue ahead on field paths alongside hedges, crossing the corner of a field via two gates and a footbridge. Reaching the church driveway, turn left to visit Baddesley Clinton Manor. Then retrace your steps, pass the church, until you reach Hay Wood Lane. Turn right back to the parking area.

Where to eat and drink

There are no pubs along the route but you will find refreshment at The Barn Restaurant at Baddesley Clinton Manor. The Case is Altered pub nearby serves real ale but no food, although you can take your own food and eat in the courtyard or gardens (open lunchtimes Thursday to Sunday and every evening).

What to look out for

Hay Wood was once part of the ancient Forest of Arden and later owned by Baddesley Clinton Estate. Today, it is commercially managed by the Forestry Commission. They have retained a mix of woodland and you'll see the track is lined with oak, rowan, birch and holly.

While you're there

The National Trust's Packwood House stands in hidden countryside less than 3 miles (4.8km) from Baddesley Clinton Manor. The building was created by Graham Baron Ash and contains fine collections of 16th-century textiles and furniture. It is most famous for its exceptional collection of 17th-century yew trees said to represent the Sermon on the Mount.

AROUND THE TOWN OF STRATFORD-UPON-AVON

DISTANCE/TIME	2.5 miles (4km) / 1hr 30min
ASCENT/GRADIENT	Negligible
PATHS	Riverside paths and pavements
LANDSCAPE	Historic streets
SUGGESTED MAP	OS Explorer 205 Stratford-upon-Avon & Evesham
START/FINISH	Grid Reference: SP205547
DOG FRIENDLINESS	On lead along streets
PARKING	Recreation Ground pay-and-display car park
PUBLIC TOILETS	At car park

This gentle walk along the banks of the River Avon takes you past the weir and Holy Trinity Church, before a stroll through the town to see some of its famous buildings, which include the medieval 14-arched Clopton Bridge that forms a splendid gateway to the town. The Town Hall is a fine Palladian building, and Harvard House in the High Street dates from 1596. The latter takes its name from the owner's daughter, Katherine Rogers, who married Robert Harvard of Southwark in London in 1605. Their son John went on to bequeath Harvard University in the USA, and the university now owns Harvard House. The Falcon, now Hotel Indigo, was probably one of Shakespeare's regular drinking places and opposite is the old guildhall and an attractive row of timbered almshouses.

But it is because of William Shakespeare that visitors flock in their millions to Stratford-upon-Avon. Born here, in Henley Street, in 1564, he was baptised in Holy Trinity Church, and attended King Edward VI's Grammar School in Church Street. He married Anne Hathaway in 1582 and they had three children: Susannah, Hamnet and Judith. At some time in the mid-1580s, he headed for London.

By 1592, William Shakespeare was the talk of the town, counting Queen Elizabeth I and her court among his plays' many admirers. His poetry was first published around this time, and he began to accumulate serious wealth. By 1597, he was able to buy New Place, then one of Stratford's grandest properties. The early 1600s saw his theatre company gain a royal title (the King's Men), and the Bard went on to write many of his best-known tragedies, including Othello, King Lear and Macbeth.

Shakespeare began to spend less and less time in the giddy London theatre-world, and more time at home in Stratford. His son Hamnet had died, aged 11, in 1596, but his daughter Susannah had survived and married Dr John Hall in 1607. The couple lived in Hall's Croft, in the old part of the town, until after her father's death. Shakespeare died on 23 April 1616 and was buried at Holy Trinity. You can see his tomb, and that of his wife Anne Hathaway, who died in 1623.

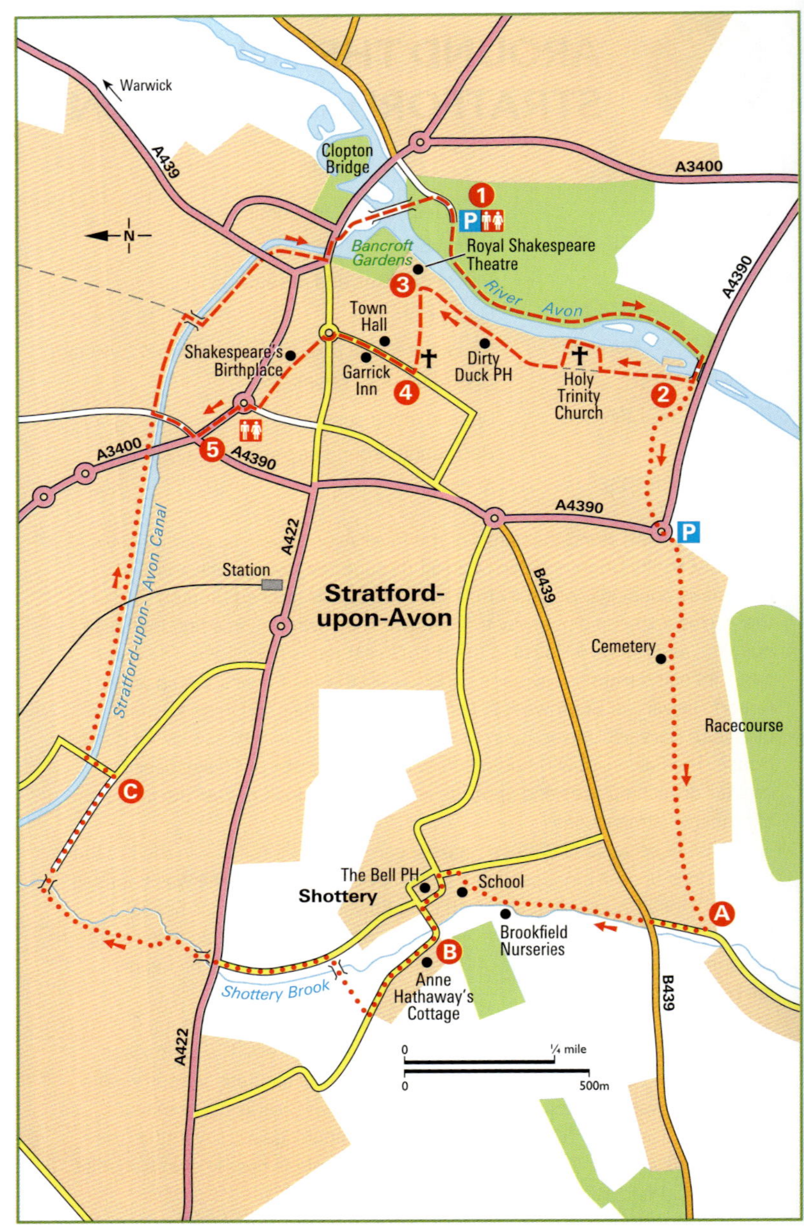

1. From the car park, walk along the banks of the River Avon opposite the famous Royal Shakespeare Theatre. Pass the weir, and continue to reach a footbridge over the river, just in front of the A4390 road bridge.

2. Go right over the footbridge and bear right past the flats that replaced the old watermill, into Mill Lane. Continue up Mill Lane and go through the churchyard of Holy Trinity Church, walking around the church to see the river

view. Leave the churchyard through the main gate into Old Town and follow the pavement. Just before reaching the turn into Southern Lane, go right into RSC Gardens and walk up through the Gardens. Continue past the ferry and stroll through the attractive Theatre Gardens by the side of the Avon, exiting into Waterside and passing by the frontage of the old theatre building.

3. Go left up Chapel Lane. At the top of the lane is the Guild Chapel to Shakespeare's Grammar School, with New Place Gardens to the right.

4. Go right along Chapel Street, passing The Shakespeare and the Town Hall into High Street. Harvard House is on the left, near the black-and-white Garrick Inn. At the end of High Street, bear left around the traffic island into Henley Street and walk along the pedestrianised area that takes you past Shakespeare's Birthplace and the museum. At the top of Henley Street, bear right and then left into Birmingham Road. Go left up to the traffic lights and cross the road at the pedestrian crossing.

5. Head right up Clopton Road for 100yds (91m), then descend to the tow path of the Stratford-upon-Avon Canal at bridge No. 66. Follow this, going southeast. Cross the canal at bridge No. 68 and continue along the tow path into Bancroft Gardens by the canal basin, where you will see an array of narrowboats and the Royal Shakespeare Theatre. Cross the old Tram Bridge to return to the car park on the right.

Extending the walk This additional 3-mile (4.8km) walk takes you to visit Anne Hathaway's cottage. Once over the footbridge at Point 2, walk ahead up the footpath away from the river that follows the line of the A4390, then arcs right and then left. Cross over Avon Meadow Close and after a short stretch of path continue through Old Town Mews, an estate road, to the roundabout on the A4390. By its side, cross the road with care, then proceed along the pavement into residential Wetherby Way. Follow the tarmac path to the right of No. 2, soon passing the cemetery hedge, and continue on a footpath through common land at the back of houses. This follows the track bed of a former railway line. At the end of the common you will come to Luddington Road, with Stratford Racecourse entrance to the left (Point A).

Go sharp right along Luddington Road up to the B439 Evesham road. Cross and walk along the signed footpath opposite, by the side of Shottery Brook. Footpaths and a pavement will take you along Hogarth Road, then follow another footpath to the driveway to Brookfield Nurseries. Go right up the driveway into Shottery. At the main road, go left past Shottery St Andrew Primary School and The Bell, then left down Cottage Lane and walk up to the picturesque cottage of Anne Hathaway (Point B). Continue past the cottage and in about 300yds (274m), go right on a tarmac footpath, passing several thatched cottages. You will emerge on the pavement in Church Lane, where you go left up to the A422 Alcester Road.

Cross the A422 and continue up a footpath opposite, to the right of Bridge House, which meanders along the side of Shottery Brook. At the end of a grassed area, bear left and go up to a residential road. Go right, then left to join a footpath alongside the Shottery Brook. Cross a road and continue ahead, to follow the left bank of the brook for 120yds (110m). Go right over a footbridge behind some swings onto the pavement of Masons Road. Follow the pavement alongside the road for some 350yds (320m), then turn left into Timothy Bridge Road (Point C).

Cross the canal bridge and descend right to the tow path which leads back into Stratford-upon-Avon. You will pass by a number of moored narrowboats and rejoin the main walk by the Clopton road bridge, No. 65 (Point 5).

Where to eat and drink

The Black Swan pub in Southern Lane, known locally as 'The Dirty Duck', is frequented by actors from the theatre. The half-timbered Garrick Inn on High Street is also a popular spot. The Bell in nearby Shottery, near Anne Hathaway's cottage, is used to welcoming walkers.

What to look out for

Back in the 1970s and 1980s, the swans virtually disappeared from the River Avon due to poisoning by lead fishing weights. Today, they have returned, and together with the ducks, add considerable interest to the many photo opportunities available. In the canal basin, narrow boats assemble to form a colourful foreground for photographs of the Gower Memorial, which depicts Shakespeare and characters from the Bard's famous plays.

While you're there

Spare time to visit some of the fantastic Shakespeare properties and indulge in the wonderful medieval atmosphere that permeates this beautiful town.

FALSTAFF

CHIPPING NORTON AND THE ROLLRIGHT STONES

DISTANCE/TIME	8.5 miles (13.7km) / 3hrs 30min
ASCENT/GRADIENT	850ft (259m)) / ▲ ▲
PATHS	Field paths and tracks, country roads, several stiles
LANDSCAPE	Rolling hills on the Oxfordshire/ Warwickshire border
SUGGESTED MAP	OS Explorer 191 Banbury, Bicester & Chipping Norton
START/FINISH	Grid reference: SP313271
DOG FRIENDLINESS	Under control or on lead across farmland, one lengthy stretch of country road and busy streets in Chipping Norton
PARKING	Long-stay car park off A44 (New Street), in centre of Chipping Norton
PUBLIC TOILETS	At car park and town centre

Commanding a splendid position overlooking the hills and valleys of the northeast Cotswolds, the Rollright Stones comprise the Whispering Knights, the King's Men and the King Stone. These intriguing stones are steeped in myth and legend. The story goes that a king was leading his army, while five of his knights stood together conspiring against him. The king met a witch nearby who told him he would be King of England if he could see the settlement of Long Compton in seven long strides. As he approached the top of the ridge a mound of earth suddenly rose up before him, preventing him from seeing the village and so the king, his soldiers and his knights were all turned to stone.

In reality, the Rollright Stones form a group of prehistoric megalithic monuments created from large natural boulders found within about 600yds (549m) of the site. The stones are naturally pitted, giving them astonishing and highly unusual shapes. The five Whispering Knights are the remains of a portal dolmen burial chamber, probably from 3800–3000 BC, long before the stone circle. The King Stone stands apart from the others. The single standing stone was almost certainly erected to mark the site of a Bronze Age cemetery around 1800–1500 BC. Finally, you come to the King's Men stone circle – a ceremonial monument thought to have been built around 2500–2000 BC.

Chipping Norton is a busy market town and its Market Square, dominated by the 19th-century Town Hall, is at its heart. Opposite the Town Hall, you'll find a museum with displays on the town's history. From the square, the town slopes down Church Street, past a row of pretty almshouses dating from 1640, towards St Mary's, a splendid church containing some fine brasses and impressive tombs. Its most unusual feature is a hexagonal porch with a vaulted ceiling. Behind the church are motte-and-bailey earthworks that show the town was of some importance in the Norman period.

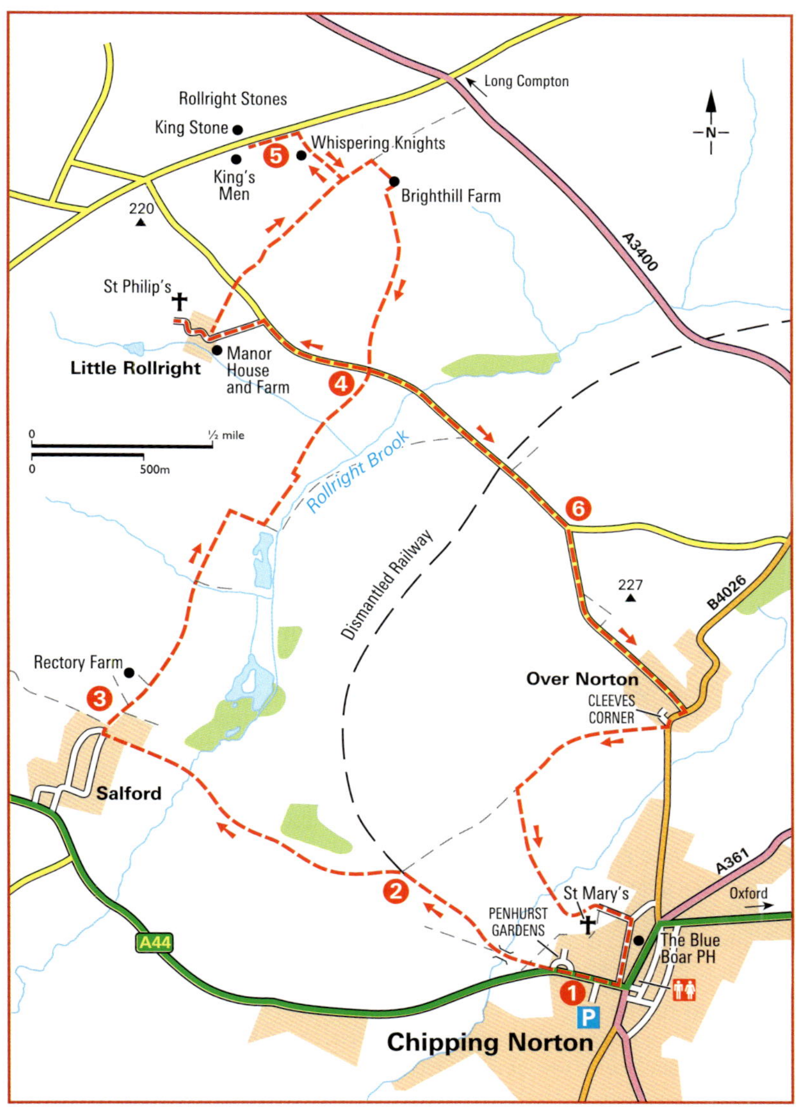

1. Follow the A44, New Street, downhill. Pass Penhurst Gardens, then veer right through a kissing gate. Skirt the left-hand edge of the recreation ground and aim for a gate. Descend to a bridge and, when the path forks, keep right. Go up the slope to a kissing gate. Cross a drive and continue to the next tarmac drive. Keep walking ahead to a kissing gate and walk along the right-hand field edge. Make for a gate and drop down to double gates on the right.

2. Go through. Turn sharp left and walk towards Salford, keeping the hedge on the left. Continue into the village and soon turn right by a sign saying, 'Rectory Farm – Trout Lakes'.

3. Follow the track to a right-hand bend. Go straight ahead here, following the field edge. Make for a gate ahead and turn right in the next field. About 100yds (91m) before the field corner, turn left and follow the path across to an opening in the boundary. Veer left, then immediately right to skirt the field. Cross a little stream and maintain your direction in the next field to reach the road.

4. Turn left, then left again for Little Rollright. After visiting the church, retrace your steps to the D'Arcy Dalton Way on the left. Follow the path up the field slope to the road. Cross over and continue on the way between fields. Head for some trees and approach a stile. Don't cross it; instead, turn left and skirt the field, passing close to the Whispering Knights.

5. On reaching the road, turn left and visit the site of the Rollright Stones. Return to the Whispering Knights, head down the field to the stile and cross it through trees. Walk ahead along a grassy path and turn right just before the next stile towards Brighthill Farm. Pass alongside the buildings to a stile, head diagonally right down the field to a kissing gate, then keep the boundary on your right and head for a galvanised gate in the bottom right corner of the field. Make for the bottom right corner of the next field, go through a gate and skirt the field, turning left at the road.

6. Keep right at the next fork and head towards the village of Over Norton. Walk through the village to the T-junction. Turn right and, when the road swings to the left by Cleeves Corner, go right on a track signposted 'Salford'. When the hedges on the left finally give way, turn left on a field edge path, with a hedge on your right. Follow the path down the slope, make for two kissing gates and then follow the path alongside a stone wall to reach the parish church. Join Church Lane and follow it as far as the T-junction. Turn right and return to the car park.

Where to eat and drink

Chipping Norton offers a variety of pubs, hotels and tea rooms. Try the rambling old Blue Boar with its views of Market Place and the town's many historic buildings. Here you'll find a good choice of dishes, including Gloucestershire sausages.

What to see

The manor house at Little Rollright was once important. It was the home of William Blower, who gave St Philip's Church its pinnacled tower in 1617. The church, which dates mostly from the 15th century, is Grade II* listed and contains two 17th-century monuments to the local Dixon and Blower families.

While you're there

Just 3 miles (4.8km) southwest of Chipping Norton is the pretty village of Churchill, the birthplace of William 'Strata' Smith, 'the Father of English Geology', who produced the first geological map of England.

25 ON THE CENTENARY WAY FROM ILMINGTON

DISTANCE/TIME	3 miles (4.8km) / 1hr 30min
ASCENT/GRADIENT	492ft (150m) / ▲ ▲
PATHS	Field paths and country lane, several stiles
LANDSCAPE	Edge of Cotswold Hills
SUGGESTED MAP	OS Explorer 205 Stratford-upon-Avon & Evesham
START/FINISH	Grid Reference: SP210440
DOG FRIENDLINESS	On lead at all times
PARKING	Playing fields car park on Mickleton Road, west of Ilmington village
PUBLIC TOILETS	None on route

Remote Ilmington is the highest village in Warwickshire, standing close to the borders of Worcestershire and Gloucestershire, and just within the Cotswolds Area of Outstanding Natural Beauty. Brimming with typical Cotswold honey-coloured stone cottages, it is a place where time seems to have stood still for centuries. The name is probably derived from a Saxon phrase describing elms on a border hill. A 10th-century record reveals its earlier name was Ylmandunes.

In 1934, Ilmington achieved a brief five minutes of fame when part of the very first Christmas broadcast by King George V was relayed to the Empire from Ilmington Manor (on Middle Street opposite the ponds), the home of the Flower family. It featured a guest appearance by local shepherd, 65-year-old Walter Walton Handy, and also included carols from the Ilmington Singers and bell ringing from the village. The local papers were delighted with the story, describing it as 'perhaps the most wonderful [feat] that has been accomplished since wireless has been brought to its present state of perfection'.

Ilmington has managed to retain its two pubs – The Red Lion and The Howard Arms – and these are enthusiastically supported by local walkers. The Ilmington Morris Dancers, carrying on a tradition that has been practised in the village for 350 years, are well known and can be seen performing regularly in the area on summer evenings.

This walk, hilly by Warwickshire standards, starts from the edge of the village. Climbing to a high point of almost 656ft (200m) near Upper Lark Stoke Farm, it offers some of the best views in the county. Having crossed farmland and strolled along a quiet country lane, you will spot the Norman church, with its fine tower, among the trees as the route drops back towards the village. The church itself is well worth a visit. It has oak pews, installed in the 1930s, which feature the unique carved mouse 'signature' of master craftsman Robert Thompson, known as the Mouseman of Kilburn. The 17th-century gabled manor house can also be seen.

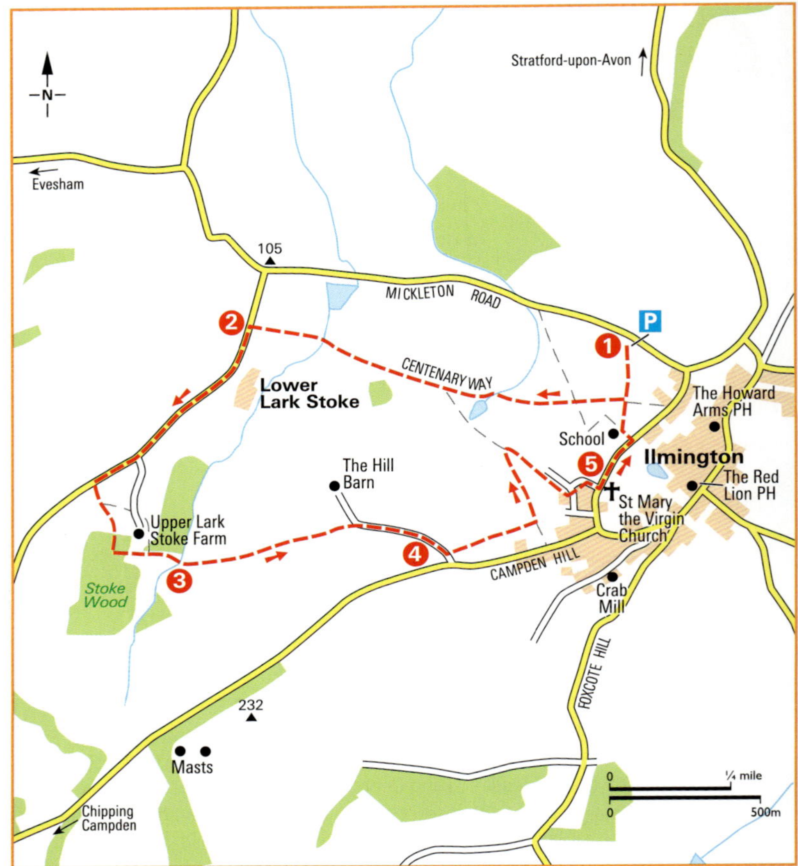

1. Cross the playing fields to go through a kissing gate to the right of a children's play area. Bear right and go through another kissing gate. Bear right again, aiming for a kissing gate in the hedge on the far side of the field. Continue in the same direction, crossing several fields. After two more kissing gates, bear left through another one, hidden from view at first. Walk gently uphill beside a hedge and then through a kissing gate, continuing in the same direction beside a fence on the right. There are fine Cotswold hill views, with an attractive farmhouse at Lower Lark Stoke ahead. Descend to go through a gate near a small pool, and bear left to walk beside the fence. Go through a gate to emerge on a driveway, along which you turn right.

2. Turn left along a tarmac lane and follow this uphill for about 0.5 miles (800m), stopping occasionally to recover your breath and to enjoy wonderful views. After the farm drive and just before the brow of the hill, go left across a field. Entering an area of young woodland just above Upper Lark Stoke Farm, keep right at a path fork. Go left just before a gate within more mature woodland and descend into a dell. Through a gate, continue downhill in the same direction to cross a small stream.

3. Bear left, uphill, to cross a footbridge and go through a gate. Keep straight ahead to climb towards the hilltop, passing to the right of a solitary tree. Over the brow, descend to a field gate. Walk beside the fence on the right and through another field gate to join a farm track. After passing the drive to The Hill Barn, over to the left, the track bends sharp right.

4. Just before reaching a road, cross a stile next to a gate on the left. Walk with the hedge on your left, descending towards Ilmington. At the bottom of the slope, go left over a stile in the trees, then right alongside a hedge. This path leads to a gate and stile, after which you turn right to follow a hedged track that leads to some buildings. Turn left, through two gates in quick succession, and then double back right, along Ilmington Grange's drive.

5. Go left at the road and then, immediately after the entrance to Ilmington Primary School, turn left through a kissing gate. Go through the gate on the right and cross the field to a kissing gate. Retracing your steps, bear left through another kissing gate and back across the playing fields to the car park.

Where to eat and drink

The Red Lion offers good food and simple bar snacks. These can be enjoyed inside the pub or outside in the covered garden area. It is also child and dog friendly. The Howard Arms pub and restaurant, once owned by the Howard family from the nearby hamlet of Foxcote, enjoys a peaceful setting on the village green and offers delicious food and a quiet pint.

What to look out for

Crab Mill is a lovely old building, built from local stone. Early in the 20th century, it was home to Lady Borwick, whose fortune came from baking powder. Later, it was occupied by Dorothy Crowfoot Hodgkin, who won a Nobel Prize for Chemistry in 1964 for her pioneering work in crystallography.

While you're there

Nearby Chipping Campden, 5 miles (8km) southwest of Ilmington, is a typical wool town built by the affluent merchants of the 14th and 15th centuries. It has many gabled Cotswold stone houses with oriel, dormer and mullioned windows, and an outstanding market hall. A visit to this wonderful old market town is almost like taking a step back into the Middle Ages.

FROM SHUSTOKE TO CHURCH END

DISTANCE/TIME	4 miles (6.4km) / 1hr 45min
ASCENT/GRADIENT	98ft (30m) / ▲
PATHS	Lakeside paths and field-edge footpaths
LANDSCAPE	Reservoir parkland, farmland and residential areas
SUGGESTED MAP	OS Explorer 232 Nuneaton & Tamworth
START/FINISH	Grid Reference: SP225909
DOG FRIENDLINESS	Under control at all times
PARKING	Shustoke car park off Coleshill Road (B4114)
PUBLIC TOILETS	None on route

The small village of Shustoke lies on the edge of Warwickshire. It was once a large parish, covering some 2,000 acres (810ha), but much of this is now under water. The village was mentioned in the Domesday survey as Scotscote and the name's origin perhaps lie in the Saxon 'sceat' meaning 'nook' or 'corner of land'. Shustoke is a divided village because of an outbreak of the plague in 1650. It used to surround St Cuthbert's Church, but the houses were moved to the west to get away from the contaminated site.

Shustoke's most famous son is Sir William Dugdale (1605–86), the author of *The Antiquities of Warwickshire*. He was born at the old rectory in Shawbury Lane, the son of a Lancashire gentleman who settled in Warwickshire after marrying late in life. William Dugdale lived at Blyth Hill in Shustoke after his marriage in 1625. He was one of a group of local gentry who took up the study of local history, and it was through this that he came into contact with members of the court of Charles I. He secured a post at the College of Arms, and spent most of the Civil War in the Royalist stronghold of Oxford, where he was able to pursue his studies in the Bodleian Library.

As well as Warwickshire, he focused his attention on English monastic houses. The first volume of his *Monasticon Anglicanum* was published in 1655, with two more huge volumes following in 1661 and 1673. *The Antiquities of Warwickshire*, the most detailed study of its day, was published in 1655. He also wrote a history of St Paul's Cathedral, published in 1658.

The Restoration was kind to Dugdale and he was able to continue with his heraldic work all over the country. He was appointed Garter King of Arms in 1677 and died, aged 80, in 1686. He was buried in the village. Today, a large part of the local land is still owned by the Dugdale family.

The beautiful Shustoke Reservoir, together with nearby Whitacre Water Works, supplies water to the bulk storage reservoirs at Coventry and Nuneaton. The reservoir is a well-used sailing venue, and is also popular with anglers and walkers.

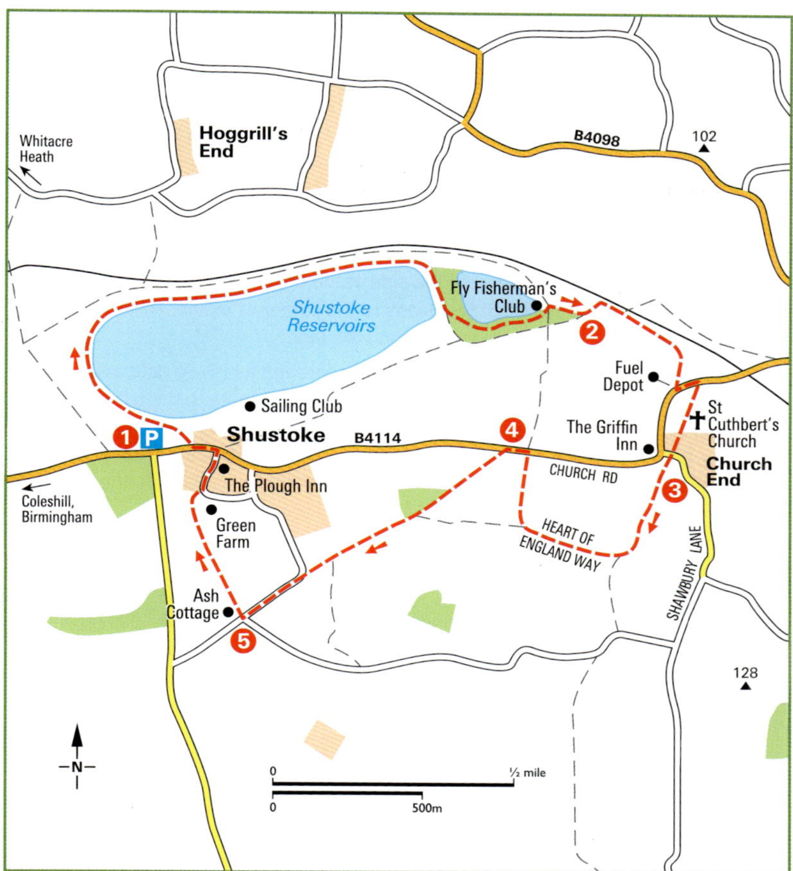

1. Leave the car park going up to the reservoir embankment and go left to follow the fingerpost of the Circular Path, which encircles the larger of the two Shustoke reservoirs. At the east end of the reservoir, go through a gate and immediately left down steps, then go right along a track. Meeting a tarmac lane, go left over a footbridge, then along a path parallel to the lane, which is a short distance to the south of the smaller reservoir – this is to protect you from the possible danger of fly fishing lines. After passing behind the buildings of the Fly Fisherman's Club, leave the reservoir complex over a stile and go right along a path in woodland and cross a footbridge.

2. Emerge from the trees via a gate and turn left. Follow the field edge to a further gate and continue along a field edge, the railway on your left, before curving round to meet the B4114 at the entrance to a fuel depot. Turn left along the road edge for 80yds (73m), then cross the road and go through a kissing gate into the pasture below St Cuthbert's Church. Walk half right up the field and go through a second kissing gate to the right-hand side of the churchyard, and take the lane past the church to Shawbury Lane.

3. Cross the lane and go through a kissing gate, situated a little to the right, into the field opposite. Following the direction of the waymarkers across two fields, via a gate and a kissing gate, to meet the Heart of England Way. Do not go through the kissing gate, but go right to a kissing gate in the field corner and follow the Way around the next two fields. Bear right at the end of the larger field to walk up to Church Road, via three kissing gates. Go left along the road for 50yds (46m).

4. At the end of a small row of cottages, turn left through a gate, and cross the field half right to a kissing gate. Take the public footpath through a small copse and then continue ahead by the side of the hedge until, via a kissing gate, you come to a farm track that leads to the corner of a lane. Through another kissing gate, continue ahead along the lane.

5. Just before you reach Ash Cottage, go right through a kissing gate and follow the footpath across a cultivated field to a kissing gate to the left of Green Farm. A final kissing gate to the right of Greenacre (cottage) leads into a lane. Continue ahead and you soon reach the Green in Shustoke, close to The Plough Inn and at the side of the B4114 (Coleshill Road). Go left, then right into the car park.

Where to eat and drink

The Plough Inn is a family pub and restaurant. Built in 1790, the building retains much of its original charm with low ceilings, nooks and crannies. They serve cask ales along with a range of home-cooked food. The Griffin Inn at Church End has a good selection of bar snacks and has a large garden area.

What to look out for

Shustoke attracts a wide range of birdlife to its valuable open water. As well as pochard, teal, widgeon and tufted duck, the occasional osprey has been sighted, dipping this way on its passage south in November. You may also spy the distinctive profile of a cormorant, patiently fishing at the water's edge.

While you're there

Not far away from Shustoke is Hoar Park Farm, an 18th-century farm complex which has been converted to accommodate a lively craft village and children's farm. There is also a country shopping area, an antiques centre, a garden centre and a restaurant, open all year round from Tuesday to Sunday.

A CIRCUIT FROM BEAUTIFUL BERKSWELL

DISTANCE/TIME	5 miles (8km) / 2hrs
ASCENT/GRADIENT	115ft (35m) / ▲
PATHS	Field paths and parkland footpaths, several stiles
LANDSCAPE	Gentle, rolling farmland and parkland
SUGGESTED MAP	OS Explorer 221 Coventry & Warwick
START/FINISH	Grid Reference: SP244791
DOG FRIENDLINESS	Off lead through Sixteen Acre Wood, otherwise under strict control
PARKING	Car park near church and primary school in Berkswell
PUBLIC TOILETS	None on route

There are few nicer places to visit in Warwickshire than Berkswell, with its red-roofed, white-timbered cottages, the beautiful church, intriguing five-holed stocks and its historic pub. The old Saxon village was mentioned in the Domesday Book and has been variously called Berchewelle, Berkeswelle, Bercleswelle and finally Berkswell. It is believed that the village took its name from the 16ft (4.8m) square well that is situated behind the almshouses. The 12th-century Church of St John the Baptist displays a wonderful two-storeyed, gabled and timbered porch that dates from the 16th century. Inside this lovely building is an old crypt conceivably dating from Saxon times, some 800-year-old stone seats along the walls and magnificent choir stalls decorated with poppy heads and the figures of three saints – Wulfstan, Dunstan and Chad.

Although the nearby five-holed stocks were probably originally built with six holes, it is more fun to believe the local legend that they were specially made to accommodate a one-legged man and his two drunken companions.

There is a 16th-century pub in the village – The Bear Inn. The fine half-timbered building was once part of the Berkswell Estate and carried the coat of arms of the Earls of Warwick. It has links dating to the Civil War – some of Cromwell's troops were stationed at Berkswell and would have undoubtedly rested and drunk here.

A 19th-century Russian cannon, which was captured during the Crimean War in 1855 by Captain Arthur Eardley-Wilmot, the lord of the manor, stands on the front terrace of the inn. It was last fired in 1897 to mark the Diamond Jubilee of Queen Victoria. Apparently, several windows in the village were shattered by the noise.

Set in beautiful farmland on the far side of the lake is Berkswell Hall, once the family home of the Eardley-Wilmots. John Eardley-Wilmot went to school with the English writer, biographer and critic Dr Samuel Johnson in the 1720s. The hall has now been converted into private residential apartments.

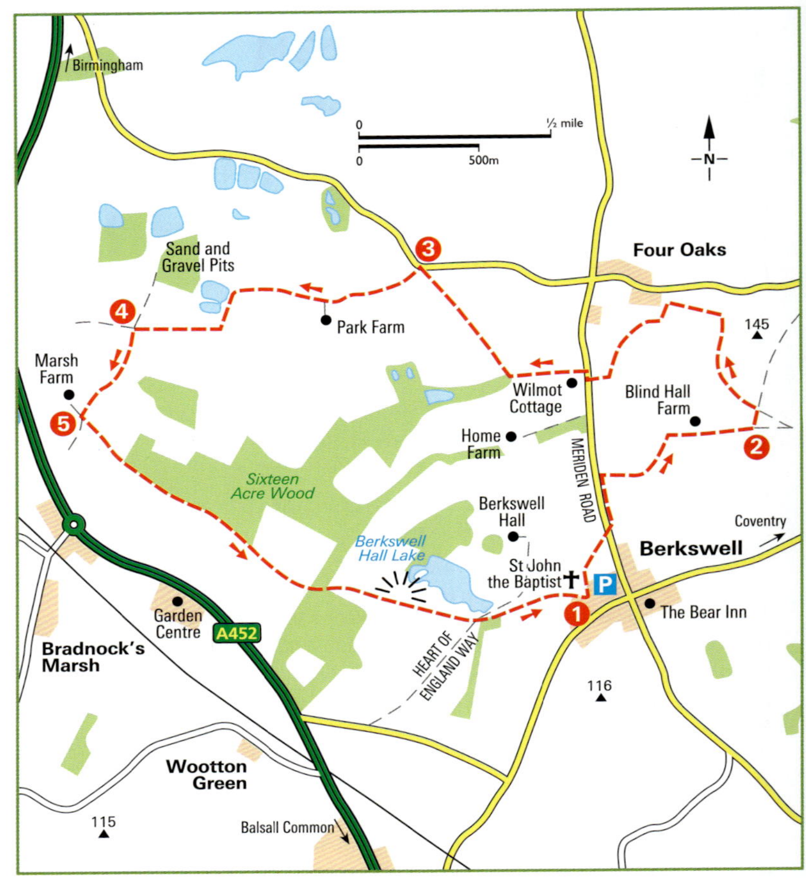

1. From the car park in the village, go right onto Church Lane and, just past the school but before the church, go right through a kissing gate. Follow the Heart of England Way to Meriden Road via four kissing gates. Go left along the road for 300yds (274m), having crossed to the pavement on the opposite side. Go right up a farm lane, passing through a kissing gate by a cattle grid and then Blind Hall Farm.

2. At the end of the lane/track go through a kissing gate by the farm gate, bear sharp left and walk along the field edge to its left corner, just past a small pond. Go left over a footbridge and then through a kissing gate and continue by the left-hand side of the hedge. The waymarked footpath weaves in and out of the hedge. After continuing ahead through a wide hedge gap, walk to the field corner and go left, skirting a small pond, to reach a kissing gate by some houses in Four Oaks. Ignore the kissing gate and bear left. In 90 paces go right over a plank footbridge and stile to cross the large, cultivated field diagonally, and exit onto Meriden Road via a kissing gate. Cross over and continue down the driveway to the right of Wilmot Cottage opposite, going through a gateway onto farmland. The path goes to the right of the hedge for two fields, crossing one stile, offering a clear view of Home Farm to the left; then, over another

stile, crosses a third field diagonally. In about 625yds (571m), through a smaller field, you will reach the corner of Mercote Hall Lane via a kissing gate.

3. Go left along Mercote Hall Lane for about 0.5 miles (800m), passing the Park Farm complex. Pass through a gate and walk along the lane past the large enclosed sand and gravel pits.

4. At the end of the pit area, at a track junction, go left along a footpath to the left of a copse, then right over a footbridge and stile. Cross to a gate and footbridge, ascend to a kissing gate and walk to the left of a hedge on the approach to Marsh Farm.

5. Just beyond the farm, turn left and follow the farm track alongside the hedge towards Sixteen Acre Wood. Cross the stile into the wood and take the track along the wood edge for some 700yds (640m). Emerging from the woodland, join the footpath for two fields, with the hedge on your left, then go through a strip of trees into former parkland via a kissing gate. Follow the path quarter-left across the cultivated field for some 650yds (594m) and you will enjoy a magnificent view of Berkswell Hall Lake. Enter trees and go left through a kissing gate to rejoin the Heart of England Way. Cross the footbridge onto a planked causeway with Berkswell Hall to your left. Continue ahead to a kissing gate. Go on through a tree belt to a kissing gate and then a gate, and back into Berkswell. Go through the churchyard along Church Lane to return to the car park.

Where to eat and drink
In Berkswell, The Bear Inn, near the junction of the Meriden and Coventry roads, has a large car park and a good beer garden. Children are allowed in the pub, but dogs are restricted to the large garden area. In the village also, near the church, is the friendly Berkswell Store and Stove Tea Room.

What to look out for
The Tsarist Russian flag in the Church of St John the Baptist displays a double-headed eagle. It was captured by Captain Eardley-Wilmot of Berkswell Hall at Kertch during his military service in the Crimean War in 1855, and now hangs in the room above the south porch.

While you're there
Take time to visit the beautiful Church of St John the Baptist in Berkswell. Can you spot master woodcarver Robert Thompson's 'signature' (carved mice) in his woodwork? There are 17 of them in the church. Look out for two of the churchyard's unusual gravestones. James Owen was beheaded in 1898 in a bizarre sawmill accident and his gravestone is a broken pillar. Carved bread, eggs and bacon appear on the memorial to a villager who died of over-eating.

A LOOP FROM LONG HILL TO ETTINGTON

DISTANCE/TIME	6 miles (9.7km) / 2hrs
ASCENT/GRADIENT	345ft (105m) / ▲ ▲ ▲
PATHS	Field paths, farm tracks and country lanes
LANDSCAPE	Gentle, rolling countryside
SUGGESTED MAP	OS Explorer 205 Stratford-upon-Avon & Evesham
START/FINISH	Grid Reference: SP251518
DOG FRIENDLINESS	On lead at all times
PARKING	Large lay-by at Long Hill on Blue Lane
PUBLIC TOILETS	None on route

Every road east of Stratford-upon-Avon appears to lead to Ettington, a small village that is bypassed by most people on their way to Banbury or Stratford. If you stop here, however, you will discover a lively place at the junction of two former turnpike roads.

Originally there were two villages – Upper Eatington and Lower Eatington, separated by a 1.5-mile (2.4km) gap. The Shirley family lived in the impressive high Victorian manor house in Lower Eatington for many years. At the end of the 18th century, they decided to landscape their estate, with the result that the village disappeared leaving just their house and the church, which became the family chapel.

The family then gave land to Upper Eatington village and a new (second) church, the Church of St Thomas à Becket, was built in 1798. At roughly the same time, Upper Eatington was renamed Ettington and the former Lower Eatington became part of the parish of Ettington. The manor house is now the prestigious Ettington Park Hotel, but its chapel has become a ruin. Unfortunately, the Church of St Thomas à Becket was built of poor-quality materials and it quickly fell into disrepair. The tower, which has become part of a residential property and remains a local landmark at the entrance to Ettington village, is all that is left. In 1903, the Church of Holy Trinity and St Thomas of Canterbury was funded by public subscription.

The walk starts from a lay-by on the Loxley Road, a mile (1.6km) or so out of the village, and follows a farm track towards Ettington. After passing the tower and Ettington church, it ascends into open countryside along a lovely stretch of footpath with fine views. The walk is completed with a stroll back up a quiet country lane.

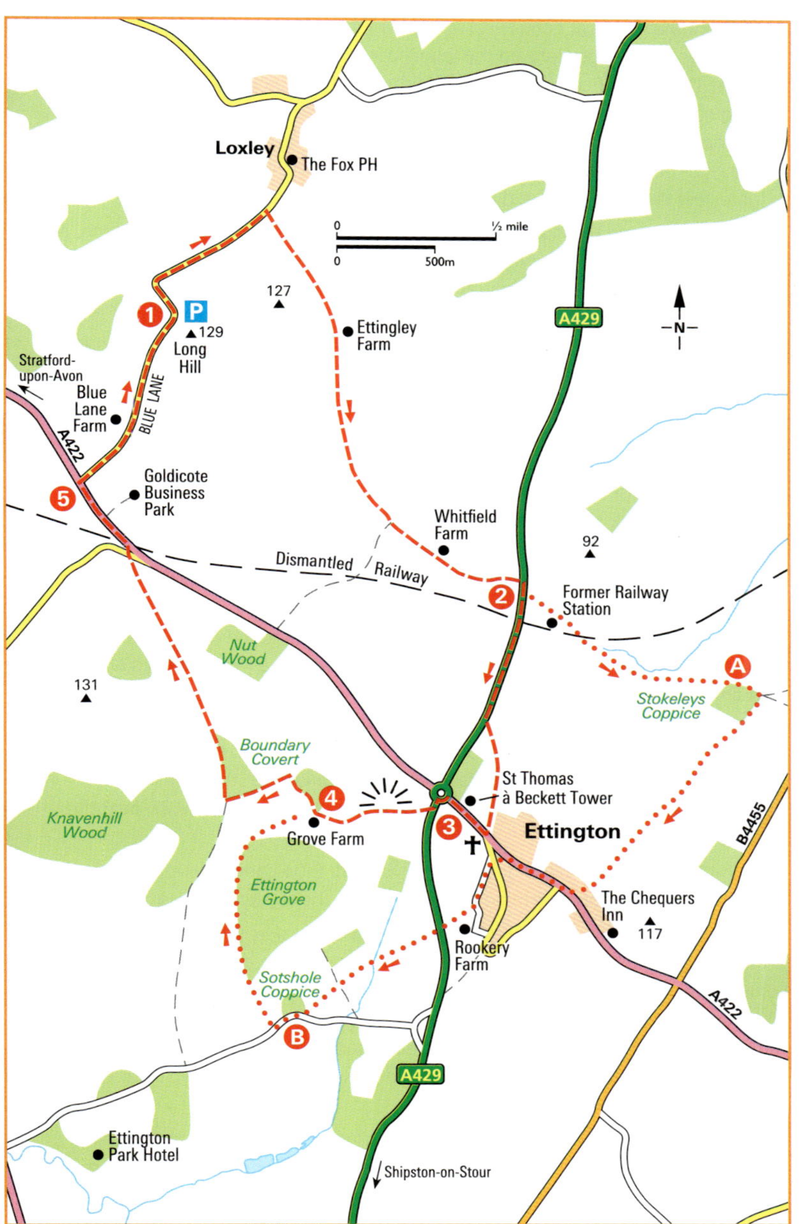

Loxley
The Fox PH
1
P
127
129
Long Hill
Ettingley Farm
Stratford-upon-Avon
Blue Lane Farm
BLUE LANE
A422
Goldicote Business Park
5
Whitfield Farm
A429
92
Dismantled Railway
2
Former Railway Station
131
Nut Wood
Stokeleys Coppice
A
Boundary Covert
St Thomas à Beckett Tower
Knavenhill Wood
4
Grove Farm
3
Ettington
Ettington Grove
The Chequers Inn
117
B4455
Sotshole Coppice
Rookery Farm
A422
B
A429
Ettington Park Hotel
Shipston-on-Stour
0   ½ mile
0   500m
N

1. From the lay-by at Long Hill, walk down the lane towards Loxley. In about 0.5 miles (800m), go right up the lane, past Hillside View and towards Ettingley Farm. Continue ahead to the right of Ettingley Farm, now a track. Through a field gate continue ahead across a field to a gate in the hedge. Descend across the next field, and at a path junction go ahead through a gate to join the path to the right of the hedge, passing to the right of Whitfield Farm. Through a kissing gate, join the farm drive and follow it down to the A429.

2. Go right along the right-hand grass verge of the A429 towards Ettington, then in about 600yds (549m) cross the busy road with care and go left through a gate in the hedge. Turn right and follow the path to the left of the hedge to reach on to the old Warwick Road. Follow this traffic-free, disused road up to the A422 in the village, which brings you to a crossroads opposite the Church of Holy Trinity and St Thomas of Canterbury.

3. Go right along the A422 Banbury to Stratford-upon-Avon road, passing by the tower of St Thomas à Becket. Just before reaching the large roundabout, cross the road and follow the grass verge along the side of the A429 for 50 paces. Cross the A429, then climb the embankment opposite and go over a plank footbridge at the top and onto a farm drive. Go left along the drive, which leads to Grove Farm, taking time to enjoy the fine view to the right.

4. Walk between the buildings of Grove Farm, then bear right along the lane/track that passes to the left of woodland. Beyond the woodland end, the track bends left. Go through a kissing gate and pass to the left of Boundary Covert. Now the farm track becomes grass underfoot as you proceed along the ridge with extensive views all around. Go right at a junction of paths and continue to the left of the covert. Go down the track past the end of Nut Wood where it soon becomes a fenced footpath. Shortly come to the Alderminster road, near Goldicote Business Park. Cross the road, then the main A422 (take care here) and go left along the wide grass verge of the A422, past the business park entrance.

5. In about 500yds (457m) go right and walk up Blue Lane towards Loxley, passing by Blue Lane Farm on the way back to the lay-by and your car.

Extending the walk This 2.5-mile (4km) extension takes you past some more of the sights in the area. Leave the main walk at the A429 (Point 2) and cross over the road with care, bearing right onto the driveway towards a farm complex, passing former railway station buildings, which closed in 1963. Bear left past some stables alongside a stream, going left at stone barns onto a farm track. Continue over the dismantled railway line, and after 30 paces, bear right over a stream into open fields.

Now go immediately left, with the stream on your left and along the side of the hedge, heading generally southeast and through a hedge gap and across a gallop. In about 500yds (457m) the path arcs right away from the stream across a cultivated field to go over a footbridge. Carry on ahead up the left side of Stokeyleys Coppice (Point A).

At the corner of the coppice, go right along the waymarked footpath, beside the coppice. Beyond the coppice, the path bears slightly right to a mid-hedge footbridge by a waymark post, then crosses the middle of a large field to another waymark post. Continue ahead beside a hedge to go between houses in Ettington. Go right along the main street, and shortly after passing the former village hall and Village Store and Post Office, go left up Church Lane.

At the top of the lane you will be in Halford Road, with the Church of Holy Trinity and St Thomas of Canterbury to your right. Go left, then bear right into Rookery Lane. In about 300yds (274m), where the lane bends sharp left, proceed ahead over a stile. Pass to the right of the Rookery Farm buildings on a metalled track, and turn right down the concrete farm track until you find the underpass for the A429. Go through the underpass and descend to a kissing gate.

Cross the field corner to another stile, then cross the next field diagonally. Go over the corner stile and continue ahead in a southwesterly direction over two cultivated fields to a country lane near Sotshole Coppice (Point B), reaching it via a stile and plank footbridge.

Go right along the lane for almost 200yds (183m), then turn right again over a stile and walk to the left of the field hedge. The clear footpath leads along the left-hand edge of Ettington Grove. At the end of the grove, bear right to cross a cultivated field, then half right, until you come out near Grove Farm and rejoin the main walk at Point 4. Go left along the farm track that proceeds to the left of woodland and complete the route.

Where to eat and drink

The Fox at Loxley is a community-owned pub that welcomes drinkers and diners to a traditional village pub that offers good-quality food. At Ettington, The Chequers Inn, an 18th-century pub and restaurant serves hearty food, craft beers, wine and cocktails. The bar and restaurant is inviting and charming, whilst the vast garden is the perfect sun spot; an ideal location for lunch, dinner or a casual bite.

What to look out for

Take a detour to see the ruins of the old church in Ettington Park, and note the epitaph to Anthony Underhill of 1587 in its tower.

While you're there

Shipston-on-Stour, a picturesque town close to the Oxfordshire/ Gloucestershire border, was once an important staging post for coaches. Several inns in the town, including the Coach & Horses, serve as a reminder of that era. The parish church of St Edmund has a lovely 15th-century tower.

HONINGTON AND THE CENTENARY WAY

DISTANCE/TIME	7.5 miles (12.1km) / 3hrs 45min
ASCENT/GRADIENT	230ft (70m) / ▲
PATHS	Field paths, tracks, quiet roads
LANDSCAPE	Pleasantly undulating fields
SUGGESTED MAP	OS Explorer 205 Stratford-upon-Avon & Evesham
START/FINISH	Grid Reference: SP262426
DOG FRIENDLINESS	On lead on country roads and across open farmland
PARKING	Honington, in the vicinity of the parish church
PUBLIC TOILETS	None on route

Hidden down country lanes and surrounded by peaceful countryside, Honington must one of the most exquisite villages in Warwickshire. Exploring it on foot reveals a picture-perfect representation of rural England, with rows of handsome houses and charming cottages built of Cotswold stone and ironstone. It comes as no surprise to learn that Honington has won countless best-kept village awards over the years. Completing the picture is the imposing Honington Hall, glimpsed across the fields in the early stages of this walk. It is open to the public but by prior appointment only. The house has been described as lying 'in a lost landscape where the Cotswolds peter out yet the Midlands has yet to begin. Here England momentarily loses a sense of direction.'

Honington Hall dates back to the late 17th-century. Situated on the banks of the River Stour, amid 15 acres (6ha) of land, the house was built by Sir Henry Parker, a London lawyer. In 1737, the estate passed to the Townsend family who carried out significant changes and alterations. The work included the creation of a great octagonal saloon, completed in 1751. Here you find classical doorways crowned with cherubs and set against blue wall panels. Above is a semi-dome, which soars to a painting of Acis and Galatea by Luca Giordano. Round-headed niches can be seen over the ground floor windows of the east front, containing busts of Roman emperors. Boasting tall chimneys, the mellow brick Caroline manor house has been described as the perfect model for a doll's house and the BBC filmed *Love in a Cold Climate*, *Our Mutual Friend* and *Martin Chuzzlewit* at the house.

At the foot of the drive is Honington's church of All Saints. Apart from a 13th-century tower, it was built around 1680 in classical style. Arthur Mee, in his renowned guides to the English shires, was less than flattering about the church's marble monument to Joseph Townsend, referring to 'perhaps the most unpleasant cherub in all England.'

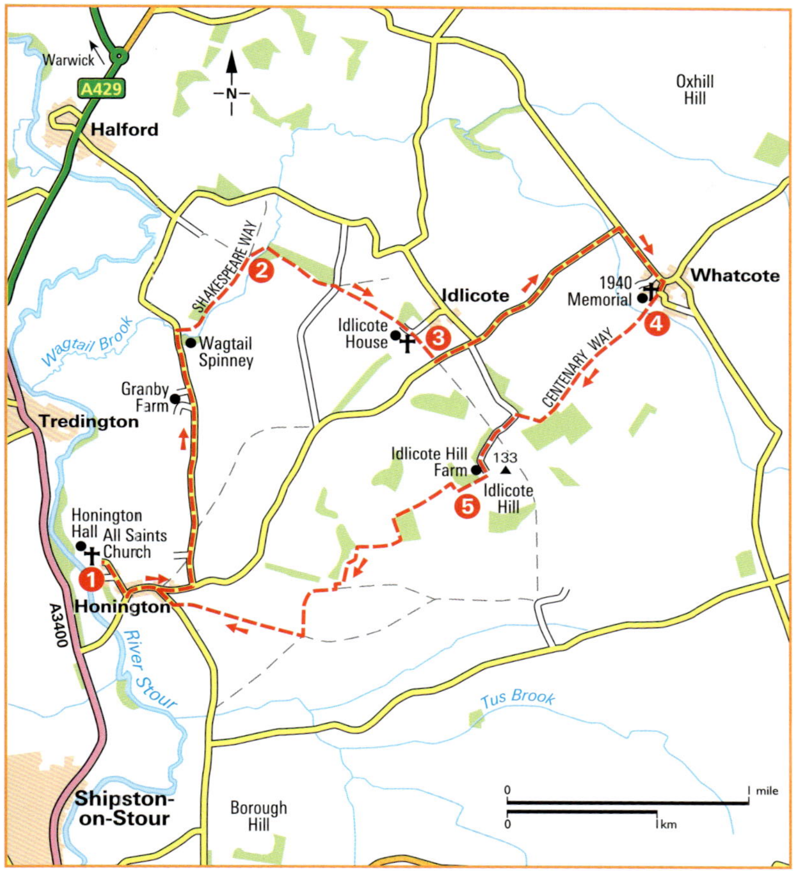

1. From Honington's parish church of All Saints walk back down the road, through the village. At the junction turn left, pass one of the entrances to Honington Hall on the left and a turning for Barcheston and Willington on the right. Take the next left turning (Granby Road, signposted to Halford) and follow the quiet country lane for about 1 mile (1.6km), passing Granby Farm and Wagtail Spinney. Cross Wagtail Brook, go through a gate on the right to join a bridleway and follow Shakespeare's Way with the brook to your right. Keep to the right of a wood and along the edge of a large field. Pass into the next pasture via a gate and continue almost to the corner.

2. Go right to cross a footbridge, then bear left round the woodland edge. At the top keep left along the field perimeter. Pass to the left of several barns, cross a farm track and keep to the bridleway as it runs southeast along the field edge. Follow a path, go through a gate and pass the buildings of Idlicote to reach Idlicote House. Visit the church, then return to where the drive bends, keep ahead for several paces, then turn right by some gates. Follow the bridleway down an elongated field to the road.

3. Turn left, pass a turning to Idlicote and Halford, continue along the lane to a T-junction and turn right into Whatcote. In the village, turn right up Church Lane and enter the church yard of St Peter's via the Lytchgate. Make for a wrought-iron kissing gate in the corner, joining the route of the Centenary Way.

4. Pass through a second gate immediately and turn right, down the field. Cross a stile and turn right, then left along the field boundary. Make for the corner and continue up the gentle slope beside woodland to the next stile. Continue on a path to the next stile, turn left after several paces to follow the field boundary, with trees on the left. Veer away from the woodland, ascending to a farm road on a bend. Turn left, following the Centenary Way to Idlicote Hill Farm.

5. Bear left then turn right south of the farm buildings and follow the obvious grassy track, which is well waymarked. On reaching the fence corner by trees, keep right. When the track forks by a pond, keep left. Bear right to a crucial junction, turning left at the waymark. After 50yds (46m), at the next sign, turn right and stay on the track until eventually you come down an open field to a T-junction. Turn right and follow the track to Honington. At the road turn right, left at the T-junction then turn right again to return to the church.

Where to eat and drink

The Royal Oak at Whatcote is a gastro-pub with a seasonal menu (open Thursday to Sunday). The Lion at nearby Tredington has a large garden and serves food Tuesday to Sunday. Alternatively, a number of eateries can be found in Shipston-on-Stour.

What to look out for

Idlicote church, set amid peaceful Warwickshire countryside, has box pews, a double-decker pulpit and an impressive roll call of past rectors dating back to 1301. The architect Sir John Soane, a professor at the Royal Academy, designed the main block of adjoining Idlicote House.

While you're there

At the eastern extremity of the walk, pause in the churchyard at Whatcote to study the monument erected in 1997. It marks the 50th anniversary of the rededication of St Peter's Church following war damage caused by German bombing here after a raid on Birmingham in December 1940.

MERIDEN – THE CENTRE OF ENGLAND

DISTANCE/TIME	5 miles (8km) / 2hrs 15min
ASCENT/GRADIENT	197ft (60m) / ▲ ▲
PATHS	Field and woodland paths, many stiles
LANDSCAPE	Gentle rolling countryside
SUGGESTED MAP	OS Explorer 221 Coventry & Warwick
START/FINISH	Grid Reference: SP251820
DOG FRIENDLINESS	Off lead through woodland, otherwise under strict control
PARKING	Old Road in Meriden, near The Queen's Head
PUBLIC TOILETS	None on route

This easy walk offers the opportunity to visit a historic place and walk through some of the most attractive woodland in the area. It's rumoured that Lady Godiva, wife of Earl Leofric of Mercia and owner of the village until AD 1066, founded the parish church of St Lawrence. You can see several timber-framed buildings and some moated farmsteads in the village.

The village claims to be the centre of England, and there is a sandstone pillar-shaped cross on the village green that carries the inscription, 'This ancient wayside cross has stood in the village for some 500 years and by tradition marks the Centre of England'.

Meriden became home to Triumph motorcycles from 1941, after the factory in Coventry was destroyed by fire during World War II. In 1973, workers blockaded the factory to prevent closure, and subsequently formed a co-operative to buy it. In turn, Triumph Motorcycles (Meriden) Ltd eventually closed in 1983, and the factory was demolished the following year. The site has since been built over by a housing estate, with road names featuring Triumph motorbike model names. A plaque commemorating the Triumph Motorcycle Factory Meriden stands by Bonneville Close.

The National Cyclists' Memorial, on the village green, is dedicated to all those cyclists who gave their lives in both World Wars – the British army had a cycling corps during Word War I. The memorial was erected with subscriptions from cyclists and cycling clubs and unveiled in May 1921 in the presence of over 20,000 cyclists. It was placed in Meriden to make it easy for cyclists to reach it from anywhere in the country, and is the site of an annual rally and commemorative service every May.

At 18th-century Forest Hall, to the west of Meriden, there is a piece of ancient turf where the Woodmen of Arden, the oldest archery society in England, holds its meetings. The turf is believed to have been undisturbed since the trees of the Forest of Arden first cast their shade over the archery butts. The society was established in 1785, and its membership is strictly limited to just 82 archers. There is also a horn here, said to have belonged to Robin Hood.

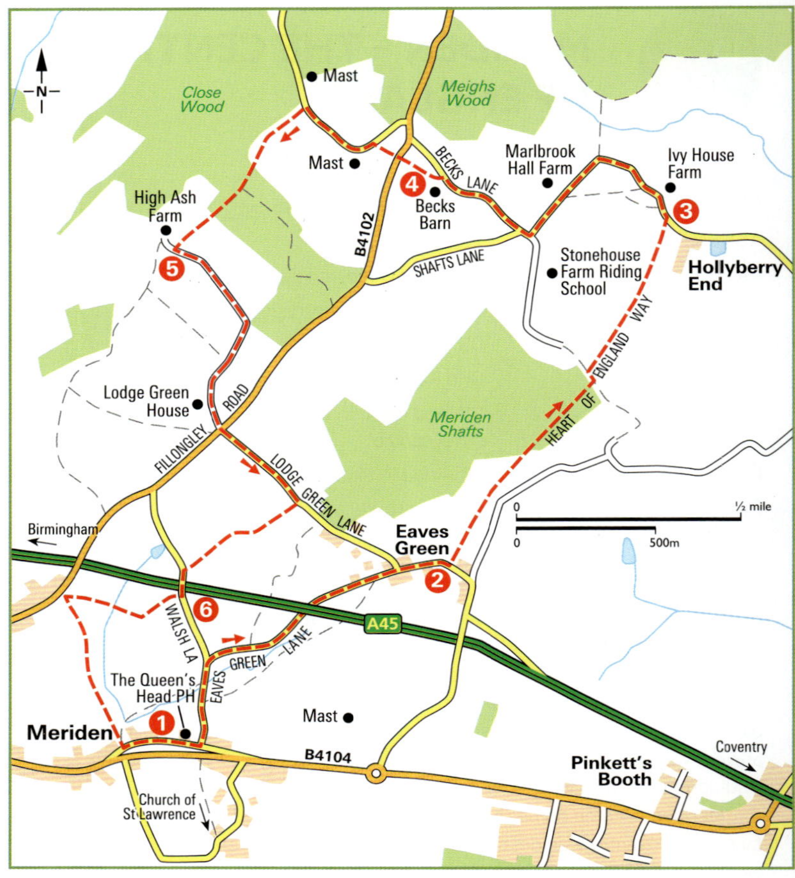

1. From The Queen's Head, walk up Eaves Green Lane, following the Heart of England Way. Ignore Walsh Lane and continue right on Eaves Green Lane. Go beneath the A45 and continue into the hamlet of Eaves Green. Continue ahead at the junction, on Showell Lane.

2. Pass Eaves Green Park Home estate and bear left through a kissing gate to a path that leads over meadows into Meriden Shafts woodland, via a footbridge and a kissing gate. Continue through another kissing gate and leave at its northeastern end via a further kissing gate. Go left along the track for 50 paces, then turn right into pastureland via a kissing gate. Continue ahead by the side of the hedge, across three fields via a gate and a stile, and on to Harvest Hill Lane in Hollyberry End via another stile.

3. Go left on the lane past Ivy House Farm. The Heart of England Way leaves the route at a sharp left bend, but you stay on the lane. After passing Marlbrook Hall Farm, bear right at the next road junction to follow Becks Lane.

4. At Becks Barn go right of the drive via a stile to a waymarked path. Two gates lead through to a further kissing gate. Cross the road and the next field to a lane via a gate near two communication masts. Go along the lane, then left over a stile to a footpath to the left of Close Wood. Skirt a pond, and cross two stiles to enter the woodland. Leave Close Wood via another stile, and continue along the path over cultivated land.

5. Pass left of High Ash Farm and left of a Dutch barn, and descend to a kissing gate by a field gate. Through this bear right, descending a lane past Lodge Green House to Fillongley Road. Cross the road and continue down Lodge Green Lane opposite. Turn right over a stile, and take the path following a line of oak trees across a cultivated field. At the end, go over a stile to the road and turn left along Walsh Lane to a bridge over the A45.

6. Immediately across the bridge, go right through a gate and take the path high above the A45. Go left through a gate into pastureland, heading for a footbridge to the right of a pond. Continue to the next field and a stile at the corner. Ignore the road and bear sharp left through a kissing gate to descend over several fields towards Meriden. Round the footpath crossing the drain at a footbridge and aim for the kissing gate. Go through this onto Old Road, and turn left to return to The Queen's Head.

Where to eat and drink
The Queen's Head is on the Heart of England Way and a well-established and friendly pub on the edge of the village of Meriden. Traditional pub lunches are available Monday to Saturday, and there's live music on Monday evenings.

What to look out for
Cross the B4104 and climb the hill to visit the Church of St Lawrence. You will be rewarded with fine views from the churchyard. If you stand near the ancient sundial or by the yew tree with the massive trunk you can see the city of Birmingham, and the view stretches out to the hills of Worcestershire, Staffordshire and Shropshire.

While you're there
The medieval cross in Meriden may not actually be the centre of England, as has been thought for over 500 years. GPS technology has identified that this point is most likely to be in the middle of a farm field some 10 miles (16.1km) away but, to many people, Meriden will always be the true centre.

POLESWORTH AND THE COVENTRY CANAL

31

DISTANCE/TIME	5 miles (8km) / 2hrs
ASCENT/GRADIENT	115ft (35m) / ▲
PATHS	Canal tow paths, field paths and residential areas, several stiles
LANDSCAPE	Gentle rolling farmland
SUGGESTED MAP	OS Explorer 232 Nuneaton & Tamworth
START/FINISH	Grid Reference: SK262024
DOG FRIENDLINESS	Off lead along tow path, otherwise under control
PARKING	Hall Court car park on Bridge Street
PUBLIC TOILETS	None on route

This trip to Polesworth allows you to experience a fragment of monastic England and to see a beautiful, ancient abbey church and vicarage. These buildings date back to AD 827 and form part of a nunnery built by Egbert, who is often claimed to have been the first Saxon king of all England. His daughter Editha was the abbess. The abbey's dovecote can be found tucked away behind the village library. The superb 14th-century nunnery gate now has two residential flats in its upper storey.

The influence of the local squirearchy can be seen all around Polesworth. Nearby Pooley Hall was built by Sir Thomas Cockain in 1506, although there are records of an earlier Saxon hall on the site. The stones in the walls and the beams in the roof were taken from the ancient abbey, following its dissolution. Sir Henry Goodere became lord of the manor and there are stories connecting him with Michael Drayton (1563–1631), the poet, who was born in Hartshill. In his early years, Drayton was a page-boy to Sir Henry at Pooley Hall, and William Shakespeare is said to have been a page-boy here too. Drayton was a regular companion of Shakespeare.

Although the population of Polesworth is around 9,000 people, it retains a village atmosphere with the old part of town largely untouched and its public houses intact. The River Anker and the Coventry Canal offer a quick step into the countryside, although it has been many years since local people were able to skate along these gentle backwaters – this used to be a favourite wintertime activity for villagers.

The walk starts near the library and takes you over the River Anker onto the tow path of the Coventry Canal. After the canal's bridge No. 49 you'll leave the tow path, crossing fields and lanes to the village of Dordon, before returning along Common Lane back into Polesworth.

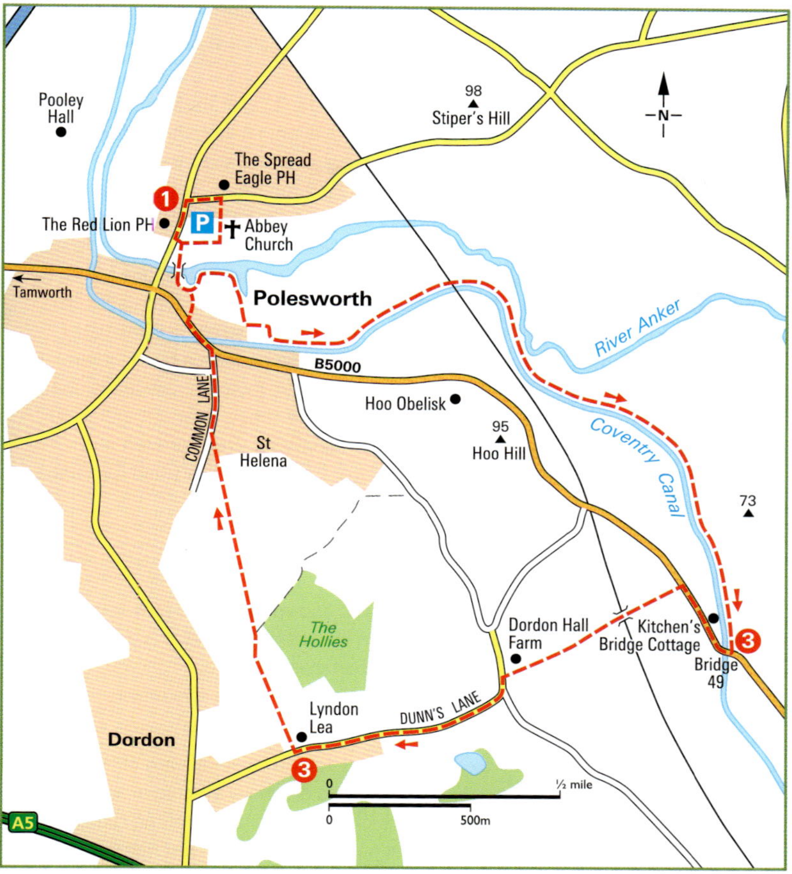

1. From the car park at Hall Court, walk towards The Red Lion and left into Bridge Street, walking towards the bridge. After about 95 paces, turn left by a shop into an alleyway that leads to a public footpath junction and turn right to take the path signed to the River Anker. Cross the footbridge over the river, then another, and bear left through the pleasant gardens, keeping by the river bank on a footpath. Leave the river and head for a sports pavilion. Beyond it turn left on a path beside the bowling green that arcs gently right towards bridge No. 51 over the Coventry Canal. Descend to the canal and turn left along its pleasant tow path, which you now follow for the next 1.5 miles (2.4km). Before walking beneath the railway line look up to your right and on the far bank you will see the obelisk on Hoo Hill. Stiper's Hill is visible to the left. Continue beneath the main electrified railway line and follow the tow path

2. Leave the Coventry Canal's tow path when you get to bridge No. 49 and ascend to the road, going left over the canal bridge and generally northwest past Kitchen's Bridge Cottage. Soon after passing the cottage, look out for a signposted gap in a hedge on the left and proceed through this to cross the footbridge over the railway line via two stiles. Now climb the hill, passing through the farm gate to the left of the buildings of Dordon Hall Farm, and

continue up to the road. Over a stile, go left along the road, then soon turn right when you reach a road junction, following the signpost to Dordon. This will take you along Dunn's Lane into the village.

3. Immediately after passing a house called Lyndon Lea, at the crest of the hill, turn to the right down a track that leads to a gate onto a footpath over open farmland. Follow this footpath, heading generally northwards, towards the prominent trees of The Hollies. Continue left past the trees, crossing a stile. Ignore a kissing gate and continue ahead along a hedged path. Soon you will find yourself walking along a surfaced farm track that becomes Common Lane, on the approach to Polesworth village. Take the pavement of the lane through a residential estate until you reach the B5000 Tamworth–Grendon road. Turn left and cross the road with care, as it can be busy, and stroll over the canal bridge. Turn right at Polesworth Garage down to the park area by the River Anker and cross back over the footbridge. The public footpath now leads up to a junction of paths where you go right, towards the abbey. Bear left and leave through the Old Nunnery Gateway onto the High Street. Now turn left and continue along the High Street, past the Nethersole Apartments and turn left again into Bridge Street to return to Hall Court car park.

Where to eat and drink
There are several good pubs in Polesworth and you will pass by a couple along the route of the walk. The Red Lion is a good local that has a lunch menu. The Spread Eagle, on the High Street, has a large beer garden, sometimes with a large marquee for functions, sa well as live music.

What to look out for
Look up to the right, midway through Point 1, for a close-up view of Hoo Obelisk on the far bank of the canal. This was originally erected in around 1848, close to the London Railway Line on the opposite side of the canal, but was moved in the 20th century for safety reasons. The inscription reads: 'Site of the Chapel of St Leonard at Hoo demolished 1538 30th Henry VIII'.

While you're there
Spare a little time to visit the old Abbey Church (closed Mondays) and see the 13th-century stone low-relief figure that is believed to be the effigy of the first abbess, Osanna. She lies on the tomb of Sir Richard Harthill with her feet on a stag, attired in a wimple and long straight gown with hanging sleeves. The church tower was built in memory of Harthill.

AROUND CHARLECOTE AND WELLESBOURNE

DISTANCE/TIME	6 miles (9.7km) / 2hrs 15min
ASCENT/GRADIENT	33ft (10m) / ▲
PATHS	Field paths and farm tracks
LANDSCAPE	Gentle rolling countryside
SUGGESTED MAP	OS Explorer 205 Stratford-upon-Avon
START/FINISH	Grid Reference: SP263564
DOG FRIENDLINESS	Under control at all times
PARKING	National Trust car park at Charlecote Park
PUBLIC TOILETS	None on route

This walk starts in the delightful village of Charlecote, about 5 miles (8km) from Stratford-upon-Avon. There is an opportunity to visit the superb Charlecote Park house, which has been the home of the Lucy family since 1247. The route passes along the banks of the pretty River Dene to the edge of the village of Wellesbourne and then crosses farmland and farm lanes on its return to Charlecote, passing close to 19th-century Charlecote Mill.

Charlecote Park is an Elizabethan mansion that is largely hidden from the road by a fine parapeted gatehouse with an oriel window above its arch. The hall was rebuilt in 1558 by Sir Thomas Lucy, in the shape of the letter E, and is surrounded by a wonderful deer park. For more than 200, years fallow deer were bred from stock and roamed freely in the large park. Thirty deer were reintroduced in 2002 and, while numbers have increased, they are still outnumbered by the 100 or so Jacob sheep.

It was at Charlecote Park that a youthful William Shakespeare is alleged to have been arrested for deer poaching. This is often cited as being the reason for his departure from Stratford for London in the mid-1580s. The story continues that the Bard got his own back on Sir Thomas Lucy and made him the butt of the world's laughter by depicting him as Mr Justice Shallow in his play The Merry Wives of Windsor. Whether there is any truth in this story is debatable. Doubters will always point to the fact the deer park had not yet been developed at Charlecote in Shakespeare's day. What is certain is that Sir Thomas Lucy was locally unpopular as a Justice of the Peace, and the subject of several mocking ballads being sung in and around the pubs of Stratford at the time. Shakespeare would certainly have known of these and could easily have adopted the caricature for his play.

By the road on the edge of the grounds of Charlecote Park is St Leonard's Church. It stands on the site of an earlier 12th-century church that was demolished in 1849. Originally the church was part of the estate, paid for by Mrs Mary Elizabeth Lucy who laid the church's foundation stone. Inside, the church is the Lucy Chapel, which holds the 17th-century tombs of three Sir Thomas Lucys.

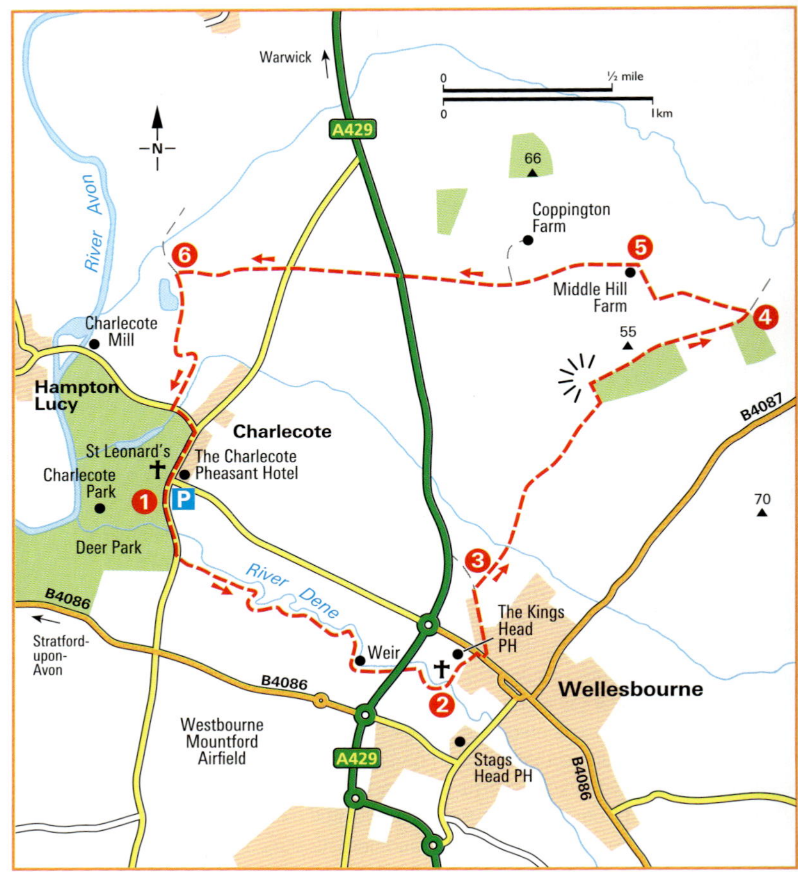

1. From Charlecote Park car park, go left along the grass verge and cross over the River Dene. In about 100yds (91m), go left along a wide track that arcs left onto a clear fenced path by the side of the river. Follow this for about 1.5 miles (2.4km), passing a sewage farm, via a kissing gate, towards the village of Wellesbourne. You will pass a pleasant weir and go beneath the A429 before you come to a footbridge near St Peter's Church.

2. Go left over the footbridge and up a fenced path into the churchyard. Keep to the right of the church until you reach the village through the churchyard gates. Continue up the road to the left of house No. 21 – The Kings Head pub is on the left – then cross the main road in the village and walk up Warwick Road opposite.

3. In about 300yds (274m), just after passing Daniell Road, go right along a tarmac path alongside modern houses. Cross a footbridge and, going through a kissing gate, continue ahead over a cultivated field. Through another kissing gate, continue ahead to cross a plank footbridge. Continue ahead along the left side of a hedge. Bear left across the field to go through a hedge gap and continue uphill to the left of the copse of trees. At the top of the rise, turn right and then go right into the woodland. Turn left along the clear track through the trees. You will emerge from the trees for a short distance and then re-enter. As the trees to the right thin out, look for a hedge gap to the left.

4. Go through the gap and cross a cultivated field to a hedge corner. Continue ahead by the hedge to a field corner, then bear right to Middle Hill Farm.

5. At a waymark post go left, between the farm buildings, then go to the right of the farmhouse and walk along the farm access lane for about 0.75 miles (1.2km), passing the entrance to Coppington Farm on the way to the A429. Cross the road with care and go over the stile opposite onto a fenced footpath. After crossing another minor road, continue ahead along a concrete driveway to farm buildings.

6. Bear left between the buildings and then bear right through the gateway to follow the field boundary on the right. Turn left at a kissing gate (don't go through it) to a second kissing gate that leads into a large cultivated field that you walk around by the field hedge, initially alongside a long lake. Go right, through a further kissing gate, and continue to the right of the field hedge until you go through a final kissing gate onto Charlecote Road. Go left along the footway past a delightful thatched cottage into the centre of Charlecote, then turn right along the grass verge of the main street past the half-timbered houses and The Charlecote Pheasant Hotel, with St Leonard's Church opposite, to reach the Charlecote Park car park.

Where to eat and drink

The Charlecote Pheasant Hotel has a fine lounge and offers an excellent carvery. In Wellesbourne, the walk goes close to The Kings Head pub, originally known as The Wellsbourne Inn. In the 1600s, the King's Head was used as a hospital during the English Civil War. During World War II, it played host to the RAF pilots and ground crews from near-by Wellsbourne airfield. Children are allowed, but dogs are restricted to the gardens.

What to look out for

As well as visiting Charlecote Park, take some time to explore the village of Wellesbourne and seek out Chestnut Square in Wellesbourne Mountford and the thatched pub, The Stags Head. A plaque in the bus shelter records that it was here, in 1872, that Joseph Arch inaugurated the first trade union for agricultural workers. The event is remembered with an annual parade.

While you're there

Visit Charlecote Mill and see the 19th-century mill grind corn by waterpower. There has been a mill on the site since the Norman Conquest, but the present one was built in about 1800. It stopped grinding corn by waterpower in 1939 but in 1983 it was acquired by the present owner, who restored it and brought it back into full-time use. It has limited opening times (around one Sunday in every month from April to October), so check online.

EXPLORING THE TOWN OF WARWICK

DISTANCE/TIME	5 miles (8km) / 2hrs
ASCENT/GRADIENT	33ft (10m) / ▲
PATHS	Canal and riverside paths, pavements
LANDSCAPE	Canalside and historic town
SUGGESTED MAP	OS Explorer 221 Coventry & Warwick
START/FINISH	Grid Reference: SP277647
DOG FRIENDLINESS	Off lead along tow path, otherwise under control
PARKING	Bread and Meat Close car park, on east side of the racecourse
PUBLIC TOILETS	None on route

This walk offers you the opportunity to visit one of the most famous castles in England. Starting from the car park at Warwick Racecourse, a stroll along the tow path of the Grand Union Canal to the River Avon brings you to Castle Bridge. This has the classic view of Warwick Castle.

There has been a fortress on the site of the castle since 1068, but the current structure of Warwick Castle dates from the 14th century. It sits imperiously above the River Avon near the centre of the town. It is the ancestral home of the Earls of Warwick, of whom Richard Neville (1428–71), known as 'the Kingmaker', was probably the most famous.

You can spend a whole day at Warwick Castle, there is so much to see: the Bailey, Guy's Tower (128ft/39m high), Caesar's Tower (147ft/45m high), the Gatehouse, the Clock Tower and the Old Bridge over the River Avon are all truly superb. Inside you can see the tapestry of the gardens of Versailles, Cromwell's helmet and Queen Anne's travelling trunk. Outside, there are gardens that were designed by Lancelot 'Capability' Brown in the 18th century.

Tear yourself away from the castle to continue the walk through the county town. It displays a fascinating blend of Georgian and Tudor architecture. In Castle Street, you pass the timbered home of Thomas Oken, a weathly wool merchant and one of the town's benefactors. It now houses a doll museum.

St Mary's Church is up the road opposite. You can climb its great 174ft (53m) tower for a fantastic view over the town and the surrounding countryside. Inside the church is the 15th-century Beauchamp Chapel where Richard Beauchamp's tomb takes centre stage. Beauchamp was father-in-law to Richard Neville and the 13th Earl of Warwick; he lived through the reigns of three kings and was present at the burning of Joan of Arc. Also in St Mary's is the tomb of Robert Dudley, Earl of Leicester, a favourite of Elizabeth I.

Before heading back to the racecourse you'll pass Lord Leycester's Hospital. This was originally the Guild House of St George, which became the Almshouse in 1571, founded by Robert Dudley. Now it is probably the most famous medieval building in this wonderful town.

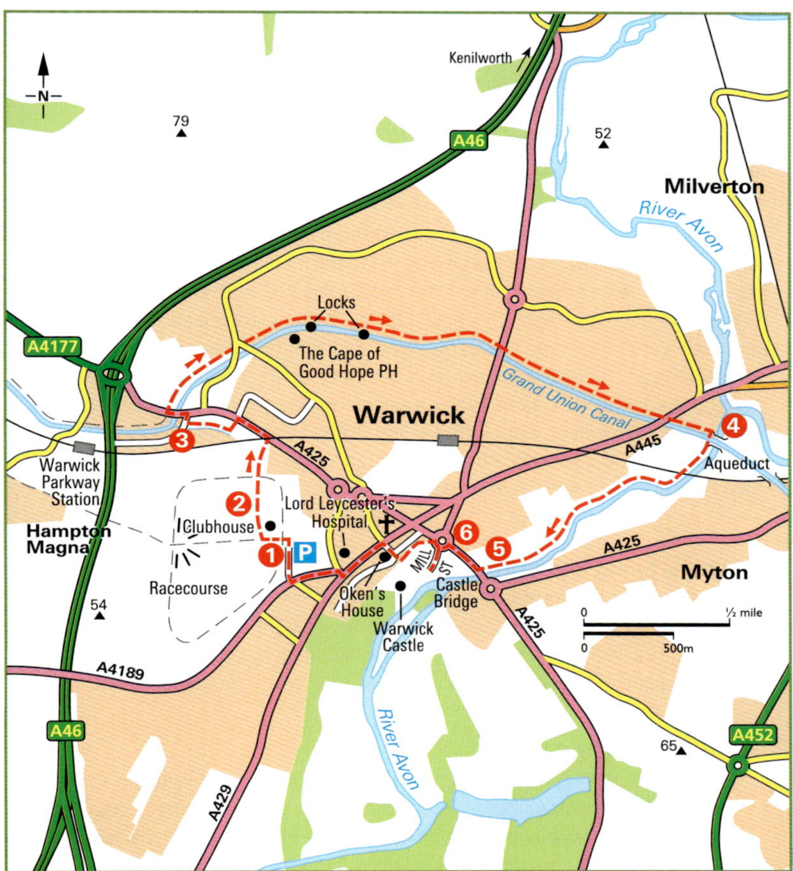

1. Walk to the far end of the car park and go left towards the golf clubhouse, the Warwick Golf Centre.

2. Beyond, go right and take the wide green track between the golf course and the driving range. In about 300yds (274m), cross over the racetrack and go through a kissing gate onto a footpath alongside modern housing. Continue ahead, and at the corner of common land go right through a kissing gate onto a lane, and descend to the road. Go left along the pavement beneath the railway bridge, then left opposite St Michael's Road through a gate (locked 6pm–8am) onto grassland by the Saltisford Canal. Follow this grassy area to the tow path, passing a large narrowboat mooring area, and climb the steps up to the canal bridge onto the pavement beside a road. Go right along the pavement, Budbrooke Road, and in 50yds (46m), you will come to the A425 and a canal bridge over the Grand Union Canal.

3. Cross the road with care. Go left over the canal bridge and, immediately across it, descend to take the tow path into Warwick, about 1.5 miles (2.4km) away. Pass a lock gate with The Cape of Good Hope pub opposite, and along the back of residential properties. After passing a supermarket on the opposite bank and just before reaching the aqueduct over the River Avon, go left down steps to join the 'Waterside Walk', turning right at the stream.

4. Proceed right under the aqueduct and follow the riverbank footpath. After 1 mile (1.6km) at Castle Bridge, climb steps onto the pavement of the A425 (Banbury) road and cross with care.

5. Stroll onto the bridge for the classic view of Warwick Castle, then turn around and follow the pavement towards Warwick town.

6. In 220yds (201m) go left and meander down picturesque Mill Street for the second favourite view of the castle. Return to the main road and go left through the main entrance gate to Warwick Castle grounds. Walk up the drive to the main gate, turn right up steps, pass the castle entrance and turn left on Castle Lane. Turn right on Castle Street and continue, passing Oken's House, to reach the tourist information centre on the corner of the High Street. Turn left here and walk along High Street, going beneath the archway of Lord Leycester's Hospital. Go right into Bowling Green Street, and in 50yds (46m) turn left down Friars Street. After 240 yds (250m), at the racecourse entrance turn right and right again into Bread and Meat Close car park.

Where to eat and drink

There are plenty of places to eat in the town of Warwick. Along the walk route The Cape of Good Hope by the side of the Grand Union Canal is a popular pub with walkers and boaters – children and dogs are welcomed. It has a patio overlooking the canal and serves locally sourced food and cask ales.

What to look out for

As you walk up Castle Street you pass a timber-framed 15th-century house. This is Thomas Oken's House. Oken was a silk and luxury goods merchant and a famous Warwick benefactor. He founded an almshouse for poor women, endowed a schoolmaster and provided money for bonfires for the young. He was Master of the Guild at the time of the 1545 town charter.

While you're there

No trip to Warwick is complete without a visit to fantastic Warwick Castle, and keep your eyes open in the Ghost Tower. It was here, in 1628, that the castle's then owner, Sir Fulke Greville, died a few weeks after being fatally stabbed in London by a manservant because he did not bequeath sufficient funds to him in his will.

A WALK TO HATTON LOCKS

DISTANCE/TIME	5 miles (8km) / 2hrs
ASCENT/GRADIENT	295ft (90m) / ▲
PATHS	Field paths and tracks, pavement, towpath
LANDSCAPE	Farmland and the Grand Union Canal
SUGGESTED MAP	OS Explorer 221 Coventry & Warwick
START/FINISH	Grid Reference: SP266655
DOG FRIENDLINESS	On lead on open farmland and in the vicinity of The Hatton Arms and the car park at the start and finish of the walk
PARKING	Car park off Old Budbrooke Road, near Warwick Parkway station
PUBLIC TOILETS	None on route

Midway round this fascinating walk to the west of Warwick is one of the area's best-known landmarks, a series of 21 locks known as the 'Stairway to Heaven.' When Hatton Locks were in constant demand in the great days of the Industrial Revolution, the working boatmen who plied Britain's inland waterways both feared and admired this engineering masterpiece.

It was at the end of 1799, with a new century about to dawn, that this canal first opened with its 21 locks. It's a distance of 2.5 miles (4km) from the top of the locks to the bottom. In those days, it was known as the Warwick and Birmingham Canal and it was constructed to transport locally mined coal to the factories and power stations of the Black Country. It was also a key component of the network of eight waterways connecting London with Birmingham and the centre of England. The private companies that owned and ran the canals vied for the best business but by now roads and railways were having a serious effect on water-based trade routes. In 1929, one company acquired the eight canals that linked London and the industrial Midlands and renamed them the Grand Union Canal. Immediately, the Grand Union Canal Company was faced with a serious challenge – to make it viable in those competitive times, it needed to implement a modernisation programme.

One of the priorities was to widen the 21 locks to enable two narrowboats to enter them and therefore speed up the process of transporting goods and cargo. The work began in 1932 and two years later, the Duke of Kent officially opened the new wide locks on the now much improved Grand Union. In the canal's heyday the boats carried coal, cement, tea, sugar and spice. The tall building seen from the bridge is known as the Signal Box. It was once used as the toll clerk's office. The windows gave him a good view of all the activity on this stretch of the canal and this way no boatman could sneak through without paying their toll – 1d per mile based on the type of cargo carried. Following the towpath on this section offers a fascinating insight into the story of one of Britain's great engineering achievements.

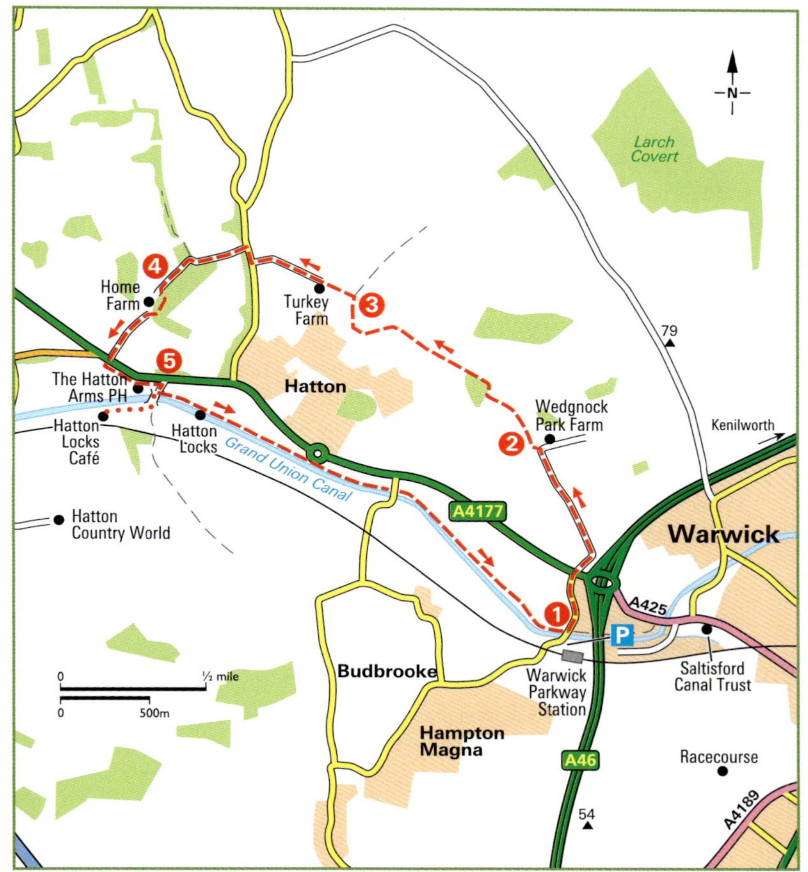

1. From the car park, take the access road to Old Budbrooke Road, turn right to cross the Grand Union Canal and walk up to the A4177. Cross over at the pedestrian lights, turn right towards the roundabout for a few paces, then turn left at the sign for Wedgenock Park Farm, following the bridleway. Soon the farm road bends left; continue on it with fields on the left and a hedge on the right. Pass several cottages and when the track sweeps right to farm outbuildings, turn left to follow the waymarked path around the left edge of the field.

2. Continue by track in the next pasture and on reaching a junction in front of trees, turn right for a few paces and then left at the corner of the wood. Follow the bridleway and pass through the gap in the field corner, keeping along the left boundary in the next pasture. Continue ahead across farmland, following the obvious path. Ascend a gentle slope towards houses and at a T-junction with a path, turn right.

3. Away to the right, in the far distance, is the tower of Warwick church. Pass a footpath on the left and continue to the top of the rise. Turn left at the bridleway sign towards Turkey Farm. Pass a pond on the right and the farm outbuildings on the left, go through double gates and follow the track to the road. Turn right, then left at the next footpath. Go through a galvanized kissing gate and walk ahead towards a spinney and a curtain of trees to the right. Keep to the right of the spinney, follow the track and bend left at the waymark towards Home Farm.

4. Just before reaching it, look for a kissing gate on the left and follow the woodland path, bypassing the farm outbuildings. Go through two more gates and follow the farm access road to the A4177. Turn left, follow the pavement beside The Hatton Arms pub and continue for about 200yds (183m) to a turning on the right for Hatton Locks.

5. On reaching the canal you have a choice. To visit the Hatton Locks Café, cross the waterway at the bridge and turn right. There is a pleasant view of The Hatton Arms over to the right. The route of the walk does not cross the canal. Instead, it turns left to follow the towpath of the Grand Union all the way to the bridge (51c) carrying Old Budbrooke Road. Leave the towpath at this point, cross the bridge and turn left for the car park where the walk began.

Where to eat and drink

The Hatton Arms is conveniently located roughly at the point where the walk begins the homeward stretch. There is a choice of bar snacks and main meals, made with fresh local produce. The pub also has a popular garden bar and a picnic area. Hatton Locks Café is open daily and serves a good selection of light meals and snacks.

What to look out for

Hatton Country World is a great place to take the children, with plenty of farm animals to see and lots of space to run around. There's also a garden centre and shopping village to wander around.

While you're there

From the walk's start and finish point you can follow the canal east towards Warwick to visit the home of the Saltisford Canal Trust. This waterway was once an arm of the Grand Union and today, by visiting the centre, you can learn all about the canal's history and the part it played in the story of Britain's once vital inland waterways.

35

AROUND KENILWORTH CASTLE

DISTANCE/TIME	4.5 miles (7.2km) / 2hrs 15min
ASCENT/GRADIENT	105ft (32m) / ▲
PATHS	Field paths and farm tracks
LANDSCAPE	Rolling countryside
SUGGESTED MAP	OS Explorer 221 Coventry & Warwick
START/FINISH	Grid Reference: SP279723
DOG FRIENDLINESS	On lead at all times
PARKING	In front of castle by Castle Green
PUBLIC TOILETS	None on route

Kenilworth Castle, now dramatic ruins, played an important part in English history. This walk starts from the castle and goes over farmland, then circles around Chase Wood to return along a track from where the best views of the castle ruins can be enjoyed. Extend the walk a little by visiting Honiley Church, rebuilt in 1707 to a design sketched – if legend can be believed – by the great architect, Christopher Wren.

Kenilworth Castle was the stronghold for lords and kings of England in the 11th and 12th centuries. Originally it was a timber fortress, and King John paid several visits to the castle, spending £1,115 between 1210 and 1216 rebuilding the outer bailey wall in stone and improving the other defences. In the 14th century, John of Gaunt transformed the fortress into a grand castle, building a great hall. The castle later passed to Henry IV. Henry V rested here after his victory at Agincourt in 1415, and it remained a royal residence until Queen Elizabeth I gave it to Robert Dudley, in 1563. It was then used to host a series of lavish entertainments for the Queen. The Civil War brought about its demise when, after a long siege, Cromwell ordered the defences to be dismantled.

The romantic ruin became a tourist destination from the 18th century onwards, and its popular fame was sealed when it became the setting for large parts of the action in Sir Walter Scott's novel *Kenilworth* (1826). Today, the castle is a Grade I listed building, and is open to the public. Be sure to climb to the top of Saintlowe Tower to be rewarded with a wonderful view.

Pleasance Mound, 'The Pleasance in the Marsh,' is situated about 0.5 miles (800m) west of Kenilworth Castle. A moated, timber-framed manor house was built for Henry V in around 1414, at the edge of the Great Mere – an artificial lake that formed part of the defences of the castle. The site was primarily used as a pleasure garden and place of entertainment in preference to the castle's more formal state apartments. It was abandoned and dismantled during Henry VIII's reign, and some of the buildings were moved to a new location within the castle walls. Historical investigations at the site of the moated island revealed the remains of a stone wall, and also identified the base of a spiral staircase and the remains of square towers built within the enclosing wall. Records show that structures here included a banqueting hall.

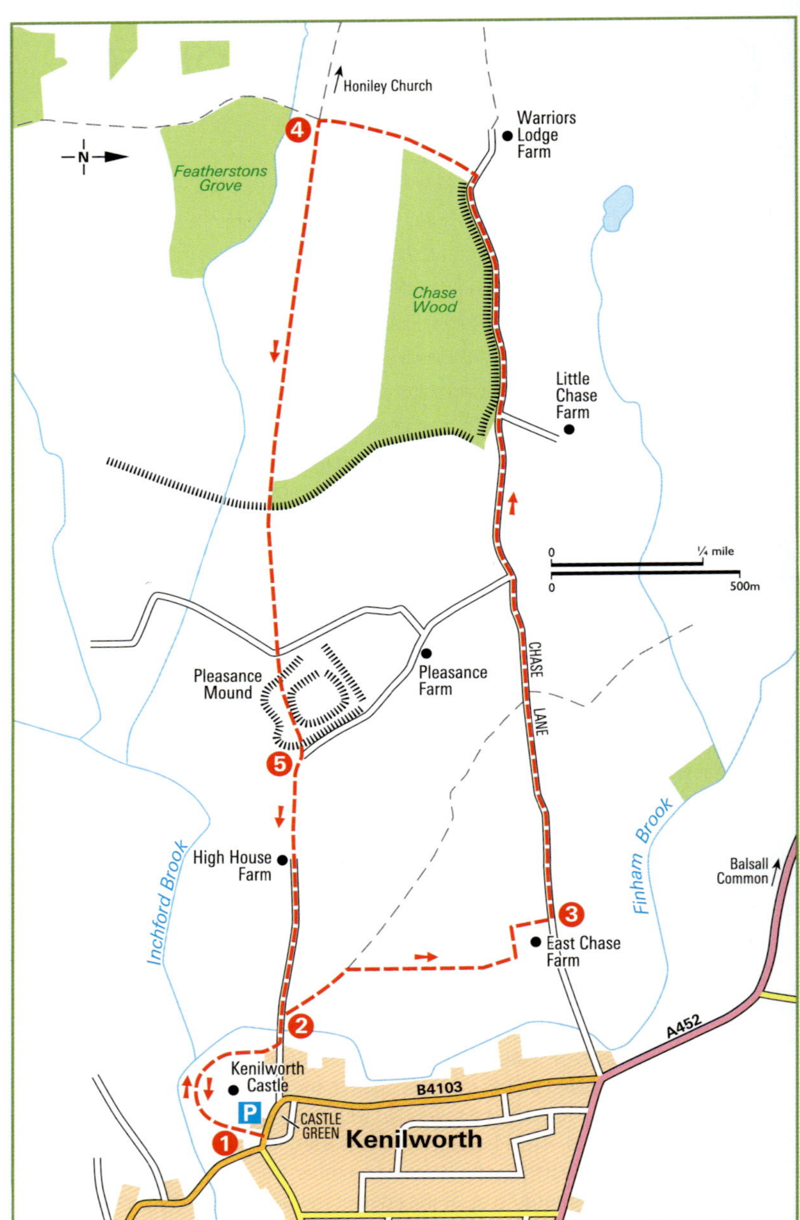

1. Walk towards the castle from the car park and go through the gate to the left of the ruins. Take the footpath that circles around the foot of the castle walls, climbing up to and crossing over the causeway, then descending to go through a kissing gate. Go ahead to pass to the left of a thatched cottage, and then onto a good wide track. Go left along this track for 195yds (150m), over a small stream, then turn right through a kissing gate into a cultivated field.

2. Follow the well-walked footpath diagonally across the field. When you reach the field corner, turn round to enjoy the fine view of the castle behind, then leave the main footpath by going right and heading up a less-used track, heading north. Walk ahead along this track over several fields and through a kissing gate, then pass to the left of East Chase Farm. Continue past the barns and then veer right towards a stile and a lane.

3. Cross the stile and head left along Chase Lane for the next 1.3 miles (2km) before passing to the right of Chase Wood. At the end of the trees, turn left on a stony farm track. After about 500yds (450m), reach a junction of footpaths. To your right, you will see Honiley Church (the footpath leading there and back will add about a further mile/1.6km to your route).

4. At the junction of footpaths, go left along a fine, wide grass track to the right of the field hedge, with Chase Wood beyond to the left. Follow this straight track for about 0.6 miles (1km), going over a footbridge. Go through two kissing gates, and continue over the Pleasance Mound earthworks to go through a further kissing gate. As you leave, you will pass an information board about the excavation.

5. Walk along the hedged footpath that leads to the farm drive to High House Farm. Continue ahead along the drive. As you reach the brow of the hill you can enjoy another classic view of Kenilworth Castle. This spectacular view continues as you descend the other side of the hill. Just before reaching the thatched cottage again, turn right onto a well-walked footpath that circles around the walls of the castle. Pass through a kissing gate and cross the castle causeway, then descend the footpath leading back to the car park.

Where to eat and drink

There is a tea room for visitors to the castle. The Queen and Castle, with its large garden and courtyard, and The Clarendon Arms, both by Castle Green opposite the castle in Kenilworth, are two popular eating places.

What to look out for

If you complete this walk in the spring you can expect to see a carpet of bluebells in Chase Wood. Look out for the views of Kenilworth Castle as you complete the walk and pause from time to time at different points along the walk. After draining part of the lake around the castle, Henry V built a summer house on 'The Pleasance'.

While you're there

Explore the Elizabethan garden at Kenilworth Castle. Based on contemporary drawings, this is a recreation by English Heritage of the original terrace gardens designed for Robert Dudley, complete with formal paths between geometric beds, and four dramatic, spiky obelisks. There's also an elegant aviary, and a central fountain.

LONG COMPTON AND THE ROLLRIGHT STONES

DISTANCE/TIME	5 miles (8km) / 2hrs
ASCENT/GRADIENT	673ft (205m) / ▲ ▲ ▲
PATHS	Field paths and country lanes, several stiles
LANDSCAPE	Rolling countryside on edge of Cotswold Hills
SUGGESTED MAP	OS Explorer 45 The Cotswolds
START/FINISH	Grid Reference: SP289323
DOG FRIENDLINESS	Under control at all times
PARKING	Two lay-bys, either side of sign for King's Men stones
PUBLIC TOILETS	None on route

This short, hilly walk offers the chance to visit the Rollright Stones, set up on the hills on the county border with Oxfordshire. The walk starts from Long Compton and ascends the lane up towards Little Rollright. The route passes by the famous stones and returns over farmland into the picturesque village of Little Rollright before descending back into Long Compton. This is a lovely village with fine old stone houses that line the road and an unusual lychgate to the village church. This was once a 16th-century cottage from which the lower storey has been removed. It appears like a two-storey gatehouse with an arch beneath.

Several myths surround the Rollright Stones, including one that the stones are all men turned to stone. The story goes that a king encountered a witch close to where the stones stand. She told him to take seven strides to the top of the hill, pronouncing, 'If Long Compton thou canst see, King of England shalt thou be!" When the eager king got to the top of the hill, he couldn't see Long Compton because a spur of land obstructed the view. The witch then turned the monarch and his hapless followers all to stone – thus creating the King Stone and the King's Men. The Whispering Knights are said to have been traitors who were plotting against the King.

The Rollright Stones comprise around 70 monoliths positioned in three sets. The King Stone is on the Warwickshire side of the road while the Whispering Knights and the group called the King's Men are on the other side, in Oxfordshire. The stones, which are much older than those found at Stonehenge, are all worn rough by the winds and centuries of rain. The King Stone is the largest at nearly 9ft (2.75m), and this is said to be placed in such a position that when seen from the centre of the King's Men circle on 21 June each year, the rising sun is immediately in line with the stone. The stones in the King's Men circle measure from between 4ft (1.2m) to 7ft (2.1m). Originally there were about 105 stones forming a continuous wall except for one narrow entrance. Here and there the stones are so close they almost touch. It is not clear what the stone circle was used for, but it may well have had some significance in religious and secular ceremonies.

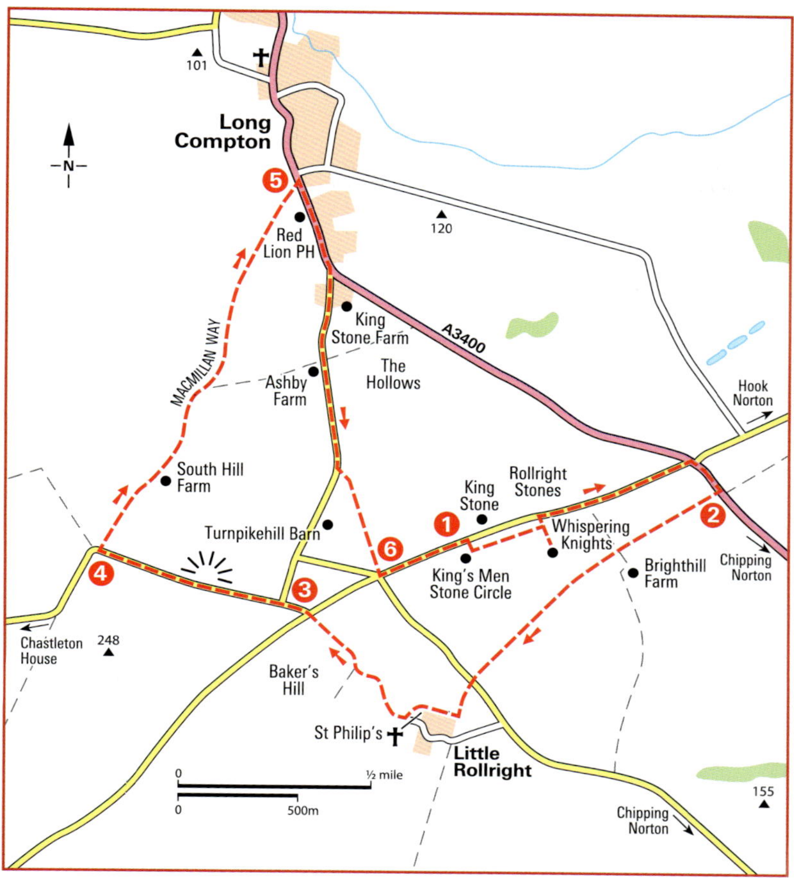

1. From the lay-by, you'll see two sets of kissing gates facing each other across the road. Go through the smaller one to visit the King Stone in the field to the north of the road. Next, cross back over the road to find the King's Men stone circle. After looking at the stone circle, continue along a grassy permissive path parallel to the road for a further 500yds (457m), then bear right along the footpath to see the third group of stones, called the Whispering Knights. Return to the road and turn right to continue along it for about another 0.5 miles (800m), then at the A3400 junction go to the right and at the brow of the hill go right again up nine steps to a field.

2. Continue ahead along a grassy path, the hedge on your left, over two fields to a stile. Cross the driveway to Brighthill Farm, and continue ahead through a copse to a double stile. Continue ahead across a cultivated field, then follow a field edge track that descends to a lane. Cross this and descend to Little Rollright via two kissing gates. At a lane turn right to curve north to the superb church. From the church ascend the footpath, signed 'Little Compton Footpath Only', up Baker's Hill to the road.

3. Over a stile cross the road to follow the lane opposite for the next 0.5 miles (800m) towards Little Compton, enjoying the view to the right over Long Compton and towards the village of Brailes.

4. Where the road bends left, go right over a stone stile (not straight onto the bridleway track) and continue ahead over a cultivated field in a generally northeast direction – the view ahead is superb. Descend to the left of South Hill Farm, and continue walking on the MacMillan Way path over several fields, passing through two gates and over a stile. The path becomes a surfaced road. Just after passing to the right of farm buildings, go left and over a stile, then continue ahead via another stile down into Long Compton. Leave the footpath through two pairs of farm gates to arrive back in the village.

5. Go right along the road to walk through the village, passing The Red Lion. Where the A3400 bends sharp left, turn right and walk up Little Rollright Road, passing King Stone Farm and Ashby Farm as you climb an area known as The Hollows. After about 0.5 miles (800m) the road bends slightly to the right, and here you go left and immediately onto a footpath with Turnpikehill Barn away to your right. Ascend the footpath to the lane near to the Rollright Stones.

6. Turn left along the lane, back towards the famous stones and the lay-bys.

Where to eat and drink

The Red Lion in Long Compton is the only pub on this route. It's a popular eating place with walkers and visitors to the area, offering morning coffee, good food, comfortable accommodation, excellent real ales and fine gardens. It is also a dog-friendly establishment.

What to look out for

Five miles (8km) southwest of Long Compton is Chastleton House, probably England's finest Jacobean house. The building has soaring gables and an elaborate state bedroom containing 'Queen Elizabeth's bed'. In the Cavaliers' Room, find out the story of Captain Arthur Jones who, on his return from the Battle of Worcester in 1651, was mistaken by Roundheads for Charles II.

While you're there

At nearby Hook Norton, 6 miles (9.7km) to the east, you will find the Hook Norton Brewery. In this part of England, Hook Norton ales are king, and the buildings at the brewery are a treat to see and visit. Here you can find out about hummellers, chondrometers, saccharometers and wort coolers. Go online to arrange a tour of this famous local brewery.

LOWER BRAILES AND SUTTON-UNDER-BRAILES

DISTANCE/TIME	5 miles (8km) / 1hr 30min
ASCENT/GRADIENT	476ft (145m) / ▲ ▲ ▲
PATHS	Field paths and country lanes, many stiles
LANDSCAPE	Rolling hills
SUGGESTED MAP	OS Explorer 191 Banbury, Bicester & Chipping Norton
START/FINISH	Grid Reference: SP308394
DOG FRIENDLINESS	Under control at all times
PARKING	On-street parking around Lower Brailes
PUBLIC TOILETS	None on route

In medieval times, Brailes was the third-largest town in Warwickshire. Today, it comprises a pair of small country villages, happily situated off main routes, away from the hustle and bustle of the modern towns and cities. This fine walk takes you over part of Brailes Hill which, at 761ft (232m), is the second-highest point in Warwickshire. From the pretty village of Upper Brailes, you walk into Lower Brailes and enjoy lovely views as you descend into open countryside. You climb above Sutton Brook and will have a wonderful valley view as you go down to Sutton-under-Brailes.

In the quaint village of Sutton-under-Brailes, time appears to have stood still. Attractive houses surround the picturesque village green and the fine old tombs in the churchyard lie beneath a magnificent spreading chestnut tree. The 13th-century church, St Thomas a Becket has a beautiful, lofty tower and a 14th- to 15th-century porch. There is a shallow recess on its north side which may once have been a chantry chapel.

It is a delight to walk through the old part of Upper Brailes, where there are a number of thatched cottages, and an ancient earthwork and burial ground called Castle Hill. Following the arrival of the Normans in the 11th century, it was used as the basis for a conventional castle of the motte-and-bailey style. From the top of its hill, you can see the distinctive marks of medieval ridge-and-furrow cultivation methods in the surrounding fields.

Lower Brailes is also a pretty place and, although it has no castle, it does contain the 14th-century Church of St George. With its splendid 120ft (37m) tower, it is sometimes referred to as the 'Cathedral of the Feldon', a potentially baffling claim to fame until you learn that 'Feldon' is an old English word for an area of rich, fertile farmland. It is without a doubt one of the finest churches in Warwickshire. Inside, you'll find some exquisite illuminated manuscripts. These date from the middle of the 13th century and are the work of William de Brailes and Matthew Paris.

Field paths lead you around the slopes of Brailes Hill between these three lovely villages, which reward you for taking time to explore on foot.

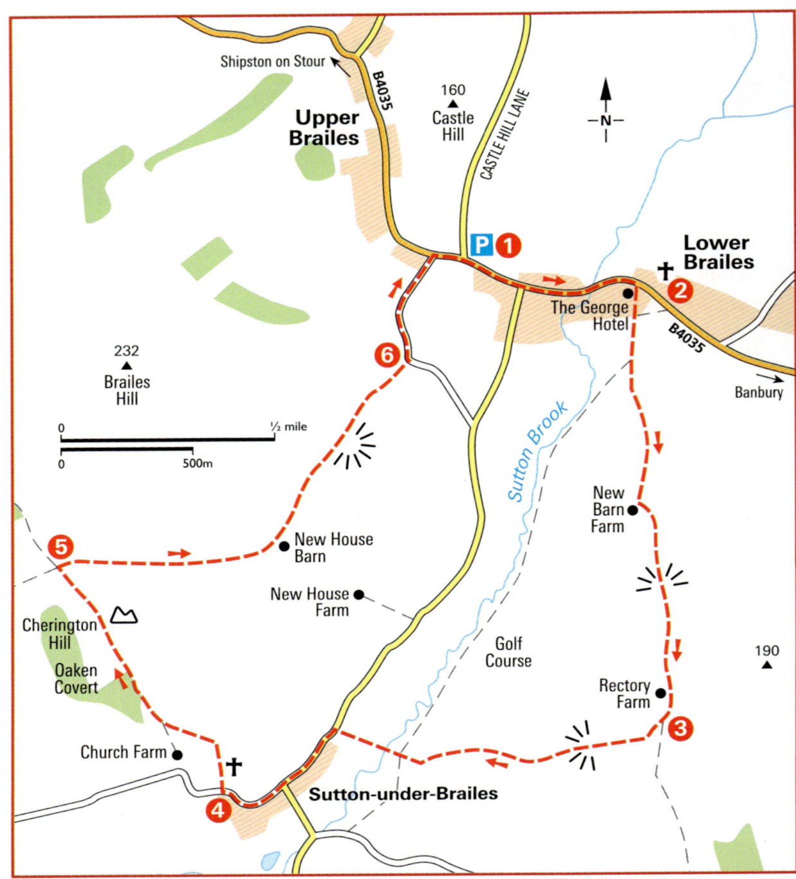

1. From the village hall in Lower Brailes, walk down to join the B4035. Turn left to stroll up through the beautiful village for about 0.5 miles (800m), passing The George Hotel, which has always been popular with local ramblers and now houses the village post office.

2. Turn right and walk down a waymarked public footpath just beyond The George Hotel. This runs beside a small Cotswold dry-stone wall, passing over a low stile, and then through a gate to cross Cow Lane into pastureland via a stile. Continue ahead, and at a footpath junction waymark post continue ahead to a double stile and footbridge in the hedge. Cross them and bear half right to the next stile, then quarter left for two further fields via a stile by a footbridge between them, heading for New Barn Farm. The footpath goes to the left of the farm complex to a gate. Through this, continue alongside the hedge to another gate. Beyond continue half left up the hill, crossing the field to a footbridge and stile. Cross the corner of the next field and continue ahead on the right-hand side of the hedge – there is a good view back over Lower Brailes. Walk up the path, then go through a hedge gap and bear right, walking above the trees surrounding the ruinous Rectory Farm.

3. Bear right at the end of the trees then half left, and now begin a gentle descent on a farm track, enjoying a wonderful view ahead over the valley as you proceed towards Sutton-under-Brailes. Pass through a field gate, the golf course now to your right, and when you reach the road at the bottom of the hill, turn left and wander through this beautiful Cotswold village, going to the right, past the village green, and heading for a stile to the left-hand side of the parish church and Church Cottage.

4. Clamber over the stile, then another, to cross an orchard and walk past the church. Go through a kissing gate and head half left across a cultivated field by Church Farm. Go through a kissing gate in the far corner onto a farm lane. Turn right up this track, passing to the right-hand side of Oaken Covert. Continue ahead through a field gate and uphill alongside a post-and-wire fence. Pass through another field gate, and with a hedge on your right you ascend Cherington Hill.

5. Just past some trees, you reach a junction of public footpaths. Go right through a metal gate and follow a tractor track heading generally eastwards. The route goes to the left-hand side of New House Barn. Continue ahead through a field gate along a track, through another gate, and continue along the top of a farm field, with more good views over the Brailes Valley to the right. At end of the field, go through a gate to descend the hedged track called High Lane, the lower part a deep sunken lane, to reach Tommy's Turn.

6. Turn left and walk down the lane, continuing your descent into Henbrook Lane. Soon you will come back out onto the High Street in Lower Brailes (the B4035). Turn right along the road for about 100yds (91m) to return to the village hall on the corner of Castle Hill Lane.

Where to eat and drink
The George Hotel, in the middle of Lower Brailes, has long been a popular eating and drinking place for walkers. Apart from fine local ales and excellent home-made food, there is a large rear garden to enjoy.

What to look out for
Make sue you wander up the B4035 and take a look around the pretty village of Upper Brailes.

While you're there
Travel to Tysoe, about 5 miles (8km) north, to explore the lovely village which William the Conqueror gave to one of his followers, Robert de Stafford. In size and importance, it ranked, along with Brailes, next to Warwick. From Upper Tysoe, you can stroll up to the parish church and enjoy a classic view of the magnificent Tudor mansion of Compton Wynyates – still the seat of the Marquis of Northampton.

HARTSHILL HAYES AND THE COUNTRY PARK

DISTANCE/TIME	4.5 miles (7.2km) / 1hr 45min
ASCENT/GRADIENT	295ft (90m) / ▲ ▲
PATHS	Lanes, field paths, woodland tracks and tow paths
LANDSCAPE	Country park and rolling countryside
SUGGESTED MAP	OS Explorer 232 Nuneaton & Tamworth
START/FINISH	Grid reference: SP317943
DOG FRIENDLINESS	Off lead in park and along tow path
PARKING	Car park at Hartshill Hayes Country Park
PUBLIC TOILETS	Hartshill Hayes Country Park

In 1978, around 136 acres (55ha) of the hillside around Hartshill were made into the fine country park that forms the basis of this walk. It strays into Warwickshire proper and includes part of the Coventry Canal. A sizeable area of woodland has developed at Hartshill, refreshingly dominated by traditional broadleaved trees such as oak, beech, sycamore, hazel and alder. Elder and holly also thrive.

Hartshill village is an old settlement, but there is little information to establish its full history. The Romans were here and may have built a military station on the hill. Hugh de Hardreshull built a motte-and-bailey castle on the hill in 1125. Robert de Hartshill, who became Lord of the Castle, was killed alongside Simon de Montfort at the battle of Evesham in 1265. Perhaps it fell into disuse then, for all traces of the fortification have long since disappeared.

The village was home to the poet Michael Drayton, a contemporary and friend of William Shakespeare. He was born in 1563 at the long demolished Chapel Cottage in Hartshill Green, and there is a plaque in his memory. His poem, *A Fine Day*, is said to draw inspiration from the local landscape. In *Polyolbion*, he described the River Anker weaving its way past his birthplace to join the River Tame.

The Coventry Canal came long after Drayton's time. It winds its way along the valley below the village linking Atherstone and the Fazeley Junction, where it joins the main canal system to connect with the Trent and Mersey. The canal reached Fazeley in 1790, happily coinciding with the completion date of the Oxford Canal and allowing it to improve a shaky financial position (under engineer James Brindley its construction had run massively over budget). It remained in a reasonably sound state until 1948, when nationalisation was followed by disuse and deterioration. In recent years, however, it has been successfully restored for pleasure craft to enjoy the scenery.

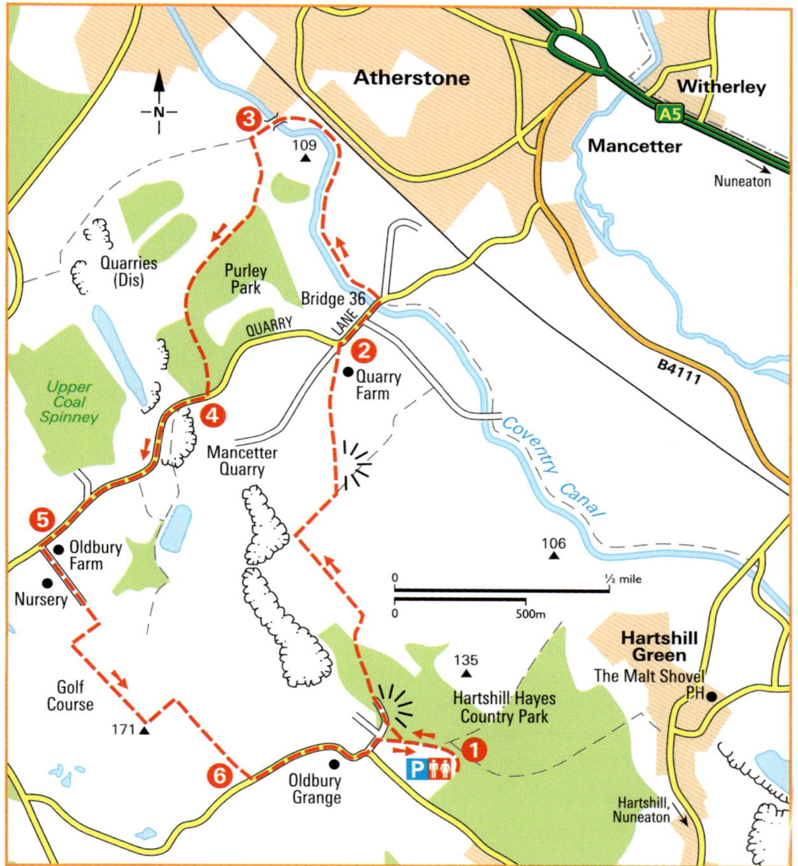

1. From the car park, enter the Hartshill Hayes Country Park at the back of the visitor centre. Pass the children's play area and take the path that arcs left (northwest) along the top of Hartshill, alongside a covered reservoir, and enjoy the super view over the surrounding area. Continue ahead on the path that then descends right into woodland. At the bottom of the woodland go over the two footbridges and then bear left to walk along a fine open path as you continue, initially to the left of the hedge, then to its right. In about 0.25 miles (400m) the path bends to the right and you will ascend northeast to the brow of the hill, from where you can overlook the Coventry Canal and get a great view. Bear left beside a kissing gate onto the path, which becomes hedged as you progress northwards towards Quarry Farm. Go through the gate to the left of the farm buildings onto Quarry Lane.

2. Turn right and stroll down the lane, bearing right at the junction until you come to bridge No. 36 over the Coventry Canal. Cross either bridge and descend right to the tow path. Go right under the bridge to walk in a northwesterly direction, and in 0.5 miles (800m) proceed beneath bridge No. 37.

3. Leave the tow path at bridge No. 38 and cross the canal onto a quiet lane. Walk up the lane for about 150yds (137m) then, just before a private house, go left through a tall kissing gate into meadowland and on into pastureland. Cross over the footbridge at the bottom of the field, then walk half right across the next field and on to a gate. This leads to a footbridge and a second tall kissing gate, and you enter the woodland of Purley Park. Follow the footpath up the right edge of the woodland. The path arcs left into the trees and you will exit on to Quarry Lane again.

4. Go right and head up the lane, past the entrance to Mancetter Quarry. Continue along the lane and in a further 600yds (549m), just past Oldbury Farm, go left.

5. Walk to the right of the farm buildings, with gardens on your right, to reach a good bridlepath beside ponds going southeast. This lovely path crosses farm land, but soon you will be following yellow-topped marker posts across a golf course.

6. Exit onto a road, via a gate, and then go left. The road passes by Oldbury Grange and Oldbury Grange Gardens. Where there is a sharp right-hand bend in the road, go left up towards the rear entrance to the gardens and enter Hartshill Hayes Country Park via two gates. Once you are in the park bear right and join the waymarked park path that takes you back to the visitor centre.

Where to eat and drink

In nearby Hartshill Green, you'll find The Malt Shovel pub serves good value food. Children and dogs may be allowed in certain rooms only. There is a garden with seating and a play area. At peak times, there is a snack bar at the country park car park.

What to see

As you return to the country park the walk takes you past Oldbury Grange, now a nursing home, which was built around 1904 by Garside Phillips, the first manager of Ansley Colliery. He bought it for his son Joseph, who himself became 'The Boss' at the pit. The Phillips family became the leading gentry in the village. Joseph's grandson is Captain Mark Phillips, the renowned horseman and former husband of Princess Anne.

While you're there

Follow the permissive footpath near Point 4 into Mancetter Quarry. There are art installations, new planting and interpretive panels explaining the development and future of these dramatic quarry workings. You can return to the main route by following the footpath to the right from a junction.

HARTSHILL HAYES AND THE COVENTRY CANAL

DISTANCE/TIME	4 miles (6.4km) / 2hrs
ASCENT/GRADIENT	330ft (100m) / ▲
PATHS	Field paths, towpath, quiet road, woodland paths in country park
LANDSCAPE	Country park, farmland and canal
SUGGESTED MAP	OS Explorer 232 Nuneaton & Tamworth
START/FINISH	Grid Reference: SP317943
DOG FRIENDLINESS	Off lead in park and on towpath
PARKING	Car park at Hartshill Hayes Country Park
PUBLIC TOILETS	Hartshill Hayes Country Park

The 100-mile (161km) Warwickshire Centenary Way offers the chance to get to the heart of the county on foot, discovering its gentle beauty and hidden landscape by simple but effective means. The route starts at Kingsbury Water Park and finishes at Upper Quinton on the Gloucestershire border. Along the way the trail makes for Hartshill Hayes Country Park, starting point for this very pleasant circular walk. It was just after midnight on the first Saturday of 1991 when five young men from the Atherstone District Scout Fellowship began their adventure. They were to walk through the night, into the next day and beyond. Their aim was to complete the Centenary Way in full. Three of them finished their trek at 4.58 the following Monday afternoon, describing the walk as 'a weekend of fierce storms and lashing rain.' Conditions may not have been very pleasant – they admitted the exercise was perhaps 'not the best way of seeing Warwickshire' – but the scouts clocked up the first recorded continuous trek along the Centenary Way, which was eventually opened to walkers in the summer of that year.

The task of planning the Centenary Way dates back over a quarter of a century. The original idea was conceived by Warwickshire County Council and was intended to be part of a programme of events marking its 100th anniversary in 1989. More than anything, the route reflects the diversity of scenery to be found within the county. Following a string of public footpaths, bridleways, canal towpaths and disused railways, the Centenary Way follows many miles of glorious countryside, passing through picturesque villages and beside ancient woodland and winding streams along the way. In the north of the county the walk explores a landscape known to George Eliot. The 19th century writer spent her formative years on the Arbury Hall estate, near Nuneaton, where her father was a land agent. The Warwickshire influence of her childhood never abandoned Eliot, whose real name was Marian Evans, though in later years she regarded much of rural England as a vanished world.

By then, the pace of life had accelerated, the railway age had dawned and a landscape once littered with farms and market towns had been transformed almost beyond recognition by the rapid development of industry. Planning

and developing a long-distance path is a long job and a major responsibility
for anyone. With funds from the Countryside Commission, the council set to
work, inviting volunteers to help by building stiles and footbridges, clearing
vegetation and erecting signposts. The Centenary Way, which is divided into
eleven sections, was officially opened at Upper Quinton, where the trail meets
the Heart of England Way.

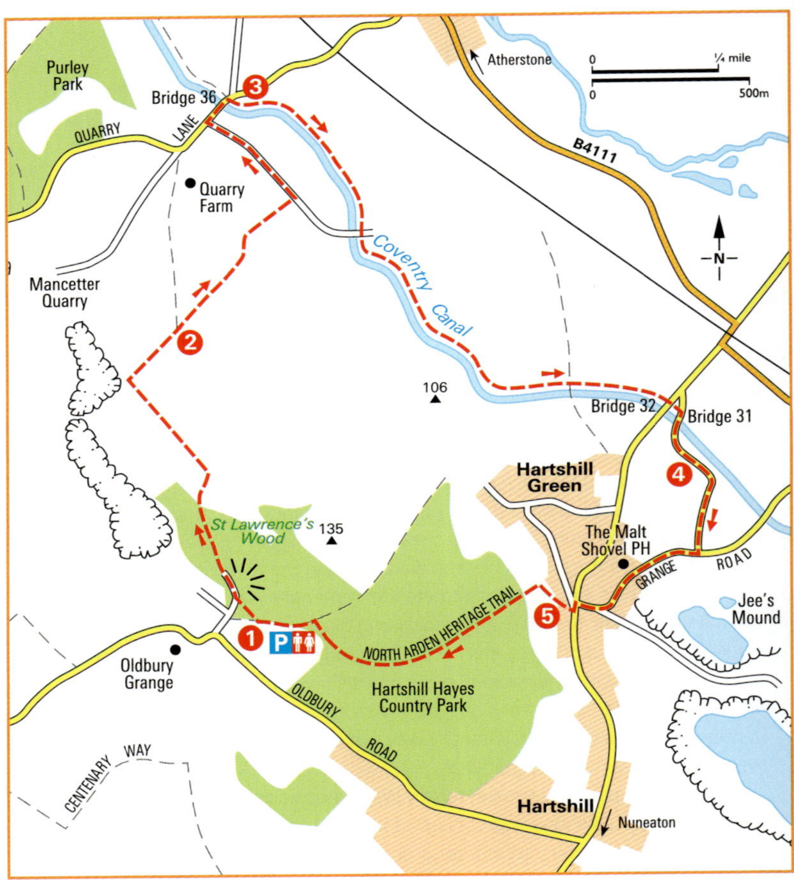

1. Pass to the rear of the refreshment kiosk and toilets and then walk
alongside a children's play area. When the path divides, keep left alongside
the boundary of a reservoir. Pass a commemorative panel and follow the path
as it descends through the trees of St Lawrence's Wood. At the bottom, avoid
the path on the right and cross two footbridges. Go down the field slope with
the quarry on your left and then bear left in the corner to pass alongside a
hedge. The path passes through a gap and then continues with the hedge on
your left. Bear right and ascend to the brow of the hill, then down to a fork by
a kissing gate.

2. Go straight on through the gate and head down through farmland with grand rural views from this breezy high ground. Make for some gates and a kissing gate in the bottom of the field and follow a track to a junction. Turn left and walk along to the road. Turn right by traffic lights and make for the towpath of the Coventry Canal.

3. Keep the waterway on your right and head for bridges 35 and 34. Continue to bridge 33, pass a footpath on the left and walk along to bridge 32. This is the site of the Hartshill Quay maintenance yard. Leave the towpath and head up towards the road. Before reaching it, turn sharp right and cross bridge 31.

4. Follow the lane uphill and at the junction at the top, turn right. Continue climbing. Pass a playground on the right and follow the lane towards Hartshill Green. Turn right beyond the Malt Shovel and make for the next road junction. Cross over, following the path to the right of the flats. When it divides, keep left and descend the steep steps to cross a lengthy footbridge.

5. This next stage of the route is part of the Quarryman's Walk and the North Arden Heritage Trail. The latter is a circular route through the countryside of North Warwickshire. Keep ahead through woodland and eventually bear right at a stone seat. Pass a wooden seat and keep on the Quarryman's Walk. Make for a kissing gate at the corner of the wood, turn left and return to the car park.

Where to eat and drink

In nearby Hartshill Green, you'll find The Malt Shovel pub serves good value food. Children and dogs may be allowed in certain rooms only. There is a garden with seating and a play area. At peak times, there is a snack bar at the country park car park.

What to look out for

To follow this route is to walk in the footsteps of our ancestors – in particular, the Romans who came here in AD 60 and made glass and pottery in kilns. Various remains have been found in the locality over the years. The writer and historian Arthur Mee claimed you could count 40 churches from the viewpoint at Hartshill Hayes Country Park.

A WALK AROUND COVENTRY

DISTANCE/TIME	3 miles (4.8km) / 1hr 30min
ASCENT/GRADIENT	16ft (5m) / ▲
PATHS	Pavements
LANDSCAPE	Historic Coventry
SUGGESTED MAP	OS Explorer 221 Coventry & Warwick
START/FINISH	Grid Reference: SP335789
DOG FRIENDLINESS	On lead at all times
PARKING	Any park-and-ride car park, then travel into city centre by bus
PUBLIC TOILETS	Library Building in Smithford Way

This short but inspiring walk guides you around the most historic parts of Coventry's centre, starting at Old St Michael's Cathedral. This became a cathedral in 1918, as a replacement for St Mary's, which had been abandoned after the Reformation. Unfortunately, it was severely damaged in the bombing raid of 14 November 1940, when so much of the city was destroyed, and it's shell remains as a memorial to that dark time.

Basil Spence was the winner of the 1950 competition to design a new cathedral, and his stark modern design has been the subject of much controversy over the years. It was a radical new approach and a complete break with tradition. The new cathedral was finally consecrated in May 1962 in the presence of Queen Elizabeth II, and you can compare the older style with the more modern during your walk.

Another impressive and important building that is well worth exploring is St Mary's Guildhall on Bayley Lane. After fleeing from London during the Wars of the Roses in 1456, King Henry VI and Queen Margaret spent most of their time in Coventry, where St Mary's Guildhall became the prime venue for entertaining royalty and their court. Amongst its many functions, the guildhall has also been extensively used as a theatre. Its raised dais made the hall suitable for public performance, and over the years it became a regular venue for visiting players. William Shakespeare is known to have performed here as a young actor in 1580. Shakespeare's last visit to Coventry was in 1608, two years before his death at the age of 52, and as you walk past the guildhall you can see a statue of the Bard above the main archway.

Lady Godiva is one of the more remarkable names associated with Coventry. Godiva was the wife of Leofric, Earl of Mercia, one of the most powerful Anglo-Saxon noblemen in 11th-century England. Leofric became so exasperated by Godiva's endless appeals to reduce Coventry's heavy and punitive taxes that he declared he would do so if she rode naked through the crowded marketplace. Godiva did exactly that – with her flowing hair covering all of her body except her legs. You will see a statue of her on her horse as you pass through the main shopping precinct.

Along the walk is Cheylesmore Manor House, which dates from the 13th century and has been lovingly renovated over the centuries by the City of Coventry. It is an outstanding example of a house from this period. It once belonged to Queen Isabella (the wife of Edward II) and in 1338 was passed to her grandson, Edward the Black Prince.

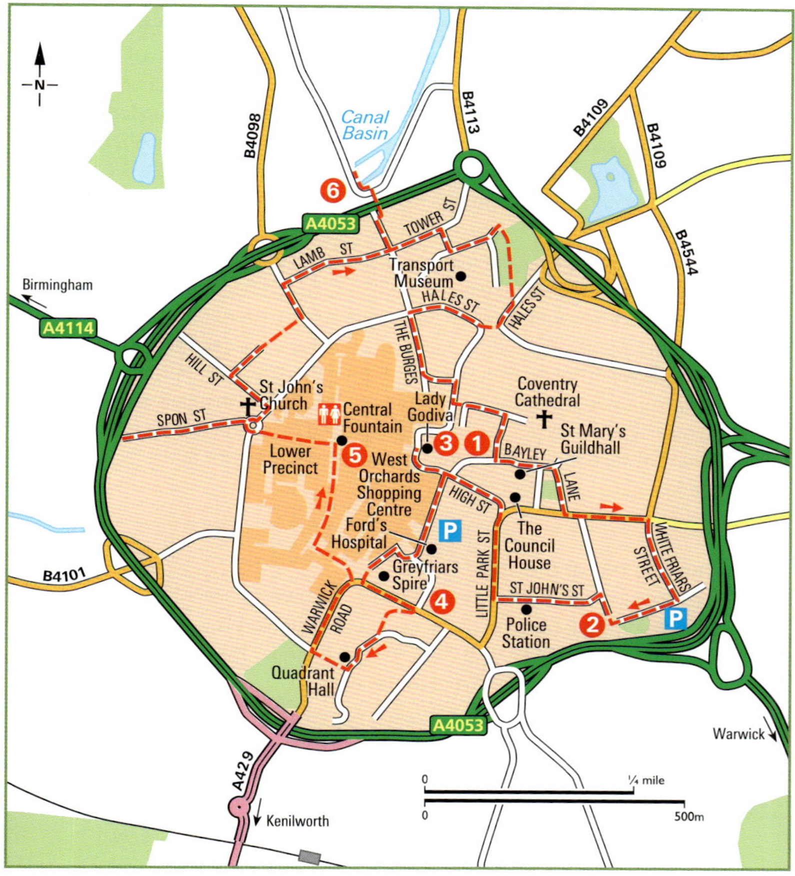

1. From the tourist information office, go left down Bayley Lane, past St Mary's Guildhall. Turn right into Earl Street, then left into Jordan Well. Cross the road and go right, down Whitefriars Street. At the bottom just before the car park, go right along cobbled Whitefriars Lane, to pass beneath Whitefriars Gateway.

2. Turn right into Much Park Street, then take the first left turn, along St John's Street to Little Park Street. Turn right down here, then left in front of the Tudor-style Council House, built in 1917. Continue left along the High Street, past the modernised Cathedral Lanes Shopping Centre to reach the Lady Godiva statue of 1949, by Sir William Reid Dick.

3. Walk back towards the High Street and go right down Greyfriars Lane. After the car park is the row of restored almshouses, Ford's Hospital. Continue along Greyfriars Lane and take the pathway to the right of the Greyfriars Spire

– all that remains of a 14th-century church – to New Union Street. Go left and cross at the crossing through the Manor Yard archway, to Cheylesmore Manor.

4. At Manor House Drive go right, and just past Quadrant Hall, go right again down a footpath to Warwick Road. Cross Warwick Road and turn right to the shopping precinct at Bull Yard. Go left into Shelton Square, then bear right and continue along Market Way into the centre of the main shopping area.

5. By the fountain, go left into Lower Precinct. At the traffic island by St John's Church, cross the road and walk down Spon Street to admire the row of medieval buildings. At the end, retrace your steps past St John's Church, and turn left into Hill Street. On your left is the Old Bablake School, founded in 1560 for the education of poor boys of Coventry. Go right along Bond Street into Belgrade Square, up the steps then turn left into Upper Well Street, then right into Lamb Street. Turn left to a footbridge over The Ringway that leads to the Canal Basin.

6. Retrace your steps over the footbridge and walk down Bishop Street. Turn left along Tower Street, right down to Cook Street, and left alongside the rear of the Transport Museum. After going beneath 15th-century Cook Street Gateway, turn right and stroll through Lady Herbert's Garden to Hales Street by the Swanswell (Priory) Gate. Pass in front of the Transport Museum right along Hales Street to a junction. Turn left up The Burges, then left around Ironmonger Row and cross the road. Go right and then left into Priory Row and down between the New and the Old Cathedrals to return to the tourist information office.

Where to eat and drink

There are plenty of places to eat and drink in Coventry. The route of this walk takes you past several of the best pubs, including The Old Windmill in Spon Street, The Town Wall Tavern in Bond Street, The Philip Larkin in The Burges and the Golden Cross in Hay Lane.

What to look out for

Coventry is a city undergoing a lot of redevelopment but most of the oldest parts are being preserved. Obtain a free street guide/map from the tourist information office before you begin your walk. There is also a very helpful booklet explaining the detailed history of each building you will pass by or visit.

While you're there

Visit the old and modern cathedrals, both dedicated to St Michael. They represent hope and rejuvenation, rather than bitterness and loss. In the modern one, there's a stunning tapestry by Graham Sutherland above the altar.

41

EDGEHILL AND RATLEY

DISTANCE/TIME	6 miles (9.7km) / 2hrs 30min
ASCENT/GRADIENT	164ft (50m) / ▲
PATHS	Lanes and field paths, several stiles
LANDSCAPE	Rolling countryside
SUGGESTED MAP	OS Explorer 206 Edge Hill & Fenny Compton
START/FINISH	Grid Reference: SP362458
DOG FRIENDLINESS	On lead at all times
PARKING	At lay-by on A422
PUBLIC TOILETS	None on route

This hilly walk takes you along the escarpment of the famous Edgehill – a prominent sandstone ridge which runs from northeast to southwest at a height of around 600ft (183m) above sea level.

Below the ridge, on the land which stretches away towards Kineton, the first major battle of the Civil War took place in October 1642. It pitted the cavaliers of King Charles I against a poorly equipped Parliamentarian army under Robert Devereux, Earl of Essex. Prince Rupert led the charge of the King's cavalry on his galloping white charger, as he would throughout the coming campaign, but on this day the outcome was inconclusive. The fighting petered out when darkness fell, the Royalists hastening back towards Banbury, the Parliamentarians to Warwick. Neither side could claim a victory. Entering the field with some 14,000 men apiece, they departed leaving around 3,000 casualties in total, and lost perhaps as many men again as deserters. You can't visit the actual battle site today, as it is hidden in a huge Ministry of Defence ammunition facility, but an Edgehill Battle Museum can be found in the grounds of Farnborough House, some 3 miles (4.8km) to the east.

The splendid Radway Tower, passed towards the end of the walk, was constructed to mark the 100th anniversary of the battle, though it wasn't completed until 1750. This 70ft (21m) octagonal folly is now occupied by the popular Castle at Edgehill Hotel and pub.

There are other monuments and views to be seen from the ridge. From Ratley, you can see an obelisk erected in 1854 by Charles Chambers to commemorate the Battle of Waterloo. At Nadbury Camp the mounds of an 18-acre (7ha) Bronze Age camp can still be seen, although the remains have been dissected by a busy road and there has been considerable damage by ploughing. The walk also takes you close to the National Trust's Upton House before descending into the medieval village of Ratley.

You'll find Ratley is a peaceful village, set away from the main Oxford road and largely unchanged since the turn of the 20th century. Its recognition in 1971 as a conservation area has helped ensure the survival of its oldest parts. Records show the manor was held by a Saxon named Ordic, before the arrival of the Normans. Most of its houses are built of honey-brown Hornton stone – a local limestone produced in the Edgehill quarry. Quarrying was once a major local industry. Today, the quarried land has been reclaimed, planted with trees and has become a nature reserve. An active farming community remains, but most local people commute to Oxford for work. Ratley's 12th-century church is near The Rose and Crown pub and has the unusual dedication of St Peter AD Vincula. Outside it is an ancient preaching cross; time has robbed it of its arms, and only the shaft remains. As you return to the start, there are superb and long views over farmland to Tysoe.

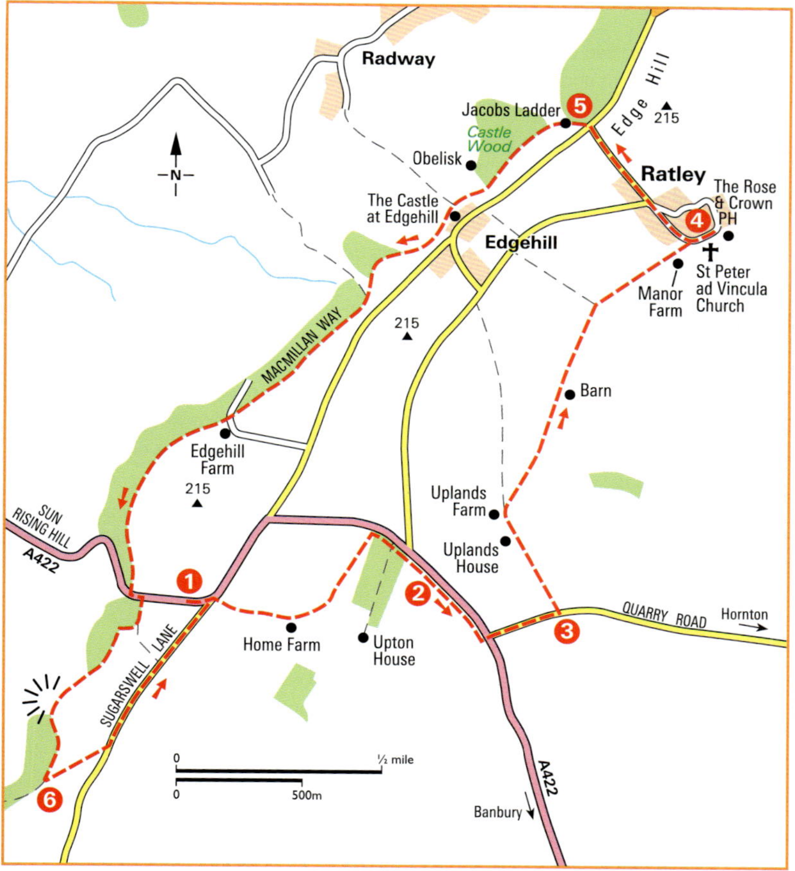

1. From the lay-by on the A422, walk east, go left and in 10yds (9m) go right again through a farm gate, following a stone wall. Then, through another gate, bear left towards Home Farm. Pass to the left of the farm buildings, then go left and aim for the far right corner of the field and two kissing gates. Continue ahead via a kissing gate through the National Trust car park to another gate and the A422. Go right along the grass verge of the busy road past the entrance gates to the 17th-century Upton House.

2. In about 600yds (549m), cross the A422 with care and go left down the lane to Hornton.

3. In a further 300yds (274m), nearly opposite Quarry Cottage, go left along a signed path. Walk to the left of the field hedge over two fields, then pass to the right of the buildings of Uplands House and Uplands Farm. Continue over a stile into open countryside, bearing right beyond a wire fence down a track to a farm gate and stile, and descend into the valley. Walk by the hedge and pass to the left of an old, dilapidated barn. Cross a stile and ascend to a junction of paths. Go left through a gate and immediately over a stile to continue ahead, descending a farm field to reach another stile in the far right corner. Head steeply half left and descend to a stone stile, to emerge in Ratley village by Manor Farm.

4. At the main road turn right to explore the village, then retrace your steps past Manor Farm and continue straight ahead on the road towards Edge Hill.

5. Cross over the road at the T-junction and descend the many steps of Jacobs Ladder into Castle Wood opposite, following the waymarkers of the MacMillan Way, and ignoring the gate into open countryside. Take the footpath along the escarpment of the famous hill. After about 0.25 miles (400m), take a right fork and shortly look right to see the Obelisk. Continue along the path, passing below The Castle Inn. Stay on this path, waymarked Macmillan Way and Centenary Way for about 1.25 miles (2km), sometimes in the edge of the wood and sometimes with the hedge on your left and trees on your right. Keep on the MacMillan Way until you reach the A422, at the top of Sun Rising Hill. Turn left along the road for about 50 paces and go right along the concrete track, initially bearing right at stables, then left before taking the footpath into a copse. Soon pass through a gate to open land with a superb view of Tysoe and the surrounding countryside. Continue through a second gate and follow a path on the edge of the woods for about 300yds (274m).

6. Go left through a farm gate and diagonally left across the field to reach Sugarswell Lane via a gate. Continue left along the lane to the A422 and the lay-by.

Where to eat and drink

The Castle at Edgehill is a splendid castellated hotel and pub. The mock castle was built as a gatehouse between 1742 and 1750 to commemorate the centenary of the Battle of Edgehill. The Rose and Crown in Ratley is a classic country pub offering hearty traditional pub food to a high standard with a wide range of drinks.

What to look out for

While in Ratley take a look at the Church of St Peter AD Vincula – 'St Peter in Chains'. One of its brass memorial plates tells us that the heiress of Simon Bury died on the 14th February 1696, aged 1697. Even in the 17th century, typographical mistakes were made.

While you're there

Upton House, a 17th-century National Trust property, was remodelled between 1927 and 1929 for the 2nd Viscount Bearsted. It contains fine collections of paintings, including works by Canaletto and El Greco. The extensive gardens are outstanding. The lower lake was formed in the mid-18th century and has a small temple with Doric columns.

42

HAWKESBURY JUNCTION

DISTANCE/TIME	4.5 miles (7.2km) / 1hr 45min
ASCENT/GRADIENT	56ft (17m) / ▲
PATHS	Lanes, field paths, woodland tracks and tow paths, several stiles
LANDSCAPE	Canalside and gentle countryside
SUGGESTED MAP	OS Explorer 221 Coventry & Warwick
START/FINISH	Grid Reference: SP361844
DOG FRIENDLINESS	Off lead along tow path, otherwise under control
PARKING	On Sutton Stop adjacent to the Greyhound pub at Hawkesbury Junction
PUBLIC TOILETS	None on route

This easy walk gives you the opportunity to share a Midlands canal experience by walking the tow paths of two of the area's most important canals. They both formed an important link in Britain's network of canals during the Industrial Revolution.

The route takes you from Hawkesbury Junction to Hawkesbury village, and then through pleasant countryside to reach the Coventry Way. After passing Hollyhurst fishery and Coalpit Fields Woodlands Nature Reserve, you join the Coventry Canal near Bedworth. Although it is quiet now, this was once a major coalmining community. You start and finish in the Hawkesbury Junction conservation area, where the elegant 50ft (15m) Britannia Foundry of Derby's cast-iron footbridge, built in 1837, spans the junction of the Coventry and Oxford canals.

Hawkesbury Junction was also known as Sutton Stop, after the name of the first lock keeper. It became a famous resting place for bargees on this part of the canal system. In 1821, an engine house was built to pump water up into the canal from a local well. The Newcomen-type atmospheric steam engine, which lifted the well water, was called Lady Godiva. It ceased pumping in 1913 and has since been transferred to the Newcomen Engine House museum in Dartmouth, Devon. Thomas Newcomen was born in Dartmouth in 1663, and Lady Godiva forms the centrepiece of his memorial museum. At Hawkesbury Junction, The Greyhound Inn and the pump house are reminders of this once busy scene. Photographers will find a classic shot through the archway of the cast-iron bridge.

The Act of Parliament to enable construction of the Coventry Canal was passed in 1768 with two objectives. The first aim was to connect Coventry with a new trade route called the Grand Trunk (today known as the Trent and Mersey Canal). The second was to provide Coventry with cheap coal from the coalfield at Bedworth, a major mining community. By 1769, the stretch of canal between Coventry and Bedworth had been completed, but because of some wrangling with the Oxford Canal Company, the Coventry Canal did not reach its point of linkage with the Grand Trunk at Fazeley until 1790. James Brindley was the original engineer for this attractive canal, but he was sacked from the job following an overspend of authorised capital.

Brindley was also the engineer of the winding 91-mile (146km) Oxford Canal, one of the earliest to be built. Its objective was to connect the Midlands with London. It reached Oxford in 1789 and was completed in 1790. Initially the link was achieved with the Coventry Canal via a mile-long (1.6km) parallel stretch of canal. In 1801, the Hawkesbury Junction was constructed to avoid this costly duplication. The price of coal in the capital, which was previously transported from Newcastle by sea, dropped almost immediately.

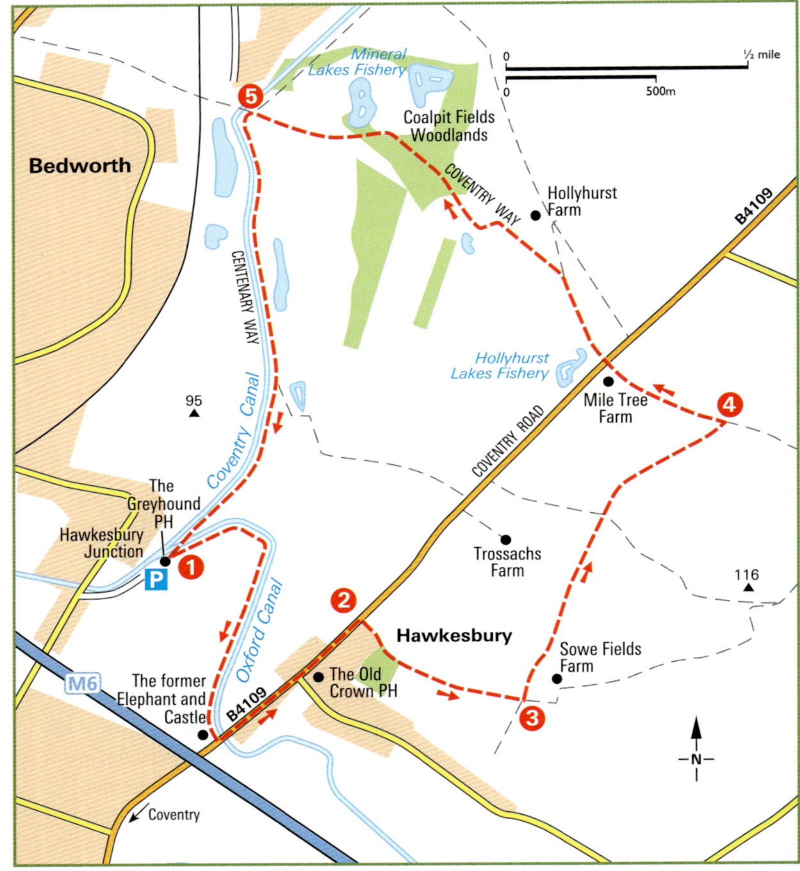

1. After parking in Sutton Stop, walk past The Greyhound pub and continue along the Oxford Canal tow path. Walk beneath the electricity pylons, past the substation and leave the canal at the first road bridge beside a house, formerly The Elephant and Castle pub. Go left, crossing the bridge over the Oxford Canal, and follow Coventry Road past The Old Crown.

2. In about 250yds (229m), just after the large sign for Nuneaton and Bedworth, go right through a gate and bearing right to skirt the house, then turn left with

the woods on the right and fields on your left. Continue along the footpath to a stile, then go left over the stile into a large field. Cross the field, heading towards a double stile at the end, but don't go over the stile.

3. Go left again and head towards another stile in the field corner, passing Sowe Fields Farm buildings on your right. Cross the stile and continue in a northeasterly direction over two stiles and through three field gates. Your route passes by Trossachs Farm (on the left) and you continue along the path by the field edge. After going over a stile and footbridge, walk diagonally over a large field, aiming to the left of an ash tree in the far corner.

4. Go over the stile, then bear sharp left to join the Coventry Way. Take the track by the field edge until you exit onto the Coventry road once again via a stile, near to Mile Tree Farm. Cross the road to a sign for Hollyhurst Lakes and turn right through gates onto a track, heading past fishing lakes generally towards Hollyhurst Farm. Follow the Coventry Way as the path arcs left at a waymark post, and follow a hedged path. Soon, through a pair of kissing gates, bear left around some barns on the right onto a grassy track which curves left alongside Coalpit Fields Woodlands. Go left over a stile and bear left along a farm track to reach bridge No. 13 over the Coventry Canal.

5. Just before reaching the bridge, go left and descend to the tow path along the pleasant canal for about a mile (1.6km). Head south along the tow path – this is part of the Centenary Way. The path arcs gently right (southwest), and soon you reach Hawkesbury Junction where large numbers of colourful narrowboats are usually moored. Cross the cast-iron footbridge to reach the pub and the end of the walk.

Where to eat and drink

The walk passes The Old Crown in Hawkesbury village, which has a large garden offering good pub food. The Greyhound at Hawkesbury Junction is attractively placed and has large gardens where children and dogs are allowed. Tables outside offer views of the canal basin.

What to look out for

The canals are heavily used by local anglers, usually with rods much taller than themselves. You may see pike, roach, perch, bream or carp being hauled onto the bank. If you stroll off the main route at Bedworth Hill Bridge you can visit two small lakes.

While you're there

Spend a little time at Hawkesbury Junction enjoying the scene with its traditionally decorated narrowboats, as their occupants visit the chandlery (a shop selling supplies for boats) or manoeuvre between the canals. This once busy industrial canal centre is now used solely for leisure purposes.

43 HARBURY AND CHESTERTON

DISTANCE/TIME	4 miles (6.4km) / 1hr 45min
ASCENT/GRADIENT	131ft (40m) / ▲
PATHS	Farm driveways and field paths
LANDSCAPE	Rolling Warwickshire countryside
SUGGESTED MAP	OS Explorer 206 Edge Hill & Fenny Compton
START/FINISH	Grid Reference: SP373597
DOG FRIENDLINESS	Under control at all times
PARKING	On-street parking near village hall in Harbury
PUBLIC TOILETS	None on route

This walk starts from one of the oldest places in Warwickshire, for Harbury was once the home of a huge ichthyosaurus that roamed the local countryside. Its skeleton and those of a plesiosaurus and several marine dinosaurs have been found in the old quarries here, as have Bronze Age cooking pots.

In about 500 BC, there was an Iron Age camp (or byrig) in these parts. It was ruled by a woman called Hereburh, and Harbury's name derives from 'the fortified place belonging to a woman called Hereburh'. The Romans were also here. Their great Fosse Way forms one of the boundaries to the west of the village, and Roman culverts can still be seen. Ridge and furrow fields reveal evidence of Saxon farmers, and an area called Temple End suggests the land was once owned by the Knights Templar.

The parish church of All Saints is mostly Norman and dates from the 13th century. It sports a sundial carrying the accusatory inscription 'Tyme flyeth, what doest thou?' The Wagstaffes were the owners of the manor from the time of Henry VIII, and inside the church is a memorial to Jane Wagstaffe who lived here during Elizabeth I's reign. Behind the church is the Tudor 'Wagstaffe School' that was founded by Jane's descendants in 1611. Today, Harbury is a delightful old village where you can see attractive cottages, imbibe in fine pubs and admire some lovely old trees.

From Harbury, the walk takes you south along peaceful country lanes, passing by attractive lakes to reach the tiny hamlet of Chesterton – a place of beauty where time appears to have stood still. The name of the hamlet is of Roman origin. The village was hit badly by the plague of 1349, and by the 15th century, there were only three families residing here.

Today, there is no shop or pub in this lovely hamlet, but St Giles' Church is rather special. Its battlemented parapet runs the entire length of the chancel, and is set on walls which are 3ft (0.9m) thick. It was founded by Richard the Forester and was presented to the priory at Kenilworth in the late 14th century. The return route takes you over pastureland and cultivated fields, passing by an old metal windpump before reaching Harbury village.

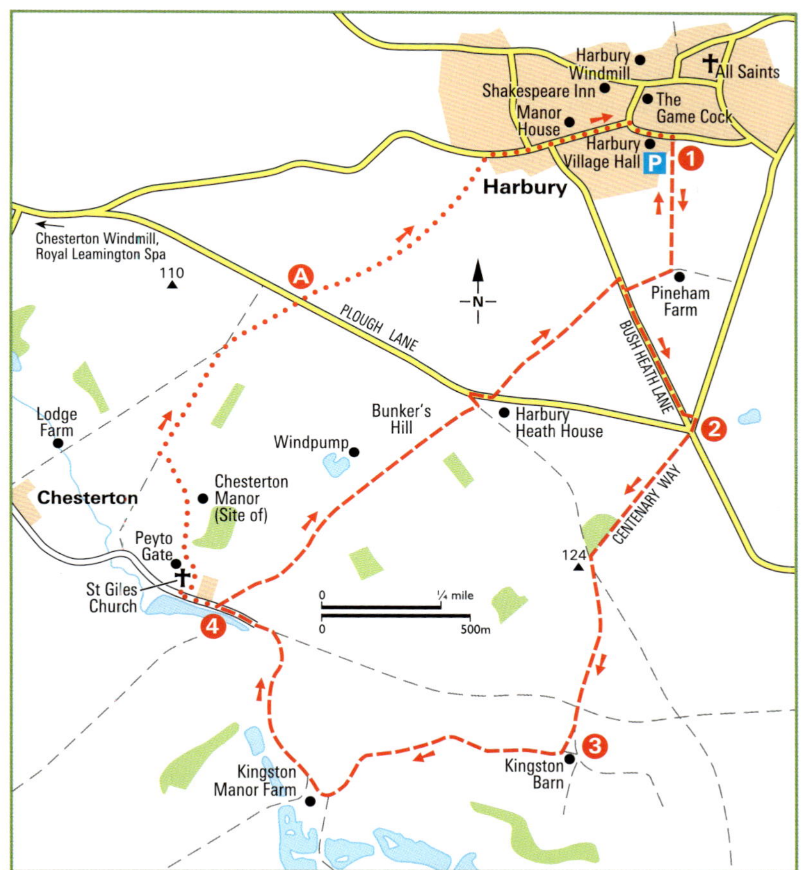

1. Walk through the car park behind the village hall and head south by football pitches to a gate in the far corner. Don't go through it, but bear right to follow the waymarkers for the Centenary Way. Cross a field to a second gate onto Bush Heath Lane. Turn left and walk down to a junction of lanes.

2. Go right here, signed 'Kingston Farm', over a cattle grid and along the grass verge of a driveway for about 600yds (549m), still following the Centenary Way. Where the Way goes off to the left, continue ahead along a quiet country lane. Soon the buildings of Kingston Barn farm will be to your left, but fork right to follow the lane as it goes to the right of the farm complex, to reach a lane going off to the right by a footpath guide post.

3. Proceed right along this lane, which weaves its way through some very attractive countryside with views of Chesterton windmill. When you reach the garden walls to Kingston Manor Farm, turn right again and continue along the lane, now heading in a northwesterly direction, passing some lakes. After about 0.5 miles (800m) of walking past the picturesque lakes, the lane arcs left up towards St Giles' Church in the hamlet of Chesterton. Through a gate or over a cattle grid, continue up the lane towards the church.

4. Some 120 paces before reaching the church gate, go right through a kissing gate and ascend over cultivated fields and pastureland, following the footpaths and heading generally northeast back towards Harbury. The footpath crosses a stile and passes to the right of an old windpump and Bunker's Hill. Over the brow of the hill head towards the left-hand of a group of houses, then left along the field edge to a gate onto Plough Lane, near Harbury Heath House. Turn right, and after 100yds (91m) turn left through a metal gate on a footpath that initially is to the right of the field hedge and later to the left, until you reach Bush Heath Lane. Go through a gate and turn right onto a lane, then after about 30 paces go left through a gate to rejoin the Centenary Way once again. The path leads towards Pineham Farm. After about 200yds (183m), go left beside a gate to return to the back of Harbury village hall.

Extending the walk This short extension explores some of Chesterton. When you reach the village leave the main walk at Point 4 and continue along the lane. Soon pass through the entrance gate to St Giles' Church.

The path goes to the right of the church, and you leave the churchyard through the gate in the far corner, to the right of a small shed, and well to the right of the ornamental Peyto gateway in the north churchyard wall. (This is a copy of one designed by Inigo Jones and built to provide a suitable entry for the Peyto family.)

Descend through the field and, passing to the left of a reed-filled pond, go over the footbridge, with a stile at each end, in the hedge below, then over another stile into the next field. Head straight uphill, and at the brow aim to the left of some rather derelict buildings – the remains of outbuildings to Chesterton Manor, largely demolished in 1802.

In the valley to the left are the buildings of Lodge Farm. Southwest of these are the remains of a medieval settlement, identified as Netherend in a document of 1319.

Go through the gate and then right, through a second. A third gate leads into a large field that you cross going northeast towards a gate in the fence ahead – the site of the manor house is to the right of here.

Through a gate, take the right of two paths, heading to the far right-hand corner of a large field, following the waymark direction. Via a gate and footbridge, exit on to Harbury Lane (Point A). Cross the lane, go over a footbridge and through a kissing gate and maintain your direction over several fields, passing through kissing gates, over footbridges and through gates until you emerge through another gate by a house in Temple End, in Harbury. Go right along the road and you will pass by the Manor House as you progress into Park Lane. Bear right into South Parade, to return to the rear of the village hall (Point 1).

From certain positions on this walk Chesterton Windmill comes into view. There are no footpaths to the windmill, but access is possible from a permissive path off a nearby road.

Where to eat and drink

You are spoilt for choice for pubs in Harbury, where good food, fine ale and a cheerful reception are available. Choose from The Crown Inn in Crown Street, The Gamecock on the corner of Chapel Street, and The Shakespeare Inn, a 16th-century part-timber framed inn close to the sail-less 18th-century windmill in the middle of the village.

What to look out for

Visit the 12th-century St Giles' Church in Chesterton. The sundial over its porch offers advice to travellers: 'See and be gone about your business.' The oldest part is now the 14th-century nave. The church is inextricably linked to the Peyto family who owned the Manor House on the hill at the back of the church. Their tombs are impressive. There is a 16th-century alabaster memorial to Humphrey Peyto and his wife Anna, with effigies of their ten children. Sir Edward Peyto supported Cromwell's Parliamentarians and successfully led the defence of Warwick Castle against the Royalists.

While you're there

Chesterton Windmill, by Harbury Lane on Windmill Hill, was probably designed by Sir Edward Peyto himself in 1632 (and influenced by Inigo Jones), and was built as a tower supported on six semicircular arches. It was used up until 1910 and contains the original machinery, which dates from 1860. Since then it has been meticulously maintained. It is owned by Warwickshire County Council and is usually open for viewing on the inside a couple of times a year – the date coincides with national Heritage Open Days throughout the country (check details online).

AROUND COMPTON VERNEY

DISTANCE/TIME	5.5 miles (8.8km) / 2hrs 30min
ASCENT/GRADIENT	260ft (80m) / ▲
PATHS	Parkland and farmland paths, stretches of road
LANDSCAPE	Rolling Warwickshire countryside and parkland
SUGGESTED MAP	OS Explorer 206 Edge Hill & Fenny Compton
START/FINISH	Grid Reference: SP307517
DOG FRIENDLINESS	On a lead on open farmland, along country roads and in the vicinity of Compton Verney
PARKING	In the vicinity of the village hall and church
PUBLIC TOILETS	None on route

The splendid Compton Verney House dates back to the early 18th century and is a Grade I listed residence built by Richard Verney, 11th Baron Willoughby de Broke. It was later remodelled, with the interiors designed by Robert Adam in the 1760s. Situated in fine parkland, the grounds were landscaped by 'Capability' Brown in 1769. Richard Greville Verney, the 19th baron, sold Compton Verney in 1921 and the estate passed to the soap magnate Joseph Watson. Sadly, Watson's tenure was short. He died from a heart attack a year later in 1922 while out hunting with the Warwickshire foxhounds in the surrounding countryside.

The Army requisitioned Compton Verney during World War II. By the end of hostilities in 1945, the house was empty. In 1993, another powerful businessman acquired the estate. This time it was Sir Peter Moores, the Littlewoods millionaire. Having rescued Compton Verney from the English Heritage Buildings at Risk register, Sir Peter implemented various changes and improvements and ultimately transformed the house into a venue for international art exhibitions. Compton Verney became an art gallery in a sumptuous country house at the heart of England.

Sir Peter was greatly impressed by German art while visiting Europe as a young man and his interest also extended to the antique treasures of China. He felt so passionately about the subject that he set about finding a suitable setting in the English shires, in which the public could share his love of art. His strong interest remains the key theme at Compton Verney and the striking collections on show include the work of Sir Joshua Reynolds and many examples of British folk art. There are six permanent collections within the house.

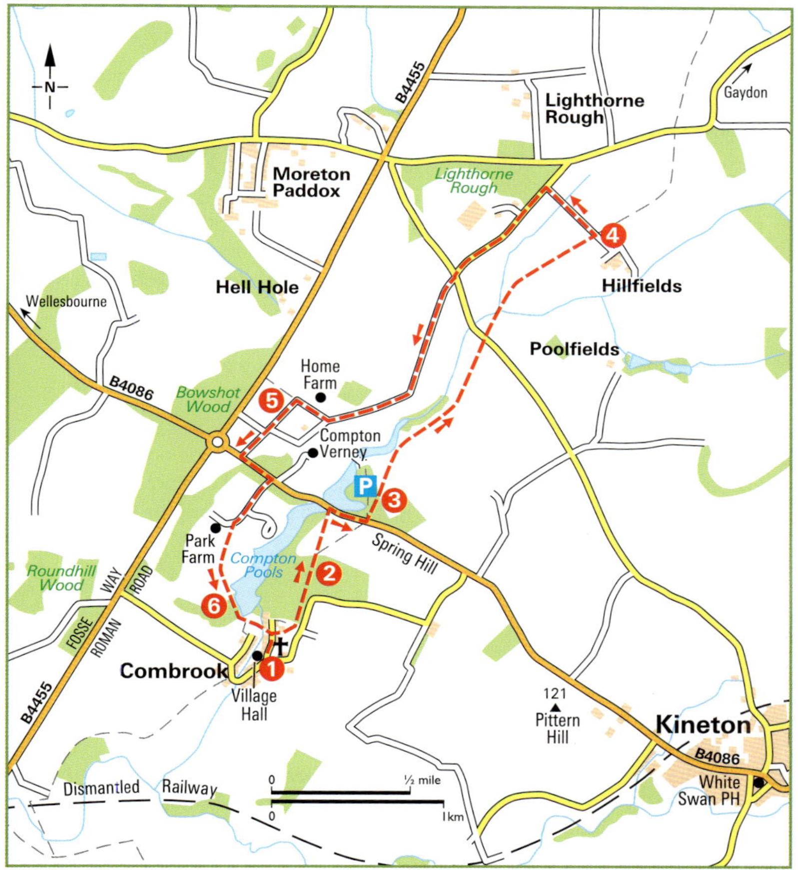

1. With the church on your right and the village hall to your left, follow the lane through the centre of Combrook. By the entrance to Chestnut House, turn right through a gate and head uphill on a path. Make for the top left corner of the field by trees and enter woodland. Keep the road parallel on your right and when it bends sharp right, keep ahead on a wide grassy path through the trees.

2. As the path sweeps right, continue straight on. Through the trees Compton Pools gradually creep into view. On reaching the edge of a field, go half right, in line with gate pillars down at the road. The splendid façade of Compton Verney is visible down by the water. Cross the road and turn right towards the entrance to Compton Verney and follow the path to the right of the entrance drive, over a footbridge.

3. Skirt the car park, keeping it on the left, following the waymarks. Make for a kissing gate leading into a field and follow the obvious path ahead to a gate in the far boundary. Compton Pools are visible down to the left. Head for the next gate, exiting to the road. Cross it to a bridleway and go straight down the field towards trees. In the corner pass through a hedge gap on the right, keep left in the next field, cross a brook and follow the path around the left perimeter of

the next pasture with a ditch beside you. Keep to the path and eventually draw
level with the trees of Lighthorne Rough.

4. On reaching the field edge, join the access road to Hillfields and turn left.
At the T-junction, turn left and follow the road to the next junction. Cross it to
follow a bridleway track. Follow the track through several gates as it gradually
curves right with Home Farm on the right and the Compton Verney buildings
on the left.

5. Pass the main farmyard and follow the track as it bends left. Go through a
gate by a cattle-grid, pass Compton Verney Lodge and reach the road. Turn
left, walk down the grassy verge and turn right at a sign for Park Farm. Follow
the drive between wooden fences and 50yds (46m) before it bends right by
several houses, go through a gate on the left. Follow the bridleway as it runs
parallel to the drive, go through a gate and head across the field to reach a
waymark. Keep ahead with the pools visible again on the left.

6. Follow the bridleway as it runs down by the water's edge, pass through a
gate into woodland and beyond the trees, pass a footpath on the right. There
are pleasant views on this final stretch over the rooftops of Combrook. Cross
a stream, make for the road and turn right, back to the centre of the village.

Where to eat and drink
There is a café at Compton Verney which is open when the house is
(Tuesday to Sunday). The surrounding area offers a choice of hostelries
including the White Swan at nearby Kineton.

What to look out for
The bridge that crosses the upper lake at Compton Verney – part of
Compton Pools – is part of a 40-acre (16ha) parkland. Up until the
18th century, the church was located at the edge of the lake but was
replaced by a place of worship closer to the main house.

While you're there
Visit The Leys in Combrook, an area of grassland flanked by ancient
woodland dropping down steeply to the village. This area is one of
very few remaining examples of surviving species-rich hay meadows.
Alternatively, The British Motor Museum at Gaydon has a collection of
over 300 cars. It tells the story of the birth, decline and rebirth of the
motor industry and the cars it produced, as well as celebrating the skills
and creativity of the people who designed and built them.

EATHORPE AND WAPPENBURY

DISTANCE/TIME	3.5 miles (5.7km) / 1hr 30min
ASCENT/GRADIENT	82ft (25m) / ▲
PATHS	Mainly field footpaths and farm tracks, several stiles
LANDSCAPE	Gentle countryside
SUGGESTED MAP	OS Explorer 221 Coventry & Warwick
START/FINISH	Grid Reference: SP392689
DOG FRIENDLINESS	Under control at all times
PARKING	Village Hall car park in Eathorpe or along road near by
PUBLIC TOILETS	None on route

This is a stroll through the attractive hidden villages southeast of Coventry. The route starts at Eathorpe, going near to the River Leam and over pleasant Warwickshire countryside to the village of Wappenbury, then crosses the river to Hunningham before returning to Eathorpe.

The name is derived from 'ea' relating to water and 'thorpe', which is a common Old Norse suffix that usually denotes a farmstead. The village is sandwiched between the old Fosse Way – the Roman Road that runs from Lincoln to Axminster in Devon – and the River Leam.

Eathorpe has two halls: the excellent Village Hall and the grander mansion of Eathorpe Hall, set in secluded parkland south of the village centre. This is a large 18th-century red-brick house once owned by Samuel Shepheard, who built the Shepheard's Hotel in Cairo. Less grandly he also rebuilt the bridge across the River Leam, which bears a commemorative inscription noting its completion date of 1862.

Early records show a variety of names for the village of Wappenbury but it is likely that it means 'Wappa's fortified place'. It was certainly once fortified, and the great earthwork ramparts can still be seen here, best preserved on the northwestern and eastern sides. Archaeologists date the great earthwork to the first century AD, some 900 years before the Danish leader Wappa came on the scene. The rampart remains surround the whole village and are believed to be the largest in the Midlands. It is assumed it was constructed to control fords across the River Leam. During excavations, four kilns dating to about AD 350 have been found, along with some items of Roman greyware. However, like so many other villages, the plague came, taking the lives of some 200 residents. Wappenbury has never recovered its original size.

The Church of St John the Baptist in Wappenbury has a 15th-century tower, and two coffin lids are the oldest stones in the village. Gravestones and murals make fascinating reading – a mural tablet inside the church here reads: 'A lingering sickness did me seize/And no physician could me ease/I fought for help but all in vain/Until the Lord did ease my pain.'

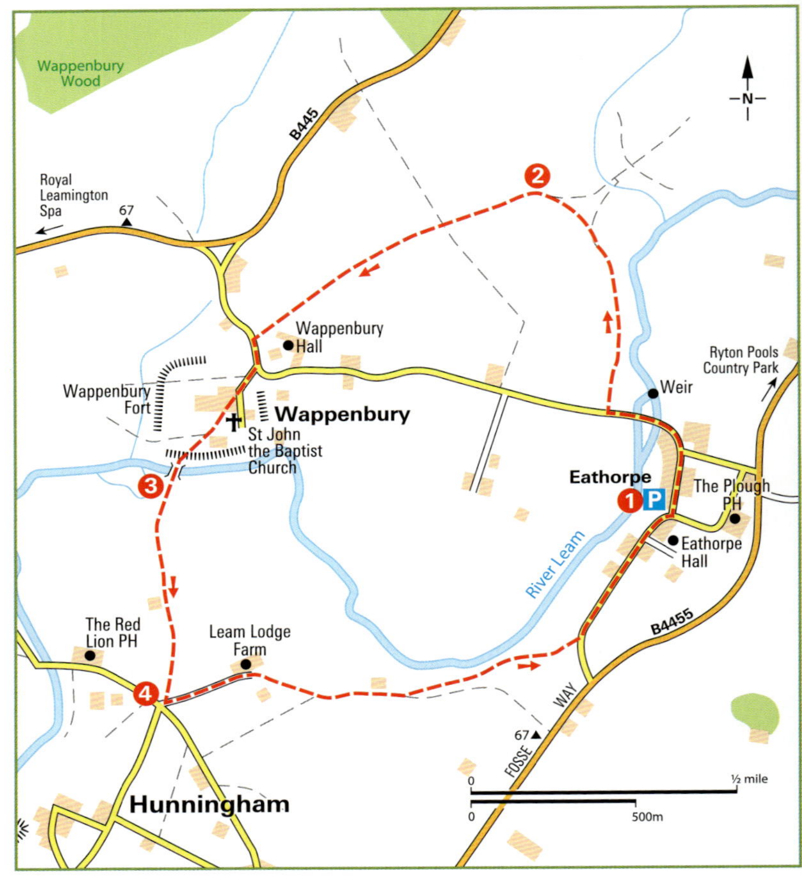

1. From the Village Hall, head through the village, initially passing a lovely pair of 17th-century thatched dwellings called Myrtle and Thyme Cottages. At the end of the village, the road bends left to pass the old watermill, and crosses the bridge over the River Leam. In 80yds (73m), go right through a kissing gate into pastureland and follow the footpath to the left of the river. You will reach a fence with a distant view of Princethorpe College, with its fine turrets. Cross the stile and aim for the gate in the far left corner of the field beside a farm gate.

2. Through the gate, follow the waymarked direction, with the hedge on your right. Continue ahead via a kissing gate at a footpath junction and alongside a hedge, with wooded grounds on the crest ahead. Go through a field gate and continue ahead to a kissing gate to the right of some conifers. Continue alongside trees until you come to a gate at the road into Wappenbury, to the right of the walls of Wappenbury Hall's grounds. Turn left along the village road until you come to the front gates of Wappenbury Hall. Go right here towards the Church of St John the Baptist – to its left you will see a fine thatched cottage called Garden Cottage. Walk along the lane to the right of the church and continue right, passing to the right of converted farm buildings. Head back into

the open countryside. Go left at a footpath fork through a gate onto a footpath. Descend to a gate onto a single-arch brick bridge, with a second (metal) footbridge beyond it.

3. Across the River Leam there is about 0.5 miles (800m) of easy walking. Passing through two gates, you reach the road in the village of Hunningham via a bridle gate. To visit The Red Lion pub turn right through the village for about 0.25 miles (400m). The pub garden looks towards the narrow, partly medieval bridge over the River Leam, mostly rebuilt around 1651.

4. If you do not visit the pub, go left and walk up the farm drive towards Leam Lodge Farm. Continue by the farm buildings and Cubbingon Sawmills, the road now no more than a good stone farm track. After following this road for about 600yds (549m), you will see that it bends to the right about 80 paces ahead of you. Look out for a stile here, leading onto a footpath going off to the left towards the River Leam once again. Walk along the footpath close to the riverbank. From the river the footpath veers right through a kissing gate. Continue along the edge of the field and left at the corner over two stiles. Veer right, and leave the next field over a stile beside an oak tree. Here you are back to the road on the edge of Eathorpe. Go left along the road, passing the entrance to Eathorpe Hall and its lodge to return to the village.

Where to eat and drink

At The Red Lion in Hunningham, an extensive menu is on offer along with beers and fine wines. Children are allowed, but dogs are restricted to the large gardens. The Hillbilly's Grill Shack at the Plough in Eathorpe is a regular haunt for walkers with a popular menu.

What to look out for

Explore the village of Wappenbury, with its idyllic thatched cottages. Impressive Wappenbury Hall was once the home of Sir William Lyons, the founder of Jaguar Motors. In the Church of St John the Baptist, see the canopied wall monument of a woman sitting sadly in a harvest field – this is a memorial to Thomas Urnbers, a patron of 19th-century scientific agriculture.

While you're there

Just four miles (6.4km) to the north of Eathorpe is the 100-acre (40ha) Ryton Pools Country Park. It's a good place to spot water birds – look for great crested grebes, swans, moorhens and Canada geese on Ryton Pool. Pagets Pool attracts dragonflies, such as the common blue and emperor dragonfly and the black-tailed skimmer.

AROUND THE DASSETTS

DISTANCE/TIME	7.25 miles (11.7km) / 3hrs 15min
ASCENT/GRADIENT	656ft (200m) / ▲ ▲ ▲
PATHS	Field paths and farm tracks, many stiles
LANDSCAPE	Hilly countryside
SUGGESTED MAP	OS Explorer 206 Edge Hill & Fenny Compton
START/FINISH	Grid Reference: SP394523
DOG FRIENDLINESS	Under control at all times
PARKING	Burton Dassett Hills Country Park car park
PUBLIC TOILETS	Near car park

This lovely walk takes you from the very top of the Dassett Hills in the Burton Dassett Hills Country Park, and through the nearby hamlets and villages of Northend, Fenny Compton, Farnborough, Avon Dassett and Burton Dassett. It's the nearest you will get in Warwickshire to wild country, with its bare hills reminiscent of the Peak District. The 100-acre (40ha) country park was opened in 1971, and is set high above the noisy M40 motorway, which didn't arrive until a couple of decades later. The park comprises a dramatic mix of rugged, grassy humps and hills with a quaint, small beacon perched on the highest point – actually the tower of a former windmill. There are a number of quarries around the side of the hills, which may date back as far as the Iron Age. Today they are covered in grass and offer welcome shelter for picnicking visitors. The view from the top of the hills is outstanding.

Initially the walk descends into Northend hamlet, before field paths lead you into the village of Fenny Compton. Fenny is an unusual, but not infrequent, prefix in the Midlands and indicates the presence of wetland. The village lies below the Dassett Hills, which give rise to at least seven springs. It was to harness these, to supply around 40 consumers in the village, that one of England's smallest water supply companies was established in 1866.

You pass by several very attractive cottages to reach the impressive Church of St Peter and St Clare – only two churches in England carry this unusual dedication. The walk continues over Windmill Hill, offering fine views over the surrounding countryside. You then descend into the village of Farnborough and find more old stone cottages. After the village of Avon Dassett, the walk then ascends into Burton Dassett, passing the 12th-century All Saints Church. Its imposing tower overlooks the battlefield of Edgehill, making it the 'Cathedral of the Hills'. Built on the slope of a hill, the floor climbs from the chancel arch with seven groups of steps. There's an elegant wall monument to John Temple, who died in 1603.

The hills of the Burton Dassett Hills Country Park are a constant theme throughout this walk and you finish with a flourish on the last of them, Magpie Hill, to enjoy the extensive views.

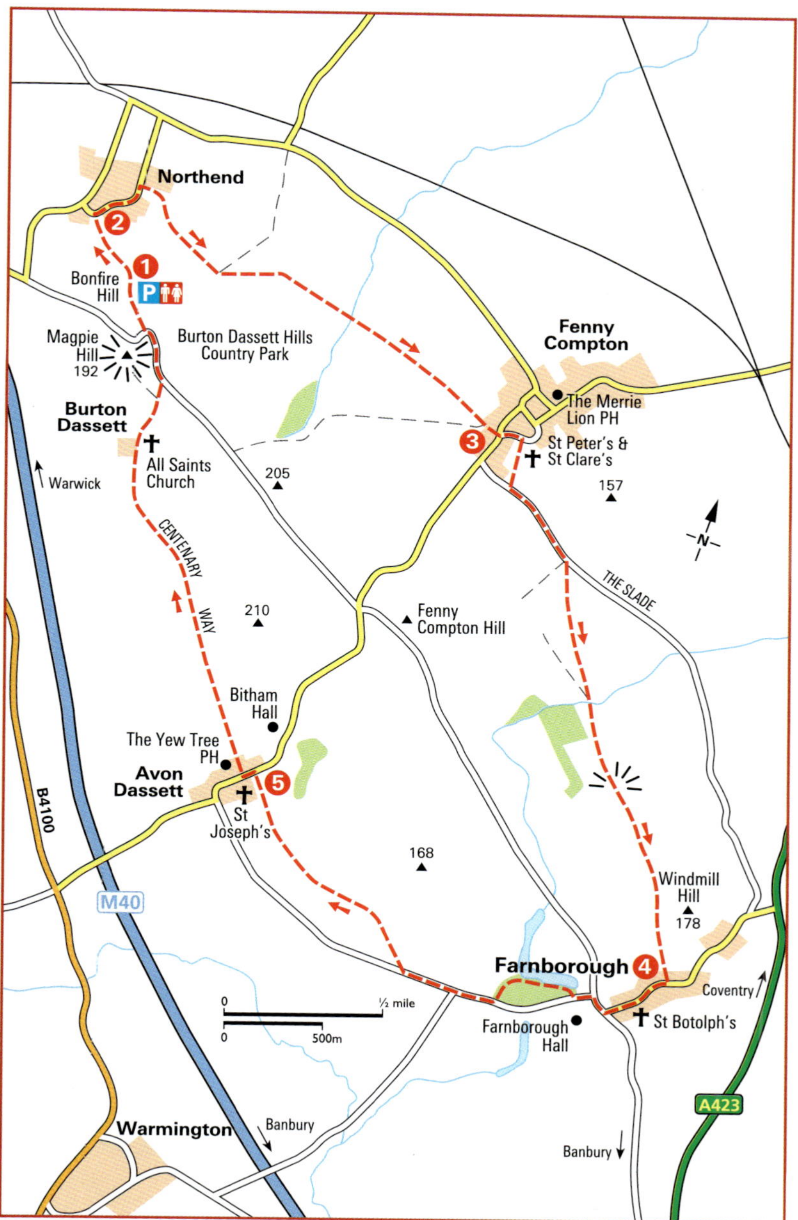

1. From the car park in the Burton Dassett Hills Country Park, descend the footpath – the Centenary Way – to the right of Bonfire Hill with its conical-roofed stone tower (once a windmill, converted to a beacon), and go through a kissing gate onto a track into the village of Northend.

2. Go right along Malthouse Lane, soon becoming Top Street, in the village for 300yds (274m), then right again just past Pype Hayes house onto a track

between gardens. Then, through a kissing gate, follow the footpath with its waymark arrows, heading generally eastwards towards Fenny Compton, crossing a mixture of pasture and cultivated fields via two kissing gates, three stiles and a footbridge.

3. Enter Fenny Compton through a gate ahead. Follow a hedged path to Grant's Close and go left into Avon Dassett road. Turn right into Church Street and right onto Dog Lane. Go past Ducketts Cottage and through the gate to the right of the village church. Now bear right and cross over pastureland to a gate in the hedge, onto a road known as The Slade. Go left along this past a large farm barn at the brow of the hill, then right over a footbridge and through a kissing gate into a large cultivated field. Go half left and follow the footpath signs, crossing this field to a second footbridge. Here go left, walk along the field edge, and at the stream bear right alongside to a hedge gap. Cross the field corner and continue beside the hedge. Over a footbridge bear half left to another. At a stile, continue ahead to the crest of Windmill Hill, with views of the windmill at Chesterton and the BT communication tower near Daventry. Descend over farm fields and a hedged footpath into the village of Farnborough, emerging via a hedged path on the main street.

4. Head right along the main street, and bear right past the public entrance gates to Farnborough Hall. Continue up the road to the left, then along the permissive footpath beside the lake, inside the trees. At the end of the woodland continue on a field-edge permissive path, to emerge back on the lane via a stile. Continue along the road for 400yds (365m), then go right over a stile and across a couple of cultivated fields into pastureland. Descend to the left of a large barn which brings you to Avon Dassett.

5. Go left past the Roman Catholic church, and in 75yds (69m) go right up Park Close, passing to the right of The Yew Tree pub and into open countryside. Up to the right is the Bitham Hall. The waymarked footpath, the Centenary Way, hugs the top of fields, crossing a large cultivated field, to arrive in Burton Dassett. Pass the church, go through the kissing gate from the churchyard, and turn right, continue up the road to the car park.

Where to eat and drink

The walk route passes near two delightful pubs. The Merrie Lion in Fenny Compton is a popular pub, just up the road from the village church. The Grade II inn dates back to 1710 and has a strong reputation for superb food and excellent beers and wines. The Yew Tree, now a community pub, has a pleasant outside garden and is situated on the track corner in Avon Dassett.

While you're there

Take the opportunity to visit the National Trust's 18th-century Farnborough Hall, which you pass along the walk route. The home of the Holbech family for some 300 years, this is a superb honey-coloured stone building with impressive plasterwork. Its extensive grounds contain charming 18th-century temples and a long terrace walk to an obelisk.

AROUND DRAYCOTE WATER TO DUNCHURCH

DISTANCE/TIME	7 miles (11.3km) / 2hrs 30min
ASCENT/GRADIENT	164ft (50m) / ▲
PATHS	Reservoir paths and field paths
LANDSCAPE	Reservoir in gentle, rolling countryside
SUGGESTED MAP	OS Explorer 222 Rugby & Daventry
START/FINISH	Grid Reference: SP466691
DOG FRIENDLINESS	Dogs not permitted around the perimeter of Draycote Water
PARKING	Pay-and-display car park at Draycote Water
PUBLIC TOILETS	At the visitor centre

The impressive Draycote Water reservoir, the largest area of open water in Warwickshire, is set in more than 600 acres (243ha) of land and attracts large numbers of wildfowl. Owned by Severn Trent Water, it was completed in 1970 as a pumped storage facility. It's refilled during winter months from the nearby River Leam, thus reducing the risk of local flooding.

A private house in Dunchurch, just east of the reservoir, is now called Guy Fawkes but was formerly The Falcon Inn. It was here that the Gunpowder Plot conspirators sought refuge from justice in 1605, after their failed attempt to assassinate King James I as he visited Parliament. Dunchurch was once a busy coaching village and The Dun Cow is the old coaching inn at the village crossroads. On the village green, you'll see the old stocks and an ancient cross. By the crossroads is a statue commemorating Lord John Scott, a local landowner and sportsman.

The 14th-century St Peter's Church has a fine tower, a Norman door and a font to match. Set inside folding doors is a monument to Thomas Newcombe, who was 'a printer to three kings' and founded the 17th-century almshouses. These now add an air of old-world charm to the hotchpotch of thatched properties in this pleasant village, which is full of floral colour in the spring and summer.

There's a fine view over the reservoir as you descend into the next village – Thurlaston. Again, a number of attractive thatched cottages catch your eye as you enter, and you pass near to a sail-less windmill (now converted into a private residence). The Church of St Edmund was completed in 1848, originally to house the village school. The site was donated by Lord John Scott (he of the statue by the crossroads in Dunchurch). The building was used as a church on Sundays, but accommodation for the schoolmaster was built into the tower. The present bell tower was added later, but the schoolmaster's accommodation remains as a private residence. Bizarrely, the bell rope still passes through one of its rooms.

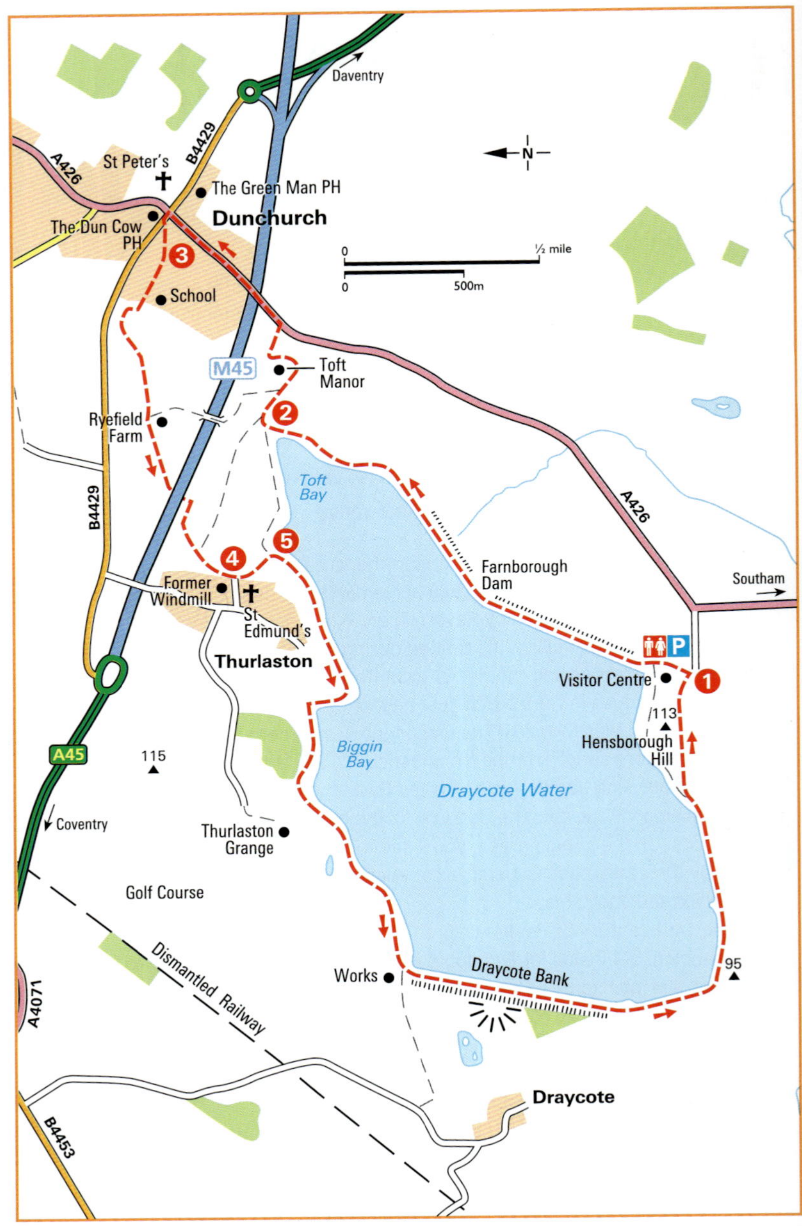

1. From Draycote Water car park proceed up to the reservoir past a sign that reads 'Visitors Centre & Reservoir', and then bear right, following the tarmac lane along the top of Farnborough Dam wall to reach the part of the Water known as Toft Bay.

2. At the end of Toft Bay, go right and leave the reservoir grounds via a gate where the perimeter road goes sharp left. Continue ahead for 50 paces, then go right to a gate and follow the waymarker signs to a footpath that climbs up towards Toft House. Over a stile, bear left along a lane and through a gate. Past Toft Manor, follow the lane round to the right and continue to the A426 Rugby–Dunchurch road. Go left along the road, cross the motorway bridge and enter the village of Dunchurch, passing a number of attractive thatched properties. The village square and St Peter's Church are to the right of the crossroads, with The Dun Cow pub immediately opposite.

3. At the crossroads go left along the pavement of the B4429 past the Dunchurch Social Club. Bear left along School Street past more thatched properties, and follow a path past the infant school down to the Dunchurch Scout Group Hall. Go right and then left along a footpath to the right of playing fields. The path bears left beside more playing fields to a kissing gate. Continue alongside a hedge, through a gate, and proceed on a track. Cross a lane and go through a kissing gate to the right of Ryefield Farm. Go ahead over pastureland, crossing another lane via two kissing gates, then pass beneath the M45 road bridge via two kissing gates before diagonally crossing the next field to a kissing gate and a gate through a third gate into Thurlaston.

4. Go to the left by St Edmund's Church and via a gate down a concrete farm track to a kissing gate and a footbridge. Enter the perimeter of Draycote Water via a gate.

5. Go right along the walkway by the side of the reservoir around Biggin Bay. To your right, you can see Thurlaston Grange, and then you will pass a golf course. Continue around the end of the reservoir, passing by the treatment works, and then stroll along Draycote Bank. To your right is the spire of Bourton-on-Dunsmore church about a mile (1.6km) away; to its right is Bourton Hall. After passing the sailing club parking area and just before reaching the yachting area, go right through a gate onto a footpath. This leads via a kissing gate up onto Hensborough Hill. Meander past the trig point, some 371ft (113m) above sea level, then head towards the visitor centre, returning to the car park via a kissing gate.

Where to eat and drink

There is the Waterside Restaurant at Draycote Water Country Park by the car park. The Green Man is on the B4429 Daventry Road. The Dun Cow at the crossroads is a popular eating place for walkers and welcomes children but not dogs (except guide dogs).

What to look out for

St Peter's Church and Bourton Hall are local landmarks to the west of Draycote Water and are clearly visible as you walk around the reservoir. Situated on Dunsmore Heath in the village of Bourton-on-Dunsmore, St Peter's has a fine 13th-century font, a Jacobean altar and a ghost in its vestry. The 18th-century Bourton Hall was restored in 1979.

While you're there

Explore Dunchurch village. It once had some 27 alehouses but now has only two pubs. The old gaol was pulled down in 1972. The last person to be held in the gaol was a Peter Murcott, who apparently spent his night there supping ale through a straw from a barrel outside the window.

48 NAPTON ON THE HILL'S HISTORIC WINDMILL

DISTANCE/TIME	2.5 miles (4km) / 1hr 15min
ASCENT/GRADIENT	213ft (65m) / ▲▲
PATHS	Field paths, farm tracks and country lanes, several stiles
LANDSCAPE	Rolling Warwickshire countryside
SUGGESTED MAP	OS Explorers 206 Edge Hill & Fenny Compton; 222 Rugby & Daventry
START/FINISH	Grid Reference: SP463612
DOG FRIENDLINESS	Off lead along tow path, otherwise under control
PARKING	On-street parking in Napton on the Hill
PUBLIC TOILETS	None on route

There has been a windmill at Napton on the Hill since 1543 – it is one of the great landmarks in Warwickshire. Next to the privately owned mill building is the former miller's stone cottage, which still houses parts of the original bread oven. Early maps of the area reveal that there were once two windmills on the hill. They drew a regular and pure supply of water from underground springs and wells. The present windmill is in good condition but not open to the public. On a good day, in fine weather, you can see seven counties from the windswept summit.

The village of Napton on the Hill, whose name derives from the old British word 'cnapton', meaning 'farm on the knap of the hill', was a substantial settlement in 1086. It was granted a charter in 1321 to hold a weekly market and an annual fair, and became a prosperous medieval village. Today, attractive mellowed brown and gold thatched houses contribute to a picturesque scene.

You could be forgiven for thinking this was a timeless image, untouched by the revolutionary industrial changes that were taking place elsewhere in the West Midlands, but even Napton succumbed to 'canal mania' towards the end of the 18th century. Britain was gripped as the whole country clamoured to invest in the new transport technology. In a two-year period in the 1790s, 37 separate Acts of Parliament were passed to enable the construction of an amazing system of 4,250 miles (6,840km) of navigable rivers and canals. The Oxford Canal, completed in 1790, was part of this and it encouraged canalside businesses to develop. Workmen were more than happy to take alcohol at The Folly Inn while they laboured in the construction of the flight of seven Napton Locks.

The 12th-century St Lawrence's Church, on the brow of the hill, was originally going to be built at the bottom of the hill, and the stone was assembled there, ready for its construction. Overnight, however, the stone was mysteriously moved to the present site, near the top of the hill – and the church was erected where it lay.

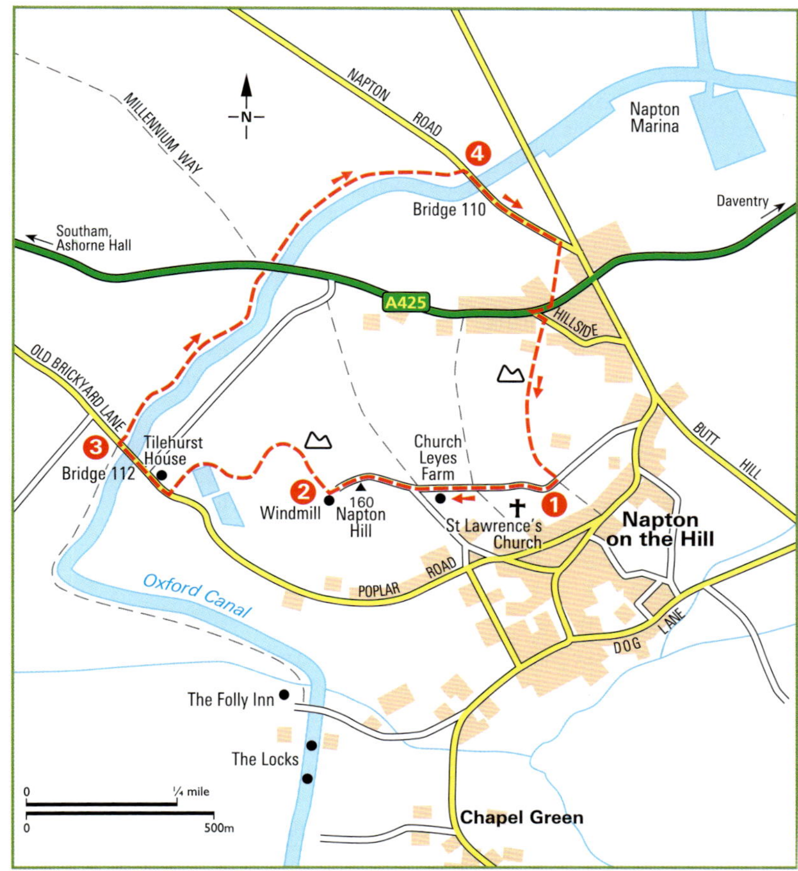

1. From St Lawrence's Church, walk around the outside of the churchyard and pass by a small car park. From here, take the track that becomes a lane and pass by Church Leyes Farm. At the lane junction, go ahead and follow the driveway towards the superb windmill which comes into view – the building and its land are private, so please respect the 'Private' signs and keep off the property.

2. Reaching wooden gates, go right along a footpath around the outside of the property, following the waymarkers. Through a gate this leads to lovely open land, and you now can go downhill, following the path that descends beside a fence line. After crossing a stile, continue steeply downhill. The path then bears sharp left and leads you past a fishing pool. Keep by the fence to reach the lane by the side of Tilehurst house, Brickyard Lane. Go right down the lane and cross bridge No. 112 over the Oxford Canal.

3. Over the bridge, descend right onto the tow path, go through a gate and then walk to the left by the canal. This is easy, pleasant walking with great views up to your right of Napton Hill with its windmill on top. Walk under the bridge with the A425 going over and carry on to the next bridge.

4. Leave the tow path at bridge No. 110 via a gate, and walk up the lane back towards the village. Just before a road junction, go right over a stile and cross the corner of a field to a further stile onto the A425 road. Bear right and cross the main road and a road called Hillside, then go through a waymarked gate and begin to climb the hill up a clear, hedged footpath. As you approach the top of the hill the path becomes less steep and you will go through two metal kissing gates and two bridle gates to reach open land once again. To your right, you will see St Lawrence's Church. Go right along the church lane back to your car to complete the walk.

Where to eat and drink

The Folly serves good food and beer in the welcoming atmosphere of a real pub. It stands by Napton Bottom Lock and is filled with charm.

What to look out for

Visit St Lawrence's Church whose squat tower has, like the windmill, withstood centuries of buffeting from the wind. The north door is called the Devil's Door and used to be opened during baptisms for the Devil to escape. At Christmas or other festivals you may hear the ringing of hand bells. Inside, there is a slate portrait of John Shuckburgh of nearby Shuckburgh Hall.

While you're there

A visit to the Nickelodeon Museum is an amazing experience. It's a remarkable working collection of vintage juke-boxes, symphoniums and many other musical machines. It once occupied the old Methodist chapel in Napton, but the number of organs grew too large and it has been moved to Ashorne Hall, about 12 miles (19.3km) to the west of here. A 1930 replica cinema shows authentic early films. People travel from all over the country for an evening meal and to recall musical memories of the past.

49 ALONG THE OXFORD CANAL

DISTANCE/TIME	5.7 miles (9.1km) / 2hrs 30min
ASCENT/GRADIENT	427ft (130m) / ▲▲
PATHS	Farmland paths and tracks, towpath and stiles
LANDSCAPE	Gently rolling countryside bisected by the Oxford Canal
SUGGESTED MAP	OS Explorers 206 Edge Hill & Fenny Compton; 222 Rugby & Daventry
START/FINISH	Grid Reference: SP463612
DOG FRIENDLINESS	Off lead along tow path, otherwise under control
PARKING	On-street parking in Napton on the Hill
PUBLIC TOILETS	None on route

The vast and complex network of Britain's inland waterways has captured our imagination in recent years. Once, these canals were clogged with cargo boats or simply derelict and forgotten – killed off as other forms of transport were ushered in. Today, a great number of these old waterways have been revived and restored and these routes have become an integral component in our recreation and leisure. The canals are an obvious destination for walkers, cyclists and boating enthusiasts. The Oxford Canal, running through the centre of England between the University City and Coventry, is a prime example of how our winding waterways have become linear recreation parks, drawing healthy numbers of visitors and boosting the local economy.

Opened towards the end of the 18th century, the Oxford Canal is 78 miles (126km) long and from near Coventry, where it meets the Coventry Canal, it runs southeast through the gently rolling Warwickshire countryside for about 15 miles (24km) to Rugby. This stretch was straightened in the 1820s and the remains of the original circuitous route can still be identified. The Oxford Canal connects with the Grand Junction section of the Grand Union Canal and then heads in a westerly direction. The two waterways coincide for the next few miles until they split at Napton, where this walk begins. Beyond Napton Hill, the canal climbs the Napton flight of nine locks to a summit level.

The next section, south of the village, heading towards the Oxfordshire border, was never straightened and is therefore one of the most convoluted stretches of waterway anywhere in the country. Acknowledged as one of the most scenic waterways in Britain, the Oxford Canal was built in several stages during a long period lasting more than 20 years. Its role was vital. The intention was to use the new canal to transport cargo from the industrial Midlands to London, via the River Thames. Today, the canal towpath is the main part of the 82-mile (132km) Oxford Canal Walk, which includes 43 locks, countless bridges and one long tunnel.

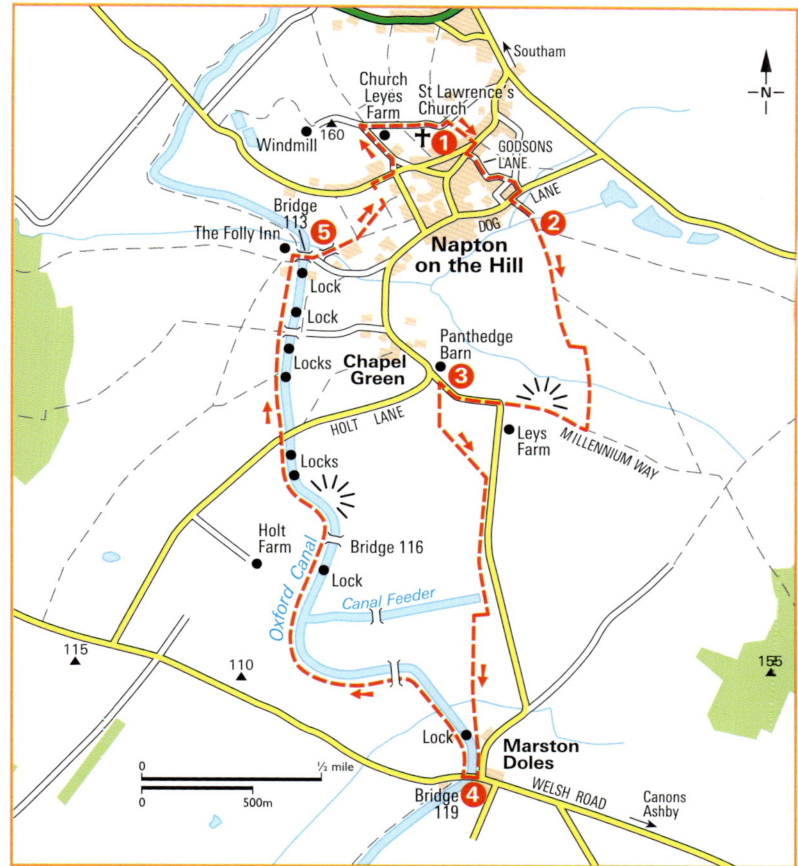

1. With your back to the church, walk along the access lane and turn right by a dog waste bin to follow the path. Descend to Vicarage Road and head right along Hackwell Street. Turn left down Godsons Lane and at the second road junction go right along Dog Lane, then almost immediately left along a waymarked bridleway between houses, heading away from Napton in a southeast direction.

2. Continue on the track for about 350 yards (320m), then ahead, passing through a series of farm gates. After the third one, go left alongside the hedge, through another field gate, then sharp right alongside a hedge to a gate. Cross the next field to a gate at a grass track and go right (enjoy the fine retrospective view of Napton on the Hill). Reach a final farm gate to the right of farm buildings. Go ahead along the road, following the Millennium Way.

3. Pass the entrance to Panthedge Barn and just before the junction of roads by the speed sign, go left over a stile and cross the field by heading diagonally left. In the next field, make for a stile in a wire fence, then maintain the same direction to a stile in the hedge ahead and walk parallel with the road hedge, going southwards. Continue over several fields and two stiles, passing to the left of a canal feeder and a derelict building, then cross meadowland via stiles and a footbridge. Keep to the right of dilapidated outbuildings, go through two gates and turn right at the road at Marston Doles.

4. Cross canal bridge No. 119 and go left, via a gate, to the tow- path, turning left to pass under the bridge. Walk beside the Oxford Canal, heading north towards Napton. Continue past the lock gates. Just after bridge No. 116, there is an exceptional view of Napton. Continue along the towpath to bridge 113, where you will find a shop and The Folly pub. Cross the bridge into Folly Lane.

5. In 50yds (46m), go left over a stile and continue across paddocks to a footbridge. Proceed ahead along a short stretch of track to a stile. Keep ahead to the next stile and cross the large field diagonally to a final stile onto Poplar Road. Go right along the road for 80yds (73m), then left opposite Howcombe Lane junction. Continue along this lane for 290yds (270m) to a junction close to Church Leyes Farm. At the junction, go right and return to St Lawrence.

Where to eat and drink

The Folly at Napton serves traditional food and occupies an attractive setting on the banks of the Oxford Canal. It gets busy during the summer months.

What to look out for

A few miles to the southeast of Napton lies Canons Ashby, an Elizabethan manor house situated in stunning 18th-century gardens. Managed by the National Trust, the house and grounds have remained unchanged since 1710 and inside are striking tapestries and Jacobean plasterwork, among other features.

While you're there

Napton's St Lawrence's church includes on the vestry door a curious grill covered by a sturdy shutter. Its function is not clear, though some sources suggest it might have once been a confessional or some kind of spy hole. Also among the relics to be found here is a wooden chest, dated 1624.

HARBOROUGH MAGNA

DISTANCE/TIME	3.5 miles (5.7km) / 1hr 45min
ASCENT/GRADIENT	49ft (15m) / ▲
PATHS	Field footpaths and tow path, several stiles
LANDSCAPE	Gentle countryside
SUGGESTED MAP	OS Explorer 222 Rugby & Daventry
START/FINISH	Grid Reference: SP478792
DOG FRIENDLINESS	Off lead along tow path, otherwise under control
PARKING	On-street parking near The Old Lion pub
PUBLIC TOILETS	None on route

Situated some 4 miles (6.4km) north of Rugby, Harborough Magna is an old village that embraces the hamlets of Harborough Parva and Cathiron. The name Harborough appears to derive from the Saxon English 'heord beorg', meaning 'the hill where flocks are kept'. Its suffix Magna (Great) was added to distinguish the village from similarly named settlements near by (Parva means 'little' in this context).

There was a priest and a mill here when William I's Domesday surveyors entered the parish in their records. Much later, the village also boasted a smithy and a wheelwright, where carts were constructed and repaired at the timber yards of William Iven. The whole area seems to have been involved in this industry at some time. Saw mills were located at Cathiron, near to the Oxford Canal, and the timber was transported via cart and canal barge to the saw mills. Plenty of cart horses were kept locally, and teams of horses could be seen hauling the larger trees from the nearby estates to Rugby Station, where they were trimmed and cut in readiness for transportation to the saw mills at Cathiron. This business has now disappeared and, along with the demise of the industrial need for the canals, pleasure boats have now taken over the Oxford Canal.

Easenhall is a quaint old village of cottages and semi-detached Victorian houses. In the past, these were used to accommodate workers belonging to the Manor House at Newbold Revel. The route passes next to the old chapel – a small, one-room former Congregational building, now the village hall.

To the southwest of the villages the route crosses the West Coast Main Line, formerly the London Midland Railway that runs from Euston to Glasgow. Before the War, prestige expresses such as the streamlined Coronation Scot or trains of maroon coaches hauled by Sir William Stanier's great pacific locomotives covered the footbridge watchers in sooty steam.

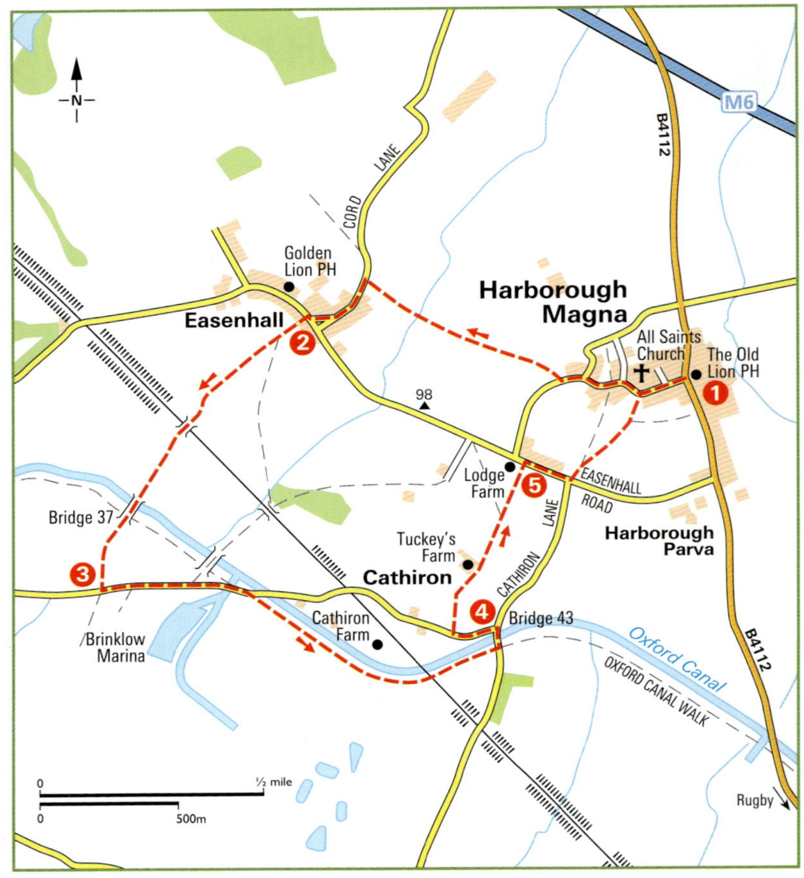

1. From The Old Lion pub, cross the B4112 and head up Main Street and into the village. Walk past All Saints Church, noting its unique clock face, and continue to the end of the village. Just after passing by Holly Cottage, go right over a stile and follow the footpath across cultivated fields towards Easenhall, climbing another stile. Cross a footbridge to reach the village, via another stile, near the thatched Campbell's Cottage. Go left through the village down to a junction of roads by the village green, with the building of the former chapel facing you. The Golden Lion public house, restaurant and hotel is further up the road to the right.

2. Cross the road and proceed up a hedged footpath to the right of The Chapel House, by the wall of the house. After negotiating a gate and a kissing gate you will come to open countryside. Continue in a southwesterly direction and through a kissing gate, following a path heading towards a prominent footbridge over the main line railway. Cross the footbridge and walk ahead over the next field. Cross bridge No. 37 of the Oxford Canal, and continue ahead across pasture and beyond another kissing gate, arriving on a lane, via a gate.

3. Go left along the lane for about 600yds (549m) until you come to bridge No. 41, where there is an easy descent via steps onto the tow path of this peaceful canal. Here you are joining the Oxford Canal Walk and you go right along the tow path, past Cathiron Farm (on the far bank). Pass under the railway, and at bridge No. 43 (Tuckey's Bridge), ascend onto a lane. Cross the bridge and go left at the lane junction.

4. In 160yds (146m), go right through a gate and follow the drive heading north towards Tuckey's Farm. Go through the gate on the right two-thirds of the way up the drive, and head to another to the right of the farm complex. Cross a drive via another gate and continue over the next field and through a kissing gate in the hedge, aiming towards houses. Leave the field via a kissing gate and footbridge onto the Easenhall Road, with Lodge Farm on your left.

5. Go right along the road, passing a row of houses. Opposite the Cathiron Lane road junction, go left and take the hedged footpath. Through a kissing gate, briefly follow the hedge and then head diagonally to the far corner of the field, aiming towards a metal kissing gate. Through this cross a footbridge and pass through another kissing gate. Cross the next field to a kissing gate by a grey house, bringing you back to Main Street in Harborough Magna. Go right along Main Street, then cross the B4112 back to The Old Lion.

Where to eat and drink

The Old Lion in Harborough Magna is a popular venue for local walkers, and dogs are welcome too. In the village of Easenhall, you will pass near the appealing Golden Lion Hotel, with its part wattle-and-daub walls. They do have an all-day menu but are closed on Thursdays.

What to look out for

If you intend walking around the lanes of Easenhall after dark, beware of the Phantom Horseman. He is apparently the ghost of a one-handed man called Broughton who died in Old Lawford Hall. Legend has it that, in an attempt to exorcise his ghost, his remains were placed in a phial and tossed into a nearby pond.

While you're there

A little further down the canal and nestled in the northwestern suburbs of Rugby, Newbold Quarry Nature Reserve is well worth a diversion. There is a car park that can be reached via Yates Avenue, a turning off the A426. The lake attracts numerous wading birds and ducks, and beneath the surface are crayfish. In the park surrounds you will find lime-loving plants and wild flowers, as well as butterflies.

Explore
the UK at
RatedTrips.com
AA